THE HISTORICAL ATLAS OF THE CELTIC WORLD

JOHN HAYWOOD

Foreword by
BARRY CUNLIFFE

with 214 illustrations, 180 in colour, including 54 maps

Thames & Hudson

For my mother

ACKNOWLEDGMENTS
Though the views expressed here are my own, I have
benefited enormously from the advice and guidance
of Professor Barry Cunliffe, Professor Vincent Megaw,
Dr Seán Duffy, Professor Steven Ellis, Dr Keith Stringer,
Dr David Shotter, Dr Alexander Grant and Simon Hall:
my grateful thanks to them all for their time and trouble.
I would also like to thank the Department of History at
Lancaster University for supporting my work through
an Honorary Research Fellowship.
John Haywood

The author is an Honorary Research Fellow in the
Department of History at the University of Lancaster
and a Fellow of the Royal Historical Society of Great
Britain. He has written many books, including
The Celts: from Bronze Age to New Age.

Barry Cunliffe is Emeritus Professor of European
Archaeology at the University of Oxford and the
author of *The Ancient Celts* and many other
books on European prehistory.

On the cover: front, clockwise from top left: Bronze ornament in the shape of
a horse; National Museum of Denmark, Copenhagen. Massive silver torc
with iron core, 29.5 cm (11 1/2 in) wide and weighing over 6 kg (13 1/2 lb)
from Trichtingen, Germany, perhaps second century BC; Landesmuseum
Württemberg, Stuttgart. Bronze figure of a stag, 1st millennium BC, from
Germany; Nuremberg, Germanisches Nationalmuseum. Silver horseman
coin of the Boii, Bratislava, Slovakia, 1st century BC; Magyar Nemzeti
Múzeum, Budapest. Pottery model of a wolf's head, shaped like the mouth
of a carynx, the Celtic War horn, from Numantia, 2nd–1st century BC;
Museo Arqueológico Nacional, Madrid. Iron Age bronze jug, once holding
wine for a ritual feast, from Waldalgesheim, Germany; Bonn, Rheinishes
Landesmuseum. *Back:* Statuette of a warrior deity from Saint-Maur-en-
Chaussée, 1st century BC. Musée Départemental de l'Oise, Beauvois.

First published in the United Kingdom in 2001 by Thames & Hudson Ltd,
181A High Holborn, London WC1V 7QX

First paperback edition 2009
Reprinted 2015

The Historical Atlas of the Celtic World © 2001 and 2009
Thames & Hudson Ltd, London

British Library Cataloguing-in-Publication Data
A catalogue record for this book is available from the British Library
ISBN 978-0-500-28831-3

Printed and bound in China by 1010 Printing International Ltd

To find out about all our publications, please visit **www.thamesandhudson.com**.
There you can subscribe to our e-newsletter, browse or download
our current catalogue, and buy any titles that are in print.

*Scythian gold beaker from
Kul'-Oba (p. 28)*

*Bronze figurine
of a Gallic priest or
Druid (p. 26)*

*Pictish silver plaque
(p. 86)*

Monastic round tower, Devenish Island (p. 102)

CONTENTS

Pipers at a Galician festival (p. 138)

*Statuette of a warrior deity from
Saint-Maur-en Chausée,
1st century BC.*

Foreword

IN 1867 A BRETON NOBLEMAN, Theodore Hersart de la Villemarqué, called together the first Interceltic Congress at St Brieuc in northern Brittany, sending out invitations to his 'kith and kin in Wales', 'brothers' in Cornwall and 'cousins' in Ireland and Scotland. La Ville-marqué was one of a small group of prominent Bretons who, angered by the repressive centralism of Paris, was attempting to establish (he would have said re-establish) the special identity of Brittany. Thirty years earlier he had published his famous *Barzaz Breiz* (*Songs of Brittany*) – a collection of folk poetry then still remembered by the Breton peasants – and now he was moving into the political arena by placing Brittany as a focus in the new nationalism that was beginning to grip the Celtic-speaking peoples of the Atlantic shores. For him, their common language and remote oceanic homelands created a quite special Celtic identity that could be traced directly back to the roots of European society. His was a powerful call – and it has gone from strength to strength.

Today, life in Brittany is greatly enriched by its Celtic heritage. The annual folk festival of Lorient brings thousands of people from all over western Europe to listen to modern Celtic music of people like Alan Stivell, who sings in French, Breton, Irish, Scottish Gaelic and Welsh. Meanwhile, the haunting and highly original piano compositions of Didier Squiban, echoing traditional Breton rhythms and the movements of the sea, are fast gaining international recognition. At a more local level the sense of community and tradition is ever present in the frequent publicly advertised *fest-noz* – originally a kind of harvest supper and now an excuse for a good party – and the annual *fêtes folkloriques* that most communes stage to raise funds for local causes. Although both are really recent re-inventions, created to meet modern needs, no one who has sat on a summer's night at an open-air communal supper and enjoyed the raucous music of the bignon and bombard, the dancing and the poetry, can fail to appreciate what it means to feel one with a deep Celtic tradition.

What I have said of Brittany applies to a greater or lesser extent to all the Celtic-speaking countries of the Atlantic. The sense of a Celtic ancestry is widely felt, and over the last 200 years many 'traditions' have been rediscovered or simply invented to create the patterns of behaviour so necessary to enhance the feeling of identity – to distinguish 'us the Celts' from 'them, the others', be it Welsh from English, Bretons from French, or Galicians from Spanish.

In all the turmoil Europe has experienced, from the emergence of nation states in the early 19th century to the regionalization and ethnic conflicts of today, the concept of Celticness has been invented and re-invented many times. Some would argue that the muddle of beliefs and half-truths has become so great that the word Celt has become entirely meaningless and is best abandoned. This is a despairing and arid view. Since the Greek historians in the 6th century BC first attempted to characterize the Celts, there have been people who have believed themselves to be Celts and others who have looked at them from a distance and offered convenient, if irreverent, stereotypes. Always there has been change – definition and redefinition – and it is this that makes the subject so eternally fascinating.

In this Atlas John Haywood presents a brilliantly balanced and entirely up-to-date picture of the Celts through time, from their distant origins far back in prehistory to the present day. It is an incomparable source, an essential companion for everyone setting out to discover the Celts, no matter where their journey begins.

BARRY CUNLIFFE

Preface

THE HISTORY OF THE CELTS, real and imagined, encompasses enormous distances of space and time, covering some 3000 years, most of Europe and, in modern times, North America and Australasia – aspects of all the great themes of European history are to be found there. Such a history positively demands to be interpreted through a historical atlas. No other medium can so graphically display the great movements, shifts of fortune and cultural changes that have affected the Celts.

The Celts have exercised a remarkable hold over the European imagination for well over two centuries now. For most of this time, the Celts have played the role of the noble savage to our well-ordered civilization. Along the way, they have been romanticized and imbued with otherworldly qualities. Yet the otherworldliness of the Celts is overplayed. In reality the ancient Celts were not so very unlike the ancient Greeks, Romans and Germans in their values and beliefs. Given time, the Celts would have developed an urban and technological civilization of their own, of that there can be little doubt. What would today's Europe be like had the Celts, rather than Rome, prevailed? Would a Celtic Europe have colonized the Americas or have experienced an industrial revolution? It is in these, and a host of other unanswerable questions that, to my mind, the real otherness of the Celts lies: they represent an unfulfilled alternative European history.

No doubt because it has been so romanticized, the Celtic identity has come in for its share of academic deconstruction in recent years. Some scholars have gone so far as to deny the very authenticity of the Celtic identity, arguing that it is simply a modern construct, a means of imposing pattern and order on an unruly past. Such arguments have considerable implications for the way millions of people today see themselves, and have inevitably caused controversy. The modern revival of Celtic identity is already having an impact on British and European politics. Where this is leading, others can decide, but at least the history of the Celts is one aspect of ancient and medieval history which cannot be dismissed by the cynics as mere antiquarianism and of no relevance to anyone's life today.

These controversies are not central to the purpose of this book, but its structure is informed by them. I accept the definition of the Celts as the ancient and medieval Celtic-speaking peoples and those modern peoples claiming descent from them, yet I hope that I have not adopted this definition uncritically. Celtic history is not a simple continuum from the Bronze Age to the 21st century. There are discontinuities in that history that are just as important as its continuities, and the organization of this book is intended to reflect them. While they spoke similar languages and shared much common culture, Continental Celts and the Celts of Britain and Ireland were different in important respects: for this reason they are dealt with separately. Both these sections finish with the end of independent Celtic-speaking communities – the absorption of Brittany into France, the English conquest of Wales and the suppression of Gaelic lordship in Ireland and Scotland. Similarly, the modern Celts are not a simple continuation of the ancient Celts. The modern Celtic identity is more a cultural identity than a national identity: it transcends national boundaries, while in all the modern Celtic countries there are substantial minorities (in some even majorities) who do not regard themselves as being Celts. It is in deference to them that there is no attempt here to chart modern national histories. Instead, the modern Celtic identity is treated primarily as a cultural and political phenomenon.

JOHN HAYWOOD

Chronology

THE ANCIENT CELTS 1200 BC – AD 500

CELTIC CULTURES
c. 750–450 BC Hallstatt Iron Age culture.
c. 450 BC–AD 50 La Tène culture.

EVENTS
c. 1200 BC The Hallstatt Bronze Age culture develops north of the Alps.
c. 750 The Hallstatt Celts adopt ironworking.
c. 700–600 Possible date of Celtic migrations to Spain.
c. 600 Foundation of Massalia: Greeks trade with the Hallstatt Celts.
c. 550 The Hallstatt culture spreads to Britain.
c. 500 Earliest written form of a Celtic language (Lepontic).
c. 500 Greek historian Hecataeus makes the earliest written reference to the Celts.
c. 450 The La Tène culture develops in Germany and France.
c. 400 The La Tène culture spreads to Britain and Transdanubia (eastern Austria and Hungary).
c. 400 Celts migrate to Italy.
390 (or 387) The Gauls sack Rome.
380 Celts raid Illyria.
369–368 Celtic mercenaries are recruited into Greek armies.
335 Alexander the Great campaigns against the Celts on the River Danube.
323 Celtic ambassadors visit Alexander the Great at Babylon.
c. 320 Celts settle in the Carpathian Mountains.
c. 310 Pytheas of Massalia visits Britain.
c. 300 Celtic settlements in southern Ukraine.
c. 300–c. 100 Beginnings of state formation in southern and central Gaul.
298 Celtic invasion of Thrace defeated at Mt Haemus.
295 Senones defeated by the Romans at Sentinum.
281 The Celts (Galatoi) defeat and kill the Macedonian king Ptolemy Ceraunos.
279 The Galatians invade Greece but are driven back from Delphi.
278 The Galatians enter Anatolia to serve as mercenaries for Nicomedes of Bithynia.
c. 278 Celts found the kingdom of Tylis in present-day Bulgaria.
274 Celtic mercenaries are recruited by Ptolemy I of Egypt.

c. 240 Attalus I of Pergamon defeats the Galatians at the Springs of Caicus.
237 The Carthaginians begin the conquest of the Celtiberians.
c. 225 Date of the earliest known Celtic coins.
225 The Romans defeat the Gauls at the battle of Telamon.
218 Celts support Hannibal's invasion of Italy.
212 Fall of the kingdom of Tylis.
206 Celtiberians regain their independence after Rome defeats the Carthaginians at Ilipa.
200–100 Fortified tribal centres (oppida) appear throughout Celtic Europe.
c. 200 BC–c. AD 200 Main period of broch building and occupation in Scotland.
191 The Romans capture Bononia, the Gauls' last stronghold in Italy.
186 The Nori of Austria become Roman allies.
139 Lusitanian war leader Viriathus is murdered by the Romans.
133 The Romans defeat the Celtiberians at Numantia.
c. 123 The Romans annex southern Gaul.
122–121 The Romans defeat the Arverni and Allobroges in southern Gaul.
113–101 Migration of the Cimbri and Teutones through Celtic Europe.
106 Tolosa (Toulouse) captured by Rome.
c. 100 Greek historian Poseidonius writes an account of the Celts based on his travels in Spain, Gaul and possibly Britain.
c. 90 A Roman merchant colony is established at Virunum, the capital of the Nori.
88 Mithridates IV of Pontus massacres the Galatian nobility.
65 Galatia becomes a client kingdom of the Roman empire.
c. 60 King Burebişta of Dacia defeats the Celtic Scordisci, Taurisci and Boii.
58 Julius Caesar begins the Roman conquest of Gaul after the Helvetii attempt to migrate into the territory of the Arverni.
55–54 Julius Caesar's raids on Britain.
52 Siege of Alesia ends Gallic resistance to Roman rule.
25 Galatia becomes a Roman province.
19–15 The Celts on the upper Danube are conquered by the Romans.
19 The Romans crush the last Celtiberian resistance in northwest Spain.

c. AD 10 The Trinovantes and Catuvellauni in Britain are united by Cunobelinus.

20 Gallic revolt under Florus and Sacrovir.

41–54 Emperor Claudius admits Gauls to the Roman Senate.

43 Claudius orders the Roman conquest of Britain.

51 Resistance ends in southern Britain after the capture of Caratacus.

54–55 St Paul's Letter to the Galatians.

60 Romans destroy the Druids of Anglesey.

60 Boudica, queen of the Iceni, leads a British rebellion against Roman rule.

61 Boudica commits suicide after her defeat by the Romans.

69 Julius Civilis rebels and attempts to create an independent 'Empire of the Gauls'.

84 The Romans defeat the Caledonians at *Mons Graupius* in northern Scotland.

87 The Romans abandon plans to conquer all Britain.

122 Hadrian's Wall built across northern Britain.

142 Antonine Wall built across northern Britain (abandoned 163).

211 Emperor Septimius Severus dies campaigning against the Caledonians.

212 Citizenship is granted to all free inhabitants of the Roman empire.

260–74 Britain and Gaul in the independent 'Gallic Empire' of Postumus.

286–96 Britain is independent under Carausius.

297 First record of the Picts in northern Britain.

c. 300 Beginning of British settlement in Brittany.

358 The Franks begin to settle in Gaul.

367 Picts, Scots and Saxons ravage Roman Britain.

c. 400 Irish king Niall of the Nine Hostages raids Britain.

c. 400 Christianity is introduced to Ireland.

c. 410 Roman rule ends in Britain.

431 Palladius is appointed first bishop of the Irish.

c. 435 St Patrick begins his mission to the Irish.

c. 440 Cunedda defeats Irish invaders in Wales.

c. 450 Many British Celts migrate to Brittany to escape the Anglo-Saxon invasions.

455 Avitus, a Gaul, becomes Roman emperor of the west.

486 Clovis, king of the Franks, defeats the last Roman ruler in Gaul at Soissons.

THE MEDIEVAL AND MODERN CELTS 500–2000

c. 500 Irish Dál Riata dynasty wins control of Argyll in Scotland.

c. 500 Battle of Mt Badon: Britons halt Anglo-Saxon expansion.

501 Death of King Fergus MacErc of Dál Riata.

563 St Columba founds the monastery of Iona.

577 Anglo-Saxons capture Bath, Gloucester and Cirencester after the battle of Dyrham.

c. 590 Urien of Rheged killed at Bamburgh.

c. 600 The Gododdin defeated by the Anglo-Saxons at Catterick.

c. 600–*c.* 800 Ireland's 'Golden Age'.

635 St Aidan begins the conversion of the Northumbrians.

635 The Bretons accept Frankish overlordship.

637 Irish and Scottish Dál Riata become independent of one another.

685 A Northumbrian attempt to conquer the Picts defeated at Nechtansmere, near Dunnichen Moss.

691 The Bretons regain full independence.

c. 790 Offa's Dyke is built to mark the Welsh border.

795 Vikings sack Iona and raid Ireland for the first time.

798 Vikings raid the Isle of Man.

c. 800 Irish monks become the first visitors to the Faroe Islands and Iceland.

841 Dublin is founded as a Viking base.

843 Kenneth MacAlpin of Dál Riata conquers the Picts.

844 Rhodri Mawr becomes king of Gwynedd.

851 Frankish king Charles the Bald recognizes Erispoë as king of Brittany.

867 Charles the Bald cedes Cotentin to King Salomon of Brittany.

870 Vikings sack Dumbarton, capital of Strathclyde.

878 Death of Doniert, the last independent king of Cornwall.

888–91 Alain the Great defeats Viking attacks on Brittany.

889 Donald II is the first to use the title 'King of Scotland'.

919 Vikings occupy Brittany.

927 Hywel Dda and other Welsh kings accept Athelstan of England as overlord.

936–39 Alain Barbetorte expels the Vikings from Brittany.

973 King Edgar of England cedes Lothian to Scotland.

1002 Brian Boru becomes High King of Ireland.

1014 Brian Boru killed at the battle of Clontarf.

1018 Owain the Bald, the last British king of Strathclyde, is killed at the battle of Carham.

1057 Macbeth is killed by Malcolm Canmore who becomes king of Scotland.

1093 Anglo-Norman conquest of Wales begins.

1110 Flemish and English settlement begins in Pembrokeshire, south Wales.

1156 Somerled rules Argyll and the southern Hebrides.

1169 Anglo-Norman mercenaries re-establish

Diarmit MacMurchada as king of Leinster.

1170 Richard FitzGilbert ('Strongbow') captures Waterford and Dublin.

1171 Irish kings submit to Henry II of England.

1183 Rory O'Connor, last High King of Ireland abdicates.

1194–1240 Reign of Llywelyn the Great (Llywelyn Fawr), king of Gwynedd.

1266 Norway cedes the Hebrides to Scotland.

1267 Treaty of Montgomery: Henry III recognizes Llywelyn ap Gruffydd as Prince of Wales.

1282 Edward I crushes a revolt by Llywelyn ap Gruffydd: end of Welsh independence.

1290 Isle of Man comes under the English crown.

1296–1328 Scottish Wars of Independence from England.

1301 Edward I gives his son the title 'Prince of Wales'.

1315–18 The English defeat the Scottish invasion of Ireland.

1354 John of Islay adopts the title 'Lord of the Isles'.

1366 Statutes of Kilkenny forbid English settlers to adopt Irish customs.

1400–10 Owain Glyndŵr's revolt in Wales.

1485 Henry VII of the Welsh Tudor family becomes king of England.

1487 France gains control of Brittany after the battle of St-Aubin-du-Cormier.

1491 Marriage of Anne of Brittany to King Charles VIII of France.

1493 The Lordship of the Isles is abolished.

1497 Cornish rebel army is defeated outside London.

1532 Brittany is formally incorporated into France.

1536 The Reformation Parliament introduces Protestantism to Ireland.

1536–42 Acts of Union make Wales officially a part of England.

1545 Donald Dubh attempts to restore the Lordship of the Isles.

1546 First printed book in a Celtic language (Welsh).

1549 Cornish rebel against the use of English in church services.

1556 First plantations of Protestant settlers in Ireland.

1593–1603 The Nine Years War in Ireland.

1601 Battle of Kinsale turns the Nine Years War in England's favour.

1603 James VI of Scotland becomes king (James I) of England.

1607 The Flight of the Earls: effective end of Gaelic Ireland.

1609 Articles of Plantation provide for the removal of the Irish to reservations.

1641 Catholic-Gaelic rebellion in Ireland.

1649–53 Cromwellian conquest of Ireland.

1688 The Glorious Revolution: Catholic King James II/VII is exiled and replaced with William of Orange.

1692 Massacre of Glencoe.

1707 Act of Union between England and Scotland.

1707 Edward Lhuyd publishes Archaeologia Britannica on the Celtic languages.

1717 The Order of Bards, Ovates and Druids is founded to 'revive' Druidism.

1745 'Bonnie Prince Charlie' lands in Scotland and begins the last Jacobite rebellion.

1746 Battle of Culloden: repression of the Highlands begins.

1760–63 James Macpherson's Ossianic poems.

1763–1886 Period of the Highland Clearances.

1777 Dolly Pentreath, the last monoglot Cornish speaker, dies.

1789 First modern eistedfodd held at Corwen.

1790 Breton Parliament is abolished.

1801 Act of Union with Great Britain abolishes the Irish parliament.

1805 Académie Celtique founded at Paris.

1822 George IV's visit to Scotland popularizes tartan.

1845 Potato blight causes famine in Ireland, the Scottish Highlands and Isle of Man.

1858 Irish Republican Brotherhood (the Fenian movement) is founded.

1860–65 Napoleon III sponsors excavations at Alesia and Bibracte.

1861 The first National Eistedfodd is held at Aberdare.

1865 Welsh colonists arrive in Patagonia.

1867 First Inter-Celtic Congress held at St Brieuc, Brittany.

1882–86 The Highland Land War (the Crofters' War).

1893 Gaelic League founded to promote the Irish language.

1900 Neo-Druids regularly celebrate the summer solstice at Stonehenge.

1916 Easter Rising in Dublin.

1922 Irish Free State becomes independent. Gaeltachts given special protection.

1925 Plaid Cymru, Welsh nationalist party, founded.

1941 Nantes is detached from Brittany by the Vichy French government.

1948 Ireland is declared a republic and leaves the Commonwealth.

1951 Mebyon Kernow, Cornish nationalist party, founded.

1974 Last native Manx speaker dies.

1992 Welsh language gains equal status with English in public administration.

1998 Good Friday Agreement gives Gaelic equal status with English in Northern Ireland.

1999 Devolution in Britain: Scottish parliament and Welsh Assembly opened.

Today, the Celts are primarily a people of Europe's Atlantic fringe, but there are in fact few European countries which do not share a Celtic past. By the time the Celts first appear in history in the 6th century BC, they were already the dominant people of western and central Europe.

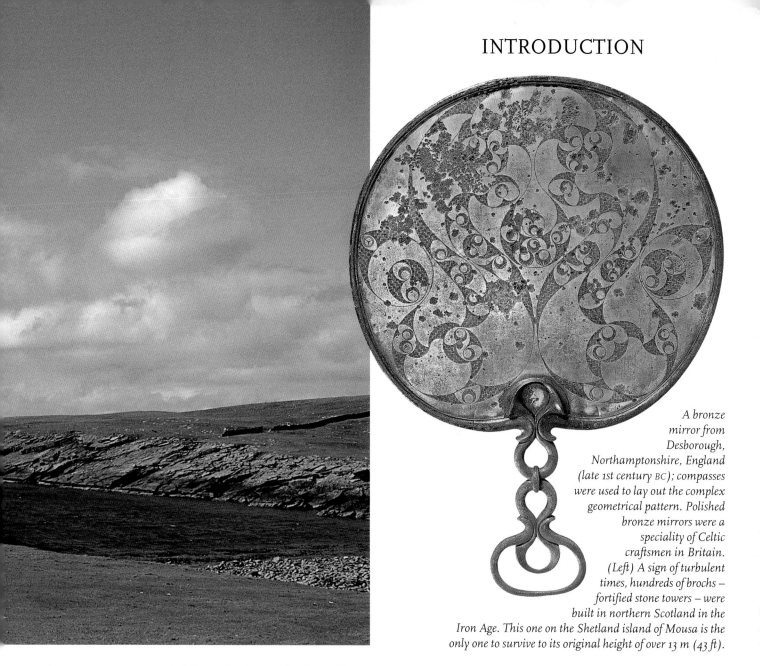

A bronze mirror from Desborough, Northamptonshire, England (late 1st century BC); compasses were used to lay out the complex geometrical pattern. Polished bronze mirrors were a speciality of Celtic craftsmen in Britain. (Left) A sign of turbulent times, hundreds of brochs – fortified stone towers – were built in northern Scotland in the Iron Age. This one on the Shetland island of Mousa is the only one to survive to its original height of over 13 m (43 ft).

THE CELTIC IDENTITY

GREAT MIGRATIONS carried the Celts into Italy, the Balkans, Greece and as far east as the steppes of the Ukraine and across the Bosporus to settle in Asia Minor. Smaller groups served as mercenaries for Greek rulers in Italy, Syria and even Egypt. Though they were always divided into many different peoples and tribes, the Celts were united across this vast area by shared culture and beliefs.

Skilled farmers and metalworkers, in the last centuries BC the Celts began to advance rapidly towards statehood and urban civilization. This process was halted when the Celts were conquered by their neighbours, the Dacians, Germans and, above all, the Romans. By the end of the 1st century AD the only independent Celts were found in Ireland and far northern Britain. With the fall of Rome, independent Celtic states re-emerged in Britain and Brittany. Converted to Christianity, the Celts played a major role in the cultural life of early medieval Europe but at the same time were thrown on to the defensive by the Franks and Anglo-Saxons. Final suppression of independent Celtic societies occurred in the early modern period (16th–18th centuries), but just at the point when it seemed that the Celts faced extinction, European intellectuals began to take a serious interest in their history and culture. Romanticized by novelists, poets, artists and nationalists, a self-conscious sense of Celtic identity began a remarkable revival which continues today. Emigration of Irish, Scots and Welsh in the 19th century to the United States and the British empire has helped spread the Celtic identity around the world, so that today it is globally recognized. Celtic history is therefore a journey through not only a considerable amount of time but also of geographical space, and it is this that makes it such a suitable subject for a historical atlas.

The Celtic Identity

Defining the Celts through this long period of history is not always easy, and some aspects of the Celtic identity – particularly the nature of the British Celts – are currently a cause of great academic controversy. Some scholars go so far as to argue that the ancient Celts are really a modern construct, others that it is the modern Celts who have been invented. Though these arguments represent extreme positions, they cannot be ignored completely, even by someone who broadly accepts the established view of Celtic history outlined above – there is certainly something to be said for both

positions. We do know that there were peoples in Iron Age Europe who called themselves Celts, but it certainly was not the case that all the peoples we now commonly regard as Celts actually saw themselves as such. Historians and archaeologists have indeed identified similarities of material culture, beliefs and language, and have imposed a degree of order and unity on what was in many ways a diverse group of peoples. Such Celtic consciousness as existed in Iron Age Europe died out after the Roman conquest, so there is also truth in the claim that the modern Celtic identity is an invention or, at least, a reinvention.

These issues are most sharply defined by the current controversy over the identity of the Celts of Britain and Ireland. None of the Celtic-speaking inhabitants of the British Isles ever described themselves as Celts before the 18th century AD. Roman writers certainly recognized similarities of language and culture between the Britons and the Gauls, but they always regarded them as separate peoples. The Britons too regarded themselves as a separate people and believed themselves to be the aboriginal inhabitants of the island. It is unlikely that the Britons were literally aboriginal, but genetic and archaeological evidence does indicate a high degree of ethnic and cultural continuity in British and

Drawing inspiration from the desert fathers rather than the Roman church, Celtic monks sought out remote sites for their monasteries, such as the island of Inishmurray off the Atlantic coast of Ireland.

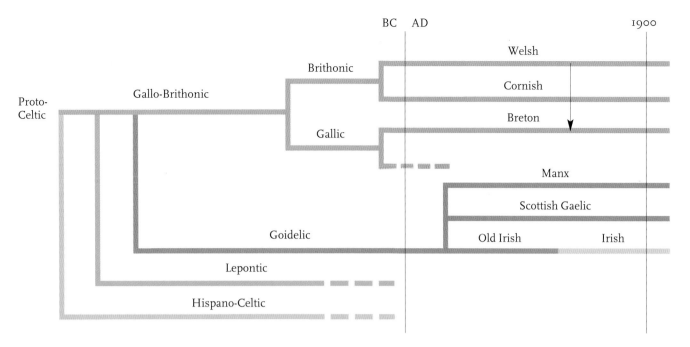

Diagram illustrating the possible development of the Celtic language group.

Irish prehistory. While the Britons and the Irish were greatly influenced by the culture of the Continental Celts, their own cultures remained distinctive. There is historical evidence of some exchange of population between Britain and the continent, but it seems increasingly likely that there were no major migrations of Celtic peoples from the continent into Britain. As a result, many archaeologists are now reluctant to use the word Celtic in relation to the British and Irish Iron Age. It is this that has made the Celtic identity one of the most contentious subjects in British archaeology. Many modern Celts have taken exception to seeing the people they regard as their ancestors being written out of (pre)history. An English plot to undermine the basis of Celtic identity and reassert Anglo-Saxon supremacy in the face of resurgent Celtic nationalism is genuinely suspected by some. While this is a somewhat paranoid over-reaction, it is disingenuous of archaeologists to claim that an attack on the Celtic identity of the ancient inhabitants of the islands has no implications for modern Celtic identity: much of its attraction is that it gives a strong sense of deep historical roots.

The Celtic Languages

Because of questions such as these, the most satisfactory way to define the Celts is not in terms of what they may or may not have called themselves, but in linguistic terms, as the group of peoples speaking Celtic languages: this embraces both the Continental Celts and the Celtic-speaking peoples of Britain and Ireland, and is the definition most widely accepted by modern Celtic-speaking peoples. A sense of Celtic identity may not have been either universal or continuous, yet the survival of Celtic languages

from prehistory into modern times provides a strong thread of continuity, and it was language issues which provided one of the focuses for the emergence of the modern Celtic identity at the end of the 18th century. In the future, language may cease to be so appropriate a way to define the Celts. There are clear signs that the Celtic identity is beginning to develop independently of its linguistic roots, as there are millions of people today who have a strong sense of being Celtic even though they do not actually speak Celtic languages on an everyday basis.

Four Celtic languages are still spoken on an everyday basis in modern Europe: Welsh, Breton, Irish Gaelic and Scottish Gaelic (not to be confused with Scots, the Scottish dialect of English). Two others – Cornish and Manx Gaelic – survived into recent historical times and are the subject of so far unsuccessful campaigns to revive them as living languages. The modern Celtic languages are divided into two groups, q-Celtic or Goidelic, which includes Irish, Scottish and Manx Gaelic, and p-Celtic or Brithonic, which includes Welsh, Breton and Cornish. The division into p- and q-Celtic is based on phonological differences, as seen, for example, between Gaelic *mac* ('son') and its Welsh equivalent *map*.

Several other forms of Celtic language are known to have existed in ancient times from the evidence of legends on Celtic coins and memorial inscriptions. The oldest recorded form of Celtic is Lepontic, which was spoken in Italy's Po valley in the 6th century BC. In Gaul Gallic was spoken, while in the Danube lands and central Europe a little known language called Eastern Celtic was spoken. Brithonic was spoken in Britain south of the Forth-Clyde isthmus. In northern Britain Pictish was spoken. The earliest records of Gaelic in Ireland date from the very early Middle Ages but a

The spectacular gold-covered bronze and iron helmet from Agris, France, epitomizes the Celtic warrior's love of display (4th century BC).

form of the language was certainly spoken there much earlier. Over most of central, northern and western Iberia, Hispano-Celtic was the language of the Celtiberians. The exact relationships between the extinct forms of Celtic are uncertain because our knowledge of them is based on very limited source material. Lepontic, Gallic and Eastern Celtic were probably all related to p-Celtic, while Hispano-Celtic was probably more closely related to q-Celtic. Pictish was a form of Brithonic which seems to have contained elements derived from an unknown non-Indo-European language.

Most Continental Celtic languages died out under Roman rule and were replaced by local Latin dialects which ultimately developed into the modern Romance languages. A form of Gallic probably survived in Armorica (modern Brittany) and, after Brithonic was introduced to the region by British settlers in the 5th century AD, contributed to the development of the Breton language. Britain was Romanized to a much lesser degree than the Celtic lands of the continent, and independent Celts always remained both there and in Ireland. The British language was influenced by Latin but survived to develop into Welsh and Cornish and influence Breton in the Middle Ages. Introduced to northern Britain and the Isle of Man, Irish Gaelic developed into its Scottish and Manx variants in the Middle Ages but Pictish died out sometime after the Picts were conquered by the Gaelic-speaking Scots in the 9th century.

Celts or Gauls?

The word 'Celt' (Greek *keltoi*) was first used in writing in the 6th century BC to describe the peoples who lived north of the Greek colony of Massalia, modern Marseille. Later, as the Greeks recognized similarities between these peoples and those of central Europe, they began to use 'Celt' more generally to describe the barbarian peoples to the north of the Alps. Eventually, the word became a synonym for 'barbarian' and was even used to describe peoples we would now regard as Germanic, such as the Franks. Despite this, the word Celt was certainly used by some Celtic-speaking peoples to describe themselves, possibly collectively, as Caesar tells us that the Gauls called themselves Celtae, but also as a tribal name (e.g. Celtici) and as a personal or family name (e.g. Celtius). There are several theories about the word's original meaning; none of them are very convincing. The Greeks used another name, 'Galatians' (Galatoi) to describe specifically the Celtic-speaking peoples who invaded Greece and Anatolia from central Europe in the 3rd century BC. The Romans habitually used the similar word 'Gaul' (Galli) when referring to the Continental Celtic-speaking peoples. Whether these words were coined by the Greeks and Romans themselves, as Caesar apparently believed was the case with the Gauls, or were derived from a word used by Celtic-speaking peoples to describe themselves is unknown, though some Celtic tribes certainly had similar sounding names (e.g. Gallaeci).

The modern usage of 'Celt' as an embracing term to include all the Celtic-speaking peoples, both on the continent and in the British Isles, past and present, was established only in the 18th century. The Scots scholar George Buchanan prepared the way for this in the late 16th century when he proposed that the ancient Britons had been Gauls. In 1704 Paul-Yves Pezron argued that the Gauls of Roman literature were the same people as the Celts of ancient Greek literature, and in 1707 the Welsh linguist Edward Lhuyd defined the Celtic language group. Lhuyd might perhaps as easily, and with as much justification, have described them as 'Gallic' languages but that word had come to be closely associated with the French, and in 1707 Great Britain was at war with France. By the mid-18th century, 'Celtic' had come to be used to describe not only the languages but also the peoples who spoke them

The Making of a Stereotype

Most of our knowledge of the beliefs and values of the ancient Celts, as well as our popular stereotypes as to what constitutes typical Celtic behaviour, derive from Classical Greek and Roman sources. Classical accounts give a fairly consistent view of the Celts. The Celts were irrationally superstitious and had savage religious practices like human sacrifice. There was a mystical order of priests called Druids, who worshipped in groves and other natural locations. They loved skill with words, and bards and poets were highly respected. They drank far too much and became quarrelsome and violent, but also had sacred laws of hospitality (which the Romans were not above treacherously exploiting). Celts were boastful and vain: a man's honour was everything and had to be defended to the death. They were warlike and aggressive but made unreliable allies. Fighting naked, Celtic warriors were fierce and impetuous in their first onrush, but if they met a stout defence they were easily discouraged and gave way to panic. Even Celtic women were fiercely assertive. To some extent these attributes are representative of what Classical writers expected of barbarians – other peoples such as the Germans are described in not dissimilar terms – but it is a credible, if stereotypical, vision.

However, Greek and Roman writers were far from objective observers of the Celts, whom they regarded as dangerous and culturally inferior. They deliberately emphasized the differences between the Celts and the Mediterranean civilizations, while largely ignoring the many similarities, and some writers had ulterior motives for exaggerating their savagery. Julius Caesar, for example, invaded Gaul to serve his own political ambitions back in Rome, but disguised his motives by emphasizing the dangers to Rome if the Celts were unchecked. Caesar also stressed the valour and martial prowess of the Celts because that magnified the significance of his own achievement in defeating them. Though they might neither like nor respect the Celts, Classical writers, therefore, were usually concerned to show them as worthy opponents for their own superior warriors. Roman writers never entirely abandoned their prejudices against the Celts but, once they had been conquered and pacified, they softened their tones and even accorded them a certain dignity. The Roman writer Tacitus used the Caledonian king Calgacus as the mouthpiece to deliver (before the battle of *Mons Graupius* in AD 84) what has become one of the most famous indictments not only of the Roman empire but of imperialism in general: 'Plunderers of the world, now they have exhausted the land by their devastations.... To theft, slaughter and plunder they have given the false name of "government". They have created a desolation and call it peace' (*Agricola*, 30). There is little reason to believe that Calgacus ever made any such statement, though Tacitus may have believed it was the kind of thing he might have said to rally his troops before a battle. Tacitus is really using the Celts as a vehicle to express concerns about the way his own society was developing, much as he did when writing about other barbarian peoples such as the Germans. It should be clear that Classical accounts need to be treated critically if they are not to be misunderstood.

A reconstructed barrow burial of the 6th century BC at Tübingen, Germany. The shallow burial chamber at its heart contained the burials of a Celtic warrior and a woman. Such elaborate burials were the preserve of persons of the highest rank.

Bronze shield decorated with the distinctive flowing scrollwork typical of insular Celtic La Tène art, and enhanced with glass settings (3rd–1st century BC). The shield was found in the River Thames at Battersea, London, where it had probably been deposited as an offering to the gods.

Romanticizing the Celts

The stereotype which Classical writers created was not intended to flatter the Celts. Yet while the unflattering stereotypes created by hostile writers for other historical peoples have been successfully challenged in recent decades – the best example of this is the Viking image: once cruel pirates, now farmers, craftsmen and merchants – the Classical stereotype of the Celt is still with us. This is undoubtedly because, to modern sensibilities, the Celtic stereotype is undeniably attractive. It was the influence of the Romantic movement that began to transform this negative image into a positive one: the noble savage, unspoiled by corrupt and decadent civilization. In our own age of unparalleled

material prosperity, declining spirituality and unsustainable human exploitation of the natural environment, the Celt as noble savage is an even more appealing figure. Today, the Celt has come to stand for those virtues which we feel our society most lacks, in particular spirituality and respect for nature. Now that war, conquest and empire-building are no longer seen as praiseworthy activities, the Celts have even gained a certain virtue as Europe's 'beautiful losers'. The truth is that, like Tacitus, we have come to use the Celts as a vehicle for expressing concerns about our own society, and in doing so have perpetuated the stereotype. In reality, the ancient Celts were much more like their neighbours than is generally recognized.

Celtic Reality

The Celts were certainly a warlike people, that much of the stereotype is undeniably true. War was necessary to maintain a social structure based on a warrior elite. In this respect they were very similar to the early German and Norse peoples, whose social structures were also based on warrior elites. For all these peoples, war was the surest way to prestige and wealth and it was for this entirely rational motive, not because of uncontrollable temper, that they had ready resort to it. This was true even of the Romans. Though often expressed in more flamboyant and fantastic terms, Celtic warrior values were similar to those found in the heroic poetry and sagas of the Germanic and Norse peoples: feasting, drinking and boasting were characteristic of them all. Celtic warfare had its own unique aspects – head-hunting, for example, and a reliance on the reckless headlong charge to break an enemy line. Warriors fought for personal glory and formal discipline was non-existent, so if their first charge failed a Celtic army really could dissolve into a disorganized panic-stricken rabble when faced by a determined opponent. But the tactic worked often enough to justify the Celts' faith in it: Highland armies were still winning battles this way during the Jacobite Rising of 1745–46.

In matters of religion the Celts were much more like their contemporaries than either hostile Classical writers or modern romantics usually allow. Like their neighbours, the ancient Celts were pagans and polytheists, though they probably did not have a clear pantheon of universal gods like the Greeks and Romans. Whatever they might have said, the Romans did not find the Celtic gods alien, as they did the animal-headed gods of Egypt, and even recognized many of them as equivalents of their own gods. Today, the Celts are often taken to represent ecologically sound values – we feel that their love of nature was somehow exceptional and that their way of life was, to use the modern jargon, 'sustainable'. But this is to view the Celts through green-tinted spectacles. The pagan Celts did show great reverence for the seasons and worshipped deities associated with natural places such

as groves, springs and rivers, but then so too did the Romans, Greeks and early Germans. All early farming peoples were close to nature – they had to be. While the Celtic way of life was, no doubt, much more sustainable than our own, it was not without cost to the environment. The source of the Celts' wealth and power was the same as it was for any ancient civilization – intensive agriculture and manpower. By the 1st century BC, many areas of Celtic Europe were nearly as densely populated and deforested as they are today.

The intellectual achievements of the ancient Greeks and Romans are still so influential today that they can easily seem to appear more 'modern' and rationalistic than they really were. But for the Greeks and Romans, like the Celts (and indeed almost all pre-modern peoples), there was no clear distinction between the natural and supernatural worlds. Mortals passed between worlds in Greco-Roman mythology, just as they did in Celtic. Greek and Roman religion was more formal than Celtic religion, but the appearance of temples in late Iron Age Gaul shows that it was developing in the same direction. Nor does the Celts'

custom of human sacrifice set them apart, as this was also common among the early Germans. To judge from Roman writers such as Caesar, human sacrifice may have been declining in Gaul in the 1st century BC, another sign of the Celts falling into line with their Mediterranean neighbours.

The aspect of Celtic religion which has attracted most attention, Druidism, is also the most characteristic. The Druids were a learned priestly caste who had to serve up to a 20-year apprenticeship in law, history, magic, medicine, poetry, astronomy and divination: the Greeks, Romans and Germans had no equivalent. However, Druids were not the monk-like ascetics they are sometimes painted. Because of their specialized knowledge and aristocratic status, Druids enjoyed great influence and were closely integrated into society. Except at sacrifices, when a single account says they wore white robes, there is no reason to believe that Druids habitually dressed differently from other Celts. Though place-names suggest it was more widespread, Classical sources only refer to Druidism in Britain and Gaul, so it is not certain that it was a universal feature of Celtic society.

Despite the importance of religion, the Celts also had a firm grasp on the things of this world. They loved beautiful objects and the prestige that came from owning and displaying them; indeed, as in other societies, status and power were largely determined by possession of them. From an early time, the Celts had a healthy appetite for the material luxuries of the Mediterranean world. In some areas, such as Noricum (modern Austria) and southern Gaul, the Celtic elite had adopted a highly Romanized way of life even before conquest by Rome. The Celts were an inventive people, with a keen interest in the practical application of technology. The Romans, who were never slow to spot a good thing, even if it had been invented by their enemies, adopted chain-mail, certain shipbuilding techniques, barrels and the design of their legionaries' helmets from the Celts.

As with religion, by the last centuries BC Celtic political institutions were also developing in the same direction as the Mediterranean world, with the appearance of kings, advisory councils ('senates'), elected magistrates and administrative institutions. The bonds of Celtic society were maintained by a system of clientage which was itself remarkably similar to that practised by the Roman aristocracy. Even the power struggles among the aristocracies of the more advanced Gaulish tribes, such as the Helvetii, mirrored those of Republican Rome. Women in Celtic society certainly enjoyed greater status, influence and sexual freedom than was the case in either Greece or Rome, and they were much more equal partners in marriage. However, there is little evidence to justify the common assertion that Celtic society was matrilinear – like its contemporaries, Celtic society was male dominated.

Compared to the stereotype, the real Celts of history do emerge as a warlike, but not irrationally violent, people. Prodigiously talented craftsmen, they were also intensely practical and inventive. They were religious, but no more or less so than their contemporaries, and they were as materialistic as any other people in world history. The ecological Celt certainly never existed. By the 2nd–1st centuries BC, the Celts were developing increasingly sophisticated political, social and economic structures, comparable to those of the Classical world. Writing and coinage, both based on Greek and Roman models, were coming into widespread use and town life, the absolute paradigm of civilization in the eyes of Greeks and Romans, had begun to appear in many areas. There is no doubt that a fully fledged Celtic urban civilization would have appeared had the Roman conquest not intervened. Had the Celts settled in Rome after they captured it in 390 BC instead of withdrawing, the history of Europe and European civilization might have been very different. As it was, the Celts were prevented from achieving their full potential, and modern western European civilization thus owes much more to Greece and Rome than it does to the peoples who dominated the continent for so long.

The Celtic Heritage

Despite this, the ancient and medieval Celts have left a heritage of art, craftsmanship and literature which is second to none. Celtic myth and legend continue to inspire Celt and non-Celt alike, while Celtic paganism, somewhat loosely it must be admitted, provides the basis for neo-Druidism and other neo-pagan religions. Lasting Celtic influence may also be apparent in a host of ancient folk customs and festivals across Europe, though with such undocumented traditions a definite link is often hard to prove.

The most important and obvious aspect of the Celtic heritage today is the contribution it has made to the modern Irish, Welsh, Scottish, Breton, Manx and Cornish identities. The origins of these identities form a large part of this book, but it is also worth considering, in passing, the Celtic contribution to the modern French and English identities. Both peoples take their names from Germanic tribes, the Franks and Anglo-Saxons, who invaded and conquered provinces of the Roman empire in the 5th century AD. In both cases the invaders were a minority, but even though the modern French and English populations must be in large part descended from the indigenous Celtic majority, neither people has ever considered itself to be Celtic. Despite this, the French celebrate their Celtic past and regard the ancient Gauls as their ancestors. In contrast the English do not generally regard the ancient Britons as their ancestors. While the Franks became assimilated to the culture and language of the native Gallo-Romans – and so came to identify

King George IV in Highland dress during his visit to Edinburgh in 1822. The visit was stage-managed by the Romantic novelist Sir Walter Scott who, virtually single-handedly, invented the idea that the kilt and its accoutrements were the traditional dress of Scotland. The painting is by David Wilkie.

Though they may sometimes help to perpetuate stereotyped folkloric visions of the Celts, festivals such as the Welsh National Eisteddfod have done much to promote and popularize Celtic culture in the modern world.

themselves with it – it was the conquered Britons who became assimilated to the culture, language and identity of the Anglo-Saxons. Conditioned by centuries of warfare to see the Britons primarily as enemies, the English have not found a place for them in their national mythology. The one aspect of the Celtic heritage which the English did adopt enthusiastically was the legend of King Arthur. As the supposed ruler of all Britain, Arthur was a suitable model for the medieval English kings, who had similar ambitions. In the 20th century, aided by a greater understanding of the origins of the legends, Arthur has been successfully reclaimed for the Celts.

Celtic Culture Today

Modern Celtic culture, especially in music and literature, enjoys a global influence and popularity out of all proportion to the size of the Celtic population. Major celebrations of Celtic culture, such as the Inter-Celtic festival in Brittany and the National Eisteddfod in Wales, attract international audiences. Although the origins of the Celts lie in prehistory, it would be a mistake to imagine that modern Celtic culture is either particularly ancient or even originally exclu-

sively Celtic. Take, for example, the three icons of Scottish Celticness, bagpipes, tartan and kilts. The bagpipes were actually invented in the Middle East in ancient times and were popular throughout Europe in the Middle Ages. Bagpipes had gone out of fashion in most of Europe by the 18th century and their survival in Scotland owes much to their adoption by the British army for Highland regimental bands. Tartans have been made and worn by many European and Asian peoples for 3000 years or more: they are so widespread simply because they are one of the easiest patterns to weave on a hand-operated loom. Clan tartans are primarily the 19th-century invention of entrepreneurial Lowland Scots textile manufacturers who realized their potential as a marketing device. The pleated kilt, or philibeg, widely regarded as traditional Highland wear, was invented only around 1727 by an English ironmaster, Thomas Rawlinson, for his employees at an ironworks at Invergarry, when he realized that their then traditional dress, the belted plaid, got in the way of their work. The kilt was then popularized in the 19th century by Scottish aristocrats whose 18th-century forebears had always worn tartan breeches called trews.

Although conservative in some respects – a consequence of centuries of political and economic marginalization – it is important to recognize that Celtic culture is not a museum piece: it has changed, invented, adapted and borrowed over the centuries just like any other culture, and it will continue to do so if it is to survive.

Though their origins lie in distant prehistory, the first Celts known to history appear in the works of ancient Greek authors of the 6th and 5th centuries BC. *Until quite recently it has been generally accepted that the Celts originated during the late Bronze Age or the early Iron Age in central Europe, from where they migrated to France, Spain, Britain, Ireland, Italy and as far east as Anatolia by the 3rd century* BC.

PART 1

The hillfort of Ipf, Bopfingen, Germany, dominates the surrounding countryside. It probably served as a centre of Celtic princely power in the late 6th century BC.

THERE IS RELIABLE contemporary written evidence of Celtic migrations into Italy, eastern Europe and Anatolia. The diffusion of the central European Hallstatt and La Tène art styles can be interpreted as evidence of similar, but undocumented, migrations in western Europe. Recently, however, this picture has changed. Archaeology and DNA analysis have been producing an increasing body of evidence of a marked degree of cultural and genetic continuity in western Europe which appears to be at odds with the accepted migration-based interpretation of Celtic history. It may actually be that Celtic-speaking peoples emerged over a much wider area of central and western Europe than has generally been thought, and at a much earlier time, perhaps in the Neolithic (*c.* 6000–2000 BC). Central Europe, France and the British Isles may have been part of this ancestral Celtic-speaking area.

If this was the case, the spread of cultures in prehistoric western Europe can be explained by everyday contacts

THE
CONTINENTAL
CELTS

Celtic warriors march to war in this engraving on an iron and bronze scabbard from a 6th-century BC burial at Hallstatt, Austria.

between peoples who already had much in common, including language, rather than by great folk movements. Though accepted by many archaeologists, this view of the origins of the Celtic languages has not found favour among linguists. For obvious reasons, the study of the prehistory of languages cannot be an exact science, so the best that can be said at present is that there is still considerable uncertainty about the ultimate origins of the Celts.

Chiefdoms and Trade Routes

The Celts whom the early Greek writers were referring to were the Hallstatt Celts of central Europe. During the early Hallstatt period, *c.* 700 BC, central and northern Europe lacked any large-scale centralized societies; the largest power-centres were the occasional small hillforts of petty chieftains. Long-distance trade routes for the exchange of essential commodities such as tin and copper (the ingredients of bronze) and salt (used as a food preservative) were already well established, however.

Beginning in the 8th century, a more aristocratic society began to emerge in central and western Europe. Small numbers of richly furnished burials begin to appear in cemeteries, indicating the emergence of a class of people who wished to distinguish themselves by their wealth even in death. Over the next 200 years, increasing numbers of hillforts were built north of the Alps and rich burials appear further and further west. These were made even more distinctive from those of the ordinary folk by being marked with earth barrows. The patronage of this social elite led to the development of the exquisite traditions of craftsmanship in bronze and precious metals for which the ancient Celts are so justly renowned. The social changes are probably linked to the introduction of iron technology, though it is far from clear how.

In the last century of the Hallstatt period there is a notable shift of wealth and power towards southwestern Germany, the Rhineland and eastern France. Spectacular graves, furnished with valuable Mediterranean imports and locally made luxury metalwork, cluster around a small number of pre-eminent hillforts, probably the seats of powerful regional chieftains. This shift may well have been a consequence of the foundation of the Greek colony of Massalia (Marseille), *c.* 600 BC, which caused trans-Alpine trade routes to decline in favour of a new route that followed the River Rhône upstream from the coast.

Warrior Culture

The Hallstatt chiefdoms abruptly disappeared *c.* 450 BC. The reasons for this are in part connected with a decline in trade with Marseille, perhaps cutting off the supply of prestige goods which underpinned the chiefs' status. Another factor was the rise of the new La Tène culture to the north. Characterized by its amazingly complex, swirling, geometrical designs, the art of the La Tène culture is instantly recognizable. The style's influence persisted for well over a thousand years and has been successfully revived by modern jewellers. Like the Hallstatt culture, the La Tène culture was the product of an aristocratic chieftainly society. It is possible that competition from the emergent La Tène chiefdoms may have been an additional factor in the decline of the Hallstatt chiefdoms.

With the appearance of the La Tène culture, the Celts begin to move more fully into the light of history. Archaeological evidence is now supplemented not just by the occasional throwaway remark, but by detailed accounts of their way of life by Greek and Roman writers. These writers often used the terms Galatian or Gaul interchangeably with Celt: all three are possibly derived from names which Celtic-speaking peoples used to describe themselves, rather than names given to them by outsiders. The Greeks and Romans were not, on the whole, very interested in the barbarian peoples of northern Europe, but the La Tène Celts could not be ignored: these barbarians were quite literally at the gates.

Gold bracelet from Rodenbach, Germany, dating to the late 5th century BC. The head at the centre is crowned with berries from the evergreen yew tree which was venerated by the Celts.

Beginning c. 400 BC, when several tribes burst over the Alps and swept into Italy, the Celtic peoples of central Europe began a series of spectacular migrations which carried them deep into the Mediterranean world. In 390 BC the Celts sacked Rome and refused to leave until the Romans handed over a vast amount of treasure. It was a traumatic experi- ence for a small city-state which was just emerging from the domination of its Etruscan neighbours, and it turned the Romans into implacable enemies of the Celts.

Celts and the Hellenistic World

Later in the same century other groups of Celts began to migrate east along the Danube, pushing into the foothills of the Carpathians and the Balkans. By 336 BC they were on the northern border of Macedonia, where they had a famous encounter with Alexander the Great. When he asked them what it was that they were most afraid of, the king was deeply disappointed to be told that it was that the sky might fall on them: Alexander had hoped they would say that it was him. Alexander's early death threw the Greek world into chaos as his generals fought among themselves over his vast empire. Taking advantage, the Celts began raiding into Macedonia in 298 BC, and in 281 BC they killed its king, Ptolemy Ceraunos, in battle. Head-hunting was an integral part of Celtic warfare and Ptolemy's head finished up being displayed on the point of a spear.

This was merely the prelude to what is the best docu- mented Celtic migration. Encouraged by their victory over Ptolemy, the Celts launched a massive invasion of Greece in 279 BC. They headed for the sacred city of Delphi, where many Greek states had their treasuries, but bad weather, constant harassment by the Greeks and divine intervention by Apollo forced them to turn back short of their objective. The Greeks, who had not had much to shout about since they were conquered by Macedonia 60 years before, com- pared this success to their victory over Xerxes' Persians in 480–479 BC. Heavy though their losses were said to be, this still left a lot of Celts in the Balkans. Some retreated to the middle Danube lands, others founded a robber-kingdom on the shores of the Black Sea, still others settled on the steppes of the southern Ukraine. The largest group accepted an invi- tation to serve in the army of King Nicomedes of Bithynia

The Dying Gaul, a Roman copy of a 3rd-century BC Hellenistic bronze original made to celebrate a victory of Attalus of Pergamon over the Galatians. Details of the statue, such as the hairstyle and the neck torc, are confirmed by contemporary descriptions and archaeology.

Bronze figure of a seated deity, with crossed legs and hoofed, deer-like feet, from Bouray-sur-Juine, Essonne, France. 1st century BC–1st century AD.

in northwest Anatolia. The Celts eventually settled in central Anatolia *c.* 275 BC, in a region which became known as Galatia from the alternative Greek name for the Celts.

It should be stressed that these migrations did not create a 'Celtic empire' in any meaningful sense. Though individual tribes did form alliances for the purpose of conquering territory, the Celts as a whole were never a single, united people, capable of conceiving of, let alone carrying out, a grand imperial master plan. The migrations were, rather, a haphazard response to the violent competitiveness which lay at the heart of La Tène society. Small-scale warfare was endemic in the Celtic world. The Celtic warrior elite positively needed war as the best means to gain wealth and prestige by bringing home plunder and the heads of defeated enemy warriors. The Celts were locked in an endless cycle of raid and reprisal. There was competition not just between tribes but between individual warriors within tribes. The stereotypical view of drunken boastful warriors fighting to the death over the hero's portion at a feast has much truth in it. In central Europe, a rising population reinforced this inherent competitiveness of Celtic society, creating internal tensions which could only be defused by the migration of part of, or even the whole of, a tribe to a new homeland.

The Seeds of Decline

The settlement of Galatia was the high-water mark of Celtic expansion. New powers were rising in Europe that would challenge the Celtic domination of the continent. Only a few years previously the Romans had begun the conquest of Italy's Celts, and in the next two centuries the Germans and the Dacians to the north and east would emerge as expansionist powers. By around the time of Christ, the Continental Celts had all been conquered by one or other of these peoples. Yet the last three centuries of Celtic independence saw some of their most brilliant achievements in arts, crafts and technology. Largely due to their skill as

farmers, the Celts became prosperous and numerous. This, and increasing contact with the Mediterranean world, led to the beginnings of urbanization and state formation. By the 1st century BC many tribes had developed monarchies or were ruled by councils and elected magistrates. Given time, there is no doubt that the Celts would have gone on to develop a sophisticated, literate, urban civilization, comparable to those of Greece and Rome. Ironically, however, it was this growing sophistication which made the Celts vulnerable.

States can marshal resources more efficiently than simpler forms of society. This can make them formidable in war, but their centralized institutions also make them easier to subjugate if they are the victims of aggression by a stronger state. If an aggressor can either replace the ruling elite or win, one way or another, its co-operation, controlling the conquered population is relatively easy. In the case of the Celts, the similarities between their political institutions and those of the Romans made their assimilation all the easier. In simpler decentralized societies,

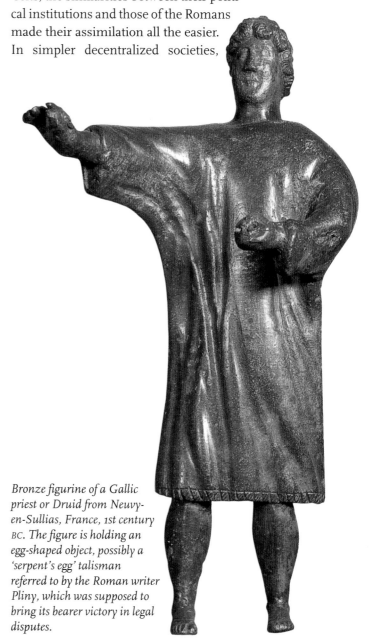

Bronze figurine of a Gallic priest or Druid from Neuvy-en-Sullias, France, 1st century BC. The figure is holding an egg-shaped object, possibly a 'serpent's egg' talisman referred to by the Roman writer Pliny, which was supposed to bring its bearer victory in legal disputes.

this is not possible, as there is no pre-eminent leadership to negotiate with, no institutions to take control of: pacification can often only be achieved using methods close to genocide. This goes a long way towards explaining why the Romans were able to conquer the Celts but failed to conquer the politically less sophisticated Germans. History has dozens of similar examples. The Romans did not, of course, conquer the Celts just because they could, they did it because Celtic wealth made it financially worthwhile and because they could never quite bring themselves to believe that the events of 390 BC would not be repeated while any Celts remained who were not under Roman rule.

It might be asked why the Celts did not unite against the common enemy? The answer is simple, the Celts not only did not but could not perceive the Romans as the common enemy because they themselves did not share a sense of common identity. Celtic tribes simply did not see it as being in their interests to fight in support of their traditional rivals. Even the greatest of Celtic war leaders, Vercingetorix, could not mobilize all the Gauls against Caesar's legions. Independence was all well and good for the stronger tribes, but for the weaker ones – the ones whose warriors' heads adorned the spears of the stronger tribes – Roman rule represented security of status and ownership for the elite and made little practical difference to the dependent peasantry. The Celts were also handicapped by their individualistic tradition of war-making. Roman generals shared the Celtic warrior's thirst for glory and the status that came with it, but the rank and file fought for pay. The reckless headlong Celtic charge was terrifyingly effective against inexperienced opponents, but if this did not work the Celtic army became simply a disorganized mass of individual warriors, suddenly vulnerable to a better-disciplined opponent.

Romanization of the Celts

The Romans did not set out to destroy Celtic culture and identity – so long as they had obedience, they were tolerant of cultural and religious diversity – but they were convinced that their own ways were the best and they encouraged their subjects to adopt them. For their part, the Celtic elite were hardly hostile to the Roman way of life – for centuries being able to drink wine like a Roman had been the ultimate status symbol. After the conquest, the Celtic elite quickly became highly Romanized in their appearance and behaviour. And to satisfy the elite's Romanized tastes, Celtic craftsmen soon adapted their own native styles to follow Classical models. The elite quickly learned to speak Latin, but many were still bilingual even in the 3rd century AD. Eventually local vernacular forms of Latin were adopted by the peasantry too and, except in Armorica (modern Brittany), Celtic languages had become extinct in continental Europe by *c.* 400. Celtic religions continued to flourish under Roman rule – the modern

King Arthur and his knights enter Camelot, from a 15th-century Flemish manuscript. The Celtic principality of Brittany played a major role in transmitting the British legends of King Arthur to medieval Europe.

myth of the otherworldly Celt has obscured how similar Celtic and Roman religious beliefs really were. What killed off this aspect of Celtic culture was an eastern mystery religion called Christianity. Whatever was left of the ancient Celtic identity was swept away by the Germanic invasions which caused the collapse of the western Roman empire in the 5th century.

The new Germanic monarchies of early medieval Europe looked to Christianity and the Roman empire for their social and political ideals, and for centuries to come the achievements of the ancient Celts were largely forgotten. Only in Brittany did a Celtic society survive into the modern period. In the 5th century the remaining Celtic-speaking population in this region was reinforced by an influx of Britons, perhaps fleeing the Anglo-Saxon invasion of Britain, perhaps merely taking advantage of the collapse of Roman power in Gaul to seize new lands. Despite having a mighty and expansionist neighbour in the kingdom of France, Brittany survived as an effectively independent principality until the end of the 15th century. It was through Brittany that the Celtic legends associated with King Arthur and his court became known in France, where they became a major influence on two of the most important cultural developments of medieval Europe: chivalry and courtly literature.

Origins of the Celtic Languages

For the purposes of this book the Celts are defined as a linguistic group. It is certain that the origins of the Celtic languages predate the first historical records of the Celts by at least 2000 years, but reconstructing the prehistory of a language is fraught with difficulties.

THE CELTIC LANGUAGES are a branch of the Indo-European family of languages, the largest and most widespread of the world's language families. Though it now has the smallest number of speakers of any Indo-European language group, *c.* 300 BC Celtic was probably the most widespread language group in Europe. Celtic exists in two forms, q-Celtic, which in ancient times included Hispano-Celtic and Goidelic (the ancestor of the modern Irish and Scottish Gaelic languages), and p-Celtic, which included Gaulish, Eastern Celtic, Lepontic and Brithonic (the ancestor of modern Welsh and Breton).

Indo-European languages were not indigenous to Europe. The earliest languages of Europe were non-Indo-European. Some, such as Etruscan and Iberian, are known from inscriptions, the existence of others is hinted at by place-names and by survivals in later languages such as Pictish, a Celtic language formerly spoken in Scotland. Modern Basque may be the lone survivor of these languages.

In conventional accounts, Indo-European languages are usually said to have originated somewhere in western Central Asia. Around 4000 BC Indo-European was introduced from the east into Europe, where it diversified into the ancestral forms of the modern European languages. Celtic emerged in central Europe and was spread into western Europe, Britain and Ireland by migrants who displaced or assimilated the indigenous inhabitants.

An alternative, and still highly controversial, account places the origin of Indo-European in Anatolia. According to this theory, Indo-European was

Scythian gold beaker from the Kul'-Oba kurgan (barrow), southern Russia. The Scythians were one of many nomadic Indo-European speaking peoples who dominated the Eurasian steppes in the last two millennia BC.

Farming reached southeastern Europe c. 7000 BC. Its spread was probably accomplished partly by migrations of farmers, partly by its adoption by hunter-gatherers whose hunting grounds were being encroached upon by the newcomers.

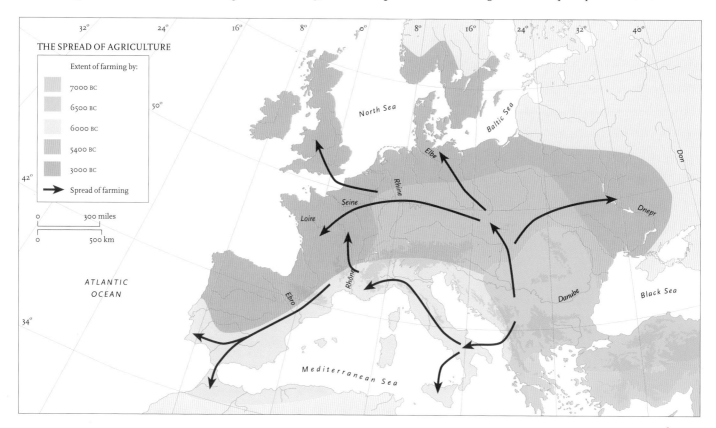

THE SPREAD OF AGRICULTURE

Extent of farming by:

- 7000 BC
- 6500 BC
- 6000 BC
- 5400 BC
- 3000 BC
- → Spread of farming

0   300 miles
0   500 km

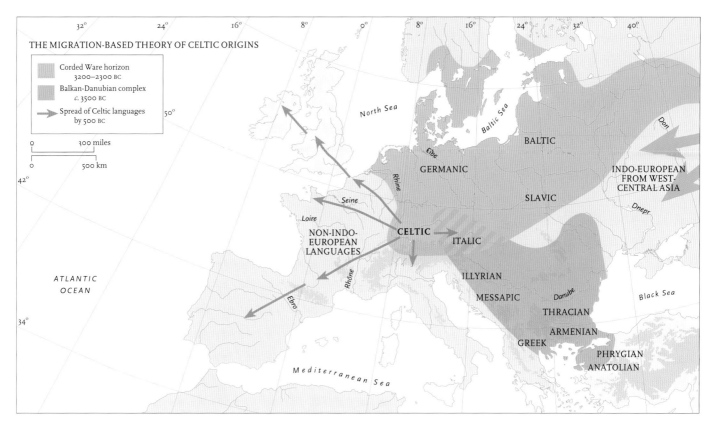

introduced to Europe from Anatolia by the first farmers who arrived *c.* 7000 BC and was then spread, along with the farming way of life, to most of western Europe by 4000 BC. Celtic languages subsequently evolved from Indo-European across much of the same area that they were spoken in at the beginning of historical times: in this interpretation there is no need to explain their spread by migrations for which there is little archaeological evidence.

(Above) Conventional theories hold that Celtic languages developed in central Europe from a form of Indo-European introduced from central Asia; they were then spread by migrations. (Below) Colin Renfrew's still controversial theory links the introduction of Indo-European languages to Europe, much earlier, with the introduction and spread of farming.

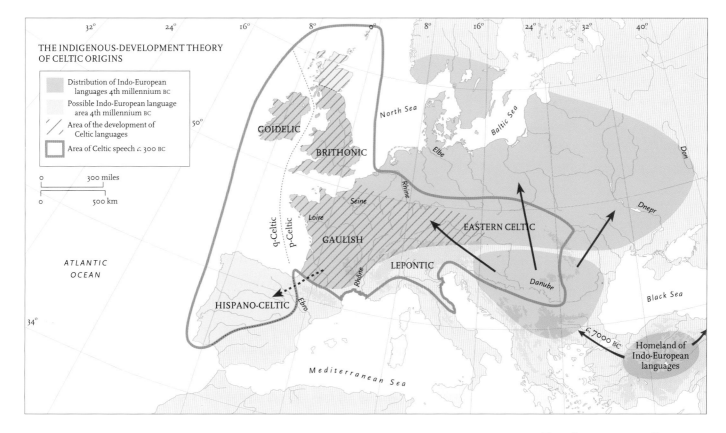

Early Bronze Age Europe and the Urnfield Culture

2000 – 750 BC

Although Celtic languages were probably already widely spoken in Europe during the Bronze Age, it was not until the period's end that a material culture – the Hallstatt culture – arose that can be firmly identified with the Celts. Nevertheless, it was during the Bronze Age that the type of aristocratic society which typified the Celts in historical times first developed in Europe.

METALS SUCH AS GOLD AND COPPER were used for ornaments in Europe from about 6000 years ago. Both metals are too soft to make useful tools and it was only with the discovery of bronze, an alloy of copper and tin, that metal tools began to replace stone ones in everyday use. The first bronze-using culture in Europe was the Únětice culture of the Elbe and Oder river basins, beginning around 2500 BC. Over the next 1000 years bronze-working spread throughout Europe. An important consequence of the introduction of bronze was a big increase in long-distance exchange. While most areas have locally available sources of stone suitable for tool-making, copper and especially tin are much less common – if they were to obtain supplies of metals, most communities had to trade.

The growth of trade created ideal circumstances for the easy transmission of ideas, so promoting considerable cultural uniformity across wide areas of Europe. By the late Bronze Age, the many distinct early Bronze Age cultures of central Europe had been replaced by the Urnfield cultures, named after their distinctive burial practices (cremations in pottery urns in often vast cemeteries).

MAP NOTES

❶ The earliest centre of European metallurgy was in the Balkan mountains: copper smelting was practised from as early as 4500 BC.

❷ The widespread Bell Beaker cultures are named after their custom of placing distinctive pottery drinking cups with their burials. The culture spans the late Neolithic and early Bronze Age.

❸ The early bronze-using Únětice culture was named after a cemetery near Prague, Czech Republic.

❹ Stonehenge, begun c. 3000 BC, fell out of use in the middle Bronze Age, c. 1500 BC.

❺ One of the largest Urnfield cemeteries, Kelheim (c. 900–800 BC) contained over 10,000 burials.

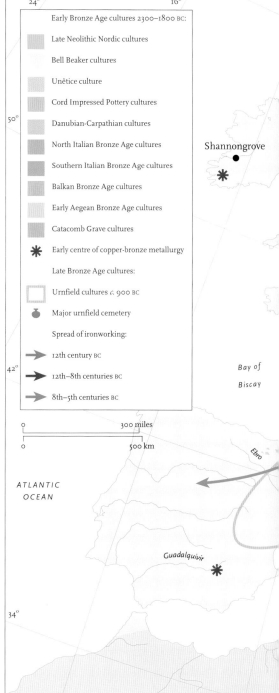

Early Bronze Age cultures 2300–1800 BC:

Late Neolithic Nordic cultures

Bell Beaker cultures

Únětice culture

Cord Impressed Pottery cultures

Danubian-Carpathian cultures

North Italian Bronze Age cultures

Southern Italian Bronze Age cultures

Balkan Bronze Age cultures

Early Aegean Bronze Age cultures

Catacomb Grave cultures

✳ Early centre of copper-bronze metallurgy

Late Bronze Age cultures:

Urnfield cultures c. 900 BC

Major urnfield cemetery

Spread of ironworking:

➡ 12th century BC

➡ 12th–8th centuries BC

➡ 8th–5th centuries BC

Shannongrove

Bay of Biscay

ATLANTIC OCEAN

300 miles

500 km

Ebro

Guadalquivir

(Right) A middle Bronze Age (c. 1300 BC) amphora decorated with a chariot, from an urnfield at Vel'ké Raškovce, Slovakia.

(Left) Gold gorget (collar) from Shannongrove, Co. Limerick, dating to the late Bronze Age, 7th century BC. Southwest Ireland was one of the earliest centres of metallurgy in the British Isles, from around the middle of the 3rd millennium BC.

Control over trade and production and use of metal tools and weapons gave social elites a means to increase greatly their power and authority. As a result, Bronze Age societies became more hierarchical, warrior elites emerged and fortifications, such as hillforts, became common. These changes are most apparent in burial customs. A minority of elite burials were richly equipped with grave goods, while the majority, those of the common people, had few or none. The needs of the elite also stimulated craftsmanship. Jewelry, fine weapons and armour, cult objects and fine tableware made of bronze, gold and silver were created so that the elite could display their superior wealth and status. Thus many of the features that characterized Celtic society in the Iron Age – hillforts, elite burials and materialistic display – have clear antecedents in the Bronze Age.

A votive hoard of bronze and gold tools and ornaments from Dieskrau, Halle, Germany.

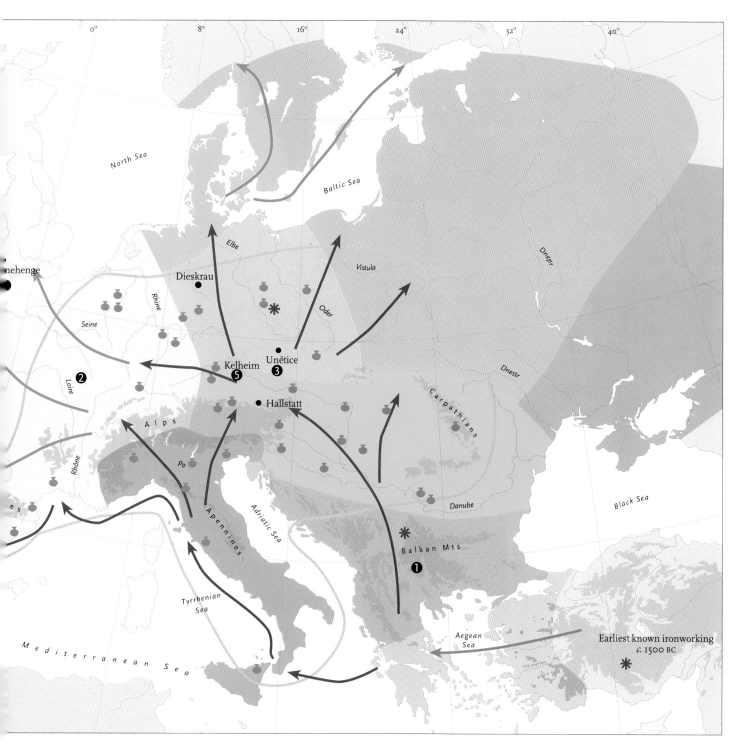

The Hallstatt Culture in Central Europe

700 – 450 BC

Impressive hillforts, superb craftsmanship, exotic Mediterranean imports and richly furnished burials characterize the Hallstatt culture of central Europe, the earliest material culture which is generally recognized as belonging specifically to the Celts.

THOUGH ITS MOST SPECTACULAR achievements date to the early Iron Age, the Hallstatt culture originated in the late Bronze Age as part of the Urnfield complex. The culture is usually divided into four periods, Hallstatt A (1200–1000 BC), B (1000–800 BC), both of the Bronze Age, C (800–600 BC) and D (600–450 BC), of the early Iron Age. Although the Hallstatt culture can be identified with the Celts, it was not identical to them. Celtic languages were probably already widespread in west and central Europe when the culture developed in the Bronze Age and even at its greatest extent in the 6th century BC there were Celtic-speaking peoples beyond its influence.

The early Hallstatt culture was similar to those of the rest of late Bronze Age Europe in that it was a society of small chiefdoms and a landscape dominated by isolated farms, villages and small forts. Major changes followed the introduction of iron into central Europe in the 8th century BC. In the region comprising modern-day Bohemia, southern Germany and northern Austria, hillforts became common, and around them appeared cemeteries of richly furnished barrow burials. Some of the richest burials even included four-wheeled funerary wagons. These developments are a sign of the emergence of a much more hierarchical and centralized society of wealthy chiefdoms, but it is far from clear what caused the transformation. An increase in trade is often cited,

Hallstatt D chiefdoms

Hallstatt C chiefdoms

Influence of Hallstatt culture
c. 500 BC

▼ Hallstatt C vehicle burials

▼ Hallstatt D vehicle burials

■ Centres of Hallstatt D chiefdoms

○ Other important fortified site

★ Hallstatt D trading centre

◉ Greek colony

Zone receiving Greek imports in the 6th century BC

0   150 miles

0   200 km

Bay of Biscay

CELTIBERIANS

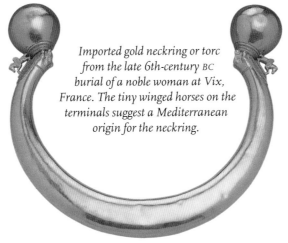

Imported gold neckring or torc from the late 6th-century BC burial of a noble woman at Vix, France. The tiny winged horses on the terminals suggest a Mediterranean origin for the neckring.

Sandstone statue of a naked warrior from Hirschlanden, Germany, late 6th century BC. It once stood as a marker on top of a high-status burial – the sword and torc were both symbols of power in the Hallstatt world.

MAP NOTES

❶ *The Hallstatt culture is named after an important large Iron Age salt-mining centre near the Austrian town of Hallstatt.*

❷ *Eberdingen-Hochdorf, one of the most richly furnished Hallstatt D 'princely' tombs, included a wagon, a bronze couch and feasting gear such as drinking horns and a Greek bronze cauldron.*

❸ *Bragny-sur-Saône was an important centre distributing Mediterranean imports such as wine, glass and pottery in Hallstatt D and early La Tène times.*

❹ *The hillfort of Mont Lassois commanded the important trade route along the Seine valley. Nearby is the famous 'princess's' grave at Vix.*

❺ *The most impressive of the Hallstatt D hillforts, Heuneburg, had, for a time in the 6th century, mud-brick fortifications which were possibly designed by a Greek architect.*

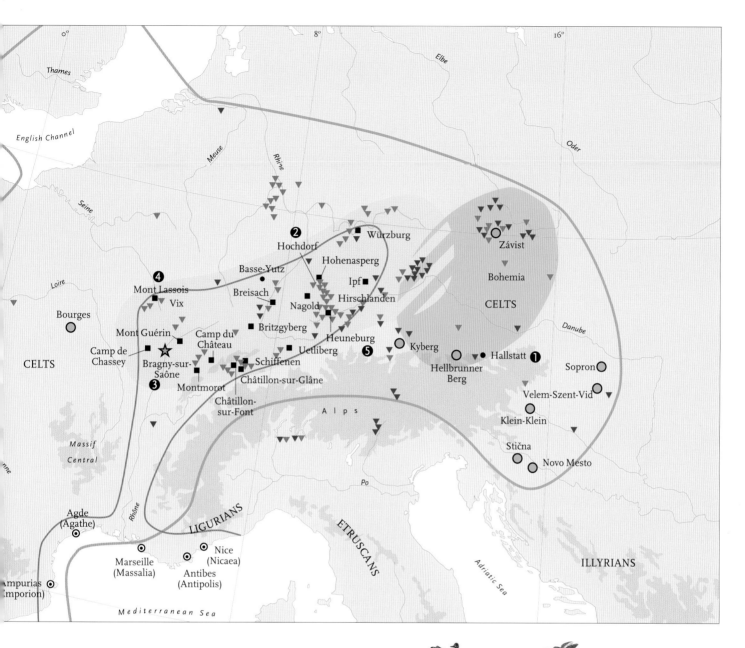

Bronze wine flagon from Basse-Yutz, Moselle, France, c. 450 BC. The flagon is based on an Etruscan prototype but has been transformed by Celtic craftsmanship and imagery.

but it is more likely that internal causes were responsible, such as a rising population and an attendant increase in wealth from agricultural production.

In the Hallstatt D period, the centre of the culture shifted to the west, to the upper Danube, the upper Rhine and eastern France. Many smaller hill-forts were abandoned while at the same time a relatively small number of large hillforts emerged as pre-eminent centres, probably the strong-holds of the powerful chiefs or 'princes' whose luxuriously equipped burials dot the surrounding countryside. The westward shift is no doubt connected with the foundation of the Greek colony of Massalia (modern Marseille) *c.* 600 BC, as most of the chiefdoms lie close to trade routes linking the Seine, Rhine and Danube valleys with the Rhône. The new trade link not only enriched the western Hallstatt chieftains but gave them access to new luxuries, most important of which was wine. Control of the distribution of these imports helped underpin the elite's status. Mediterranean imports are rarely found outside hillforts (unless as grave goods), emphasizing their elite nature. It was probably through traders' stories about these chiefdoms that the Mediterranean civilizations first became aware of the people called *Keltoi*.

The La Tène Culture in Central Europe

450 – 50 BC

The second of the great continental Celtic cultures, the La Tène developed in west-central Europe, between the River Marne and the Rhineland, in the mid-5th century BC. The culture is named after a settlement and ritual site on Lake Neuchâtel, Switzerland, first discovered in 1857.

BY 300 BC LA TÈNE had become the dominant culture across a broad swathe of Europe, from the Atlantic coast of France to the Carpathian Mountains, and its influence was felt in Spain and Cisalpine Gaul. In the 1st century BC La Tène influence spread to the British Isles, where its characteristic art style was developed in distinctive ways. Soon after the Roman conquests the La Tène culture disappeared from the continent and Britain, but the style survived in Ireland and spread back to Britain in the early Middle Ages.

The La Tène culture is defined primarily by its distinctive curvilinear art style, seen at its finest on weapons and other items of luxury metalwork. The style arose from a synthesis of Hallstatt geometrical decorative styles and Greek and Etruscan vegetal decorative styles, which were derived from imported drinking vessels. Mediterranean influence can also be seen in the techniques of craftsmanship, particularly in the spread of painted pottery. Though it was influenced by Hallstatt traditions, the La Tène culture developed on the northern and western margins of the Hallstatt heartland, in the central Rhineland, with secondary centres on the River Marne and in Bohemia. An outstanding feature of the early La Tène culture is its aristocratic warlike character, typified by its many richly furnished warrior burials. Some of these include chariots, an innovation in Celtic warfare. Hallstatt burials, in contrast, rarely included war gear. La Tène art was essentially an elite art form, designed to produce splendid vessels, jewelry, weapons and armour for display at warrior feasts and military parades.

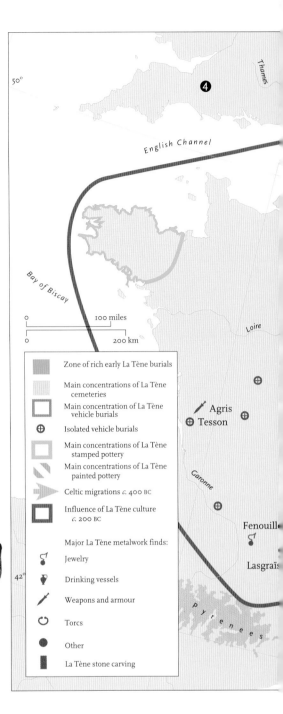

(Left) Stone carving of the head of a Celtic man or god from outside a sacred enclosure at Mšecké Žehrovice (c. 100 BC). The torc, moustache and hairstyle closely match what we know about the appearance of Celtic men from archaeological and literary sources.

Gold torc and armrings from the richly furnished 'princess's' burial at Waldalgesheim, Germany (c. 350–325 BC). They are decorated with a characteristic Classical-inspired vegetal style, from which La Tène art developed.

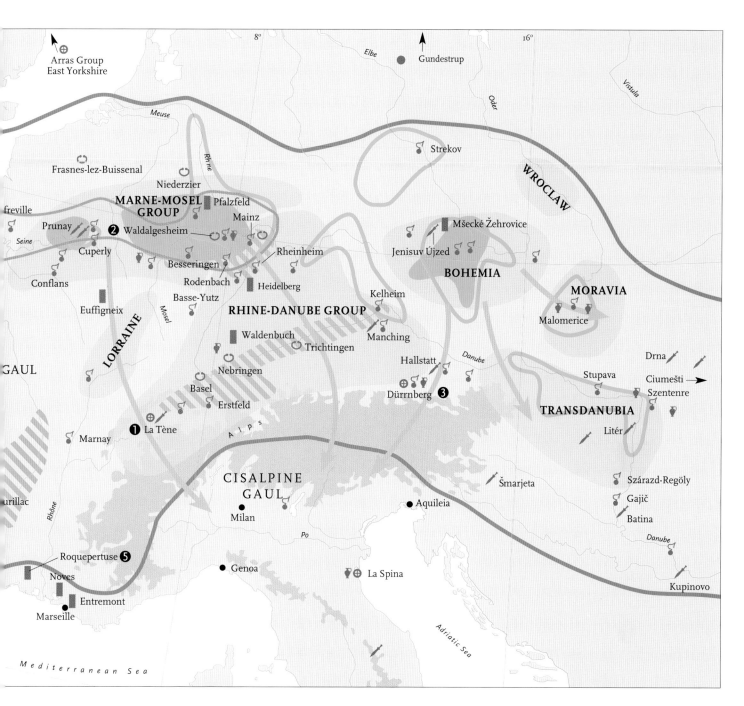

The rise of the La Tène culture was accompanied by the decline of the Hallstatt chiefdoms to the south. Changing trading patterns may have been responsible for this, or it could be that the Hallstatt chiefdoms were destroyed by the emergent La Tène warrior chiefdoms. Around 400 BC a wave of migrations began which carried the La Tène culture across central Europe and into Italy. These migrations are believed to have originated from the early La Tène centres, but the evidence is inconclusive. The Boii were among the invaders of Italy, for example, but it is not known if they actually occupied Bohemia as early as the 5th century BC. Archaeological evidence from settlements and cemeteries in Bohemia does seem to indicate a reduction in population c. 400 BC that would be consistent with migration out of that region, however. These migrations were probably a way for warrior societies to deal with internal tensions resulting from rising populations. There is no evidence for major folk movements in Gaul and Britain in the last centuries BC, so the La Tène culture must have spread there by other means.

MAP NOTES

❶ Type site for La Tène culture. Discovered in 1857, excavations in 1907–17 uncovered a vast votive deposit of finely decorated bronze and iron tools, and human sacrifices.

❷ Waldalgesheim: an outstanding 4th-century BC chariot burial of a Celtic 'princess', famous for its spectacular gold jewelry.

❸ Dürrnberg replaced Hallstatt as a salt-mining and trading centre in the 5th century BC.

❹ Insular La Tène art traditions developed in the 1st century BC.

❺ Stone carvings at Roquepertuse, Noves and Entremont mix Classical Greek influences and Celtic iconography.

The Celtic Migrations
500 – 275 BC

By the beginning of the Iron Age *c.* 750 BC Celtic-speaking peoples were probably already to be found over an area of Europe stretching from the region of modern Austria to the Bay of Biscay, and into Britain and Ireland. By the 3rd century BC migrations had spread the Celts even more widely, into Spain, Italy, eastern Europe and even Anatolia.

ALTHOUGH THEIR ROLE has been somewhat diminished by recent developments in archaeology and genetics, large-scale migrations were an important feature of Celtic history. Celtic society was highly competitive and migration was probably an effective way of relieving the internal tensions caused by population pressure and land shortage. The earliest Celtic migration for which there is some evidence crossed the Pyrenees into the Iberian peninsula in the 7th or 6th century BC. Typical elements of Celtic culture, such as the Hallstatt art style and hillforts, were introduced into Iberia as a result, along with the Celtic language. The Celts here assimilated with the native Iberians, producing a distinctive Celtiberian culture but one which was still recognizably Celtic to outside observers.

The main period of Celtic migrations began soon after the start of the La Tène period. Increasing numbers of weapons in graves suggest that La Tène society was more militarized than Hallstatt society, hence there was a greater propensity to migrate. The earliest migration of La Tène Celts was over the Alps into Italy, where they quickly overran the Po valley, weakening the Etruscans and leaving them vulnerable to Roman expansionism. In 390 BC the Celts sacked Rome, at that time still a minor power, and some groups even found their way to southern Italy, where they signed on as mercenaries with local Greek rulers.

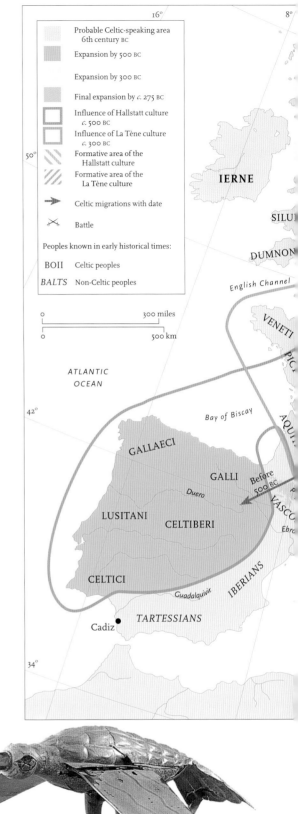

Silver plaque showing a Thracian cavalryman from Letnica, Bulgaria, 400–350 BC. The Thracians were overrun by migrating Celts in the 3rd century BC.

(Above) A wooden shield of typical Celtic shape, preserved by the dry desert atmosphere of the Fayum oasis in Egypt, where a group of Celtic mercenaries settled in the 3rd century BC.

Eagle-crowned iron helmet from a chieftain's tomb at Ciumeşti, 3rd century BC. The wings were hinged and would flap ominously and impressively when the wearer was running.

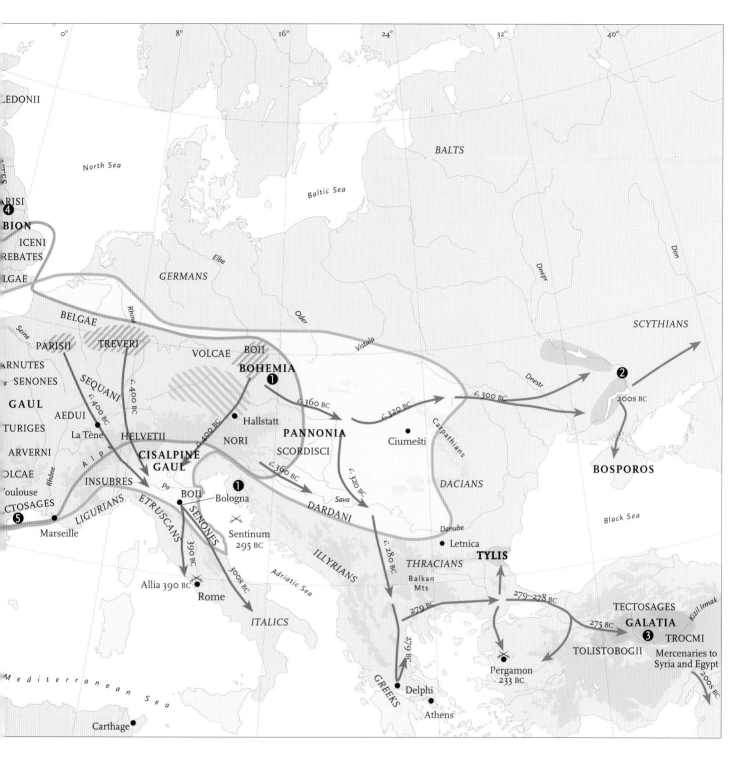

Population movements eastwards began perhaps as early as 400 BC and continued into the 3rd century BC when Celts penetrated the Carpathians. Around 300 BC groups of Celts settled on the Dnepr. A single inscription refers to an attack by Celts and Scythians on the kingdom of Bosporos and a scattering of La Tène objects across the southern steppes indicates that some Celts reached as far east as the River Don. The best-documented Celtic migration was the unsuccessful incursion into Greece in 279 BC. The survivors founded a robber kingdom at Tylis on the Black Sea; others crossed the Black Sea and settled in Anatolia, still others became mercenaries in Syria and Egypt, so bringing the Celtic world to its greatest expansion. A few years earlier, the Romans had won their first major victory over the Celts at Sentinum: over the next 300 years most of the Celtic world would be conquered by them.

MAP NOTES

❶ *Bohemia and Bologna are named after the Boii.*

❷ *Evidence for Celtic settlement on the Dnepr comes from burials and stray La Tène objects.*

❸ *Galatia kept its Celtic identity until the 4th century AD.*

❹ *Though there were probably no major migrations to Britain, tribal names such as the Parisi and Belgae indicate that there was some exchange of population with the continent.*

❺ *A branch of the Tectosages may have joined the Celtic invasion of Greece before settling in Anatolia. Loot from the invasion is said to have been sent to the tribal sanctuary at Toulouse.*

The Celtic Invasion of Greece

Despite the terror it caused, the Celtic invasion of Greece was a costly failure. The Greeks united against the Celts, or 'Galatoi' as they called them, and expelled them within a few months with heavy losses: the survivors moved on to settle in Thrace and Anatolia.

THE INVASION OF GREECE was part of the final pulse of the Celtic migrations. In the course of the 4th century, Celtic peoples had settled the middle Danube basin and by 300 BC a loose confederation of Celtic tribes had moved into the Balkans and attacked the Illyrians, Paionians and Triballi. At first, relations with the Greek world were friendly. Celtic embassies were sent to Alexander the Great, including one which attended his court at Babylon in 323 BC. No doubt emboldened by the political chaos which engulfed the Greek world after Alexander's death, the Celts began raiding Thrace and Macedonia in 298 BC. The raids were contained until Bolgios defeated and killed the Macedonian king Ptolemy Ceraunos in 281 BC.

This success encouraged the Celts to launch a massive plundering raid deep into Greece in 279 BC under Brennus (probably a legendary name) and Achichorios. However, even before it entered Greece, the force had split up as a result of internal dissent, with a large force under Leonorios and Lutorios heading into Thrace and, eventually, Anatolia. The Celts met little real opposition until they reached Thermopylae: the locals simply retreated into their walled towns, which the Celts were unable to take. As the Persians had done 200 years earlier, the Celts by-passed the Greek army at Thermopylae and advanced through the mountains intent on capturing the wealthy sacred city of Delphi. Exactly what happened next is uncertain, as the sources are contradictory. According to Greek writers, divine intervention in the form of unseasonable snow storms and rock falls saved Delphi from attack. An alternative tradition records that the Celts did in fact plunder Delphi and some of the treasure was

Alexander the Great. Before he embarked on his epic conquest of the Persian empire, Alexander secured his northern frontiers with a campaign against the Celts.

MAP NOTES

❶ *Rich burial with a Celtic war chariot: a Celtic chief's or a Thracian nobleman's who had been given, or had captured, a Celtic chariot?*

❷ *According to Greek sources, the Celt's sacking of Callium was accompanied by horrific atrocities, including mass rape.*

❸ *The temple of Athena at Larissa was hung with the shields of defeated Celtic warriors.*

❹ *Byzantium regularly paid protection money to the Celts of the kingdom of Tylis in the 3rd century.*

The Sacred Way, Delphi. The treasuries of the Greek city states, housed in the sacred city for safe keeping, were the target for the Celtic invasion of Greece.

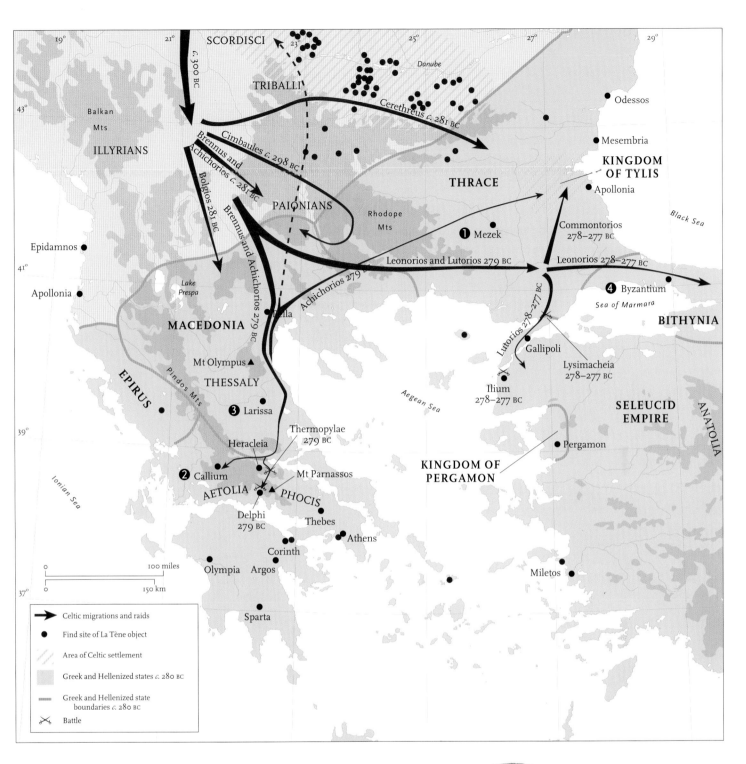

Map labels

19°   21°   SCORDISCI   c. 300 BC   23°   25°   Danube   27°   29°

TRIBALLI

Balkan Mts

43°

Cerethreus c. 281 BC

Odessos

ILLYRIANS

Cimbaules c. 298 BC

Brennus and Achichorios c. 281 BC

Mesembria

KINGDOM OF TYLIS

THRACE

Apollonia

Bolgios 281 BC

PAIONIANS

Rhodope Mts

41°

Epidamnos

Brennus and Achichorios 279 BC

Lake Prespa

Pella

MACEDONIA

Achichorios 279 BC

❶ Mezek

Commontorios 278–277 BC

Black Sea

Leonorios and Lutorios 279 BC

Leonorios 278–277 BC

❹ Byzantium

Sea of Marmara

BITHYNIA

Apollonia

Lutorios 278–277 BC

Gallipoli

Lysimacheia 278–277 BC

Mt Olympus ▲

THESSALY

EPIRUS

Pindos Mts

39°

❸ Larissa

Ilium 278–277 BC

Aegean Sea

SELEUCID EMPIRE

ANATOLIA

Heracleia

Thermopylae 279 BC

Ionian Sea

❷ Callium

AETOLIA

Mt Parnassos

PHOCIS

KINGDOM OF PERGAMON

Pergamon

Delphi 279 BC

Thebes

Athens

Corinth

Olympia   Argos

Miletos

37°

Sparta

Legend

→ Celtic migrations and raids

● Find site of La Tène object

▨ Area of Celtic settlement

▨ Greek and Hellenized states c. 280 BC

━ Greek and Hellenized state boundaries c. 280 BC

✕ Battle

0   100 miles

0   150 km

---

sent to Gaul, where it later fell into Roman hands. Whatever the truth, it is certain that Delphi suffered no serious damage. Harassed continually by the Greeks, the Celts began a disorderly retreat: Brennus himself died of wounds received in a skirmish.

Some of the survivors of the raid remained in Greece, signing on as mercenaries for King Antigonus of Macedonia; others returned to the Danube and joined the Scordisci; still others moved into Thrace and founded the kingdom of Tylis. The Celts of Tylis terrorized the Greek coastal cities for years until, finally, they were conquered by the Thracians in 213–212 BC. The whole dramatic episode of the Celtic incursion into Greece and the Balkans has left almost no trace in the archaeological record and would be unknown were it not for literary sources.

Bronze coin of the Bosporan king Leucon II showing a typical Celtic-style shield, evidence perhaps for the defeat of an otherwise unrecorded 3rd-century Celtic invasion of the Crimea?

Galatia: The Celts in Anatolia

278 BC – AD 400

The most far-flung of all Celtic settlements was on the high, dry, plateau of central Anatolia. Anatolia was not invaded by the Celts; they were invited in by Hellenistic rulers to serve as mercenaries. Once they had arrived, however, the Celts proved difficult to control.

THE CELTS, ABOUT 20,000 IN ALL, came to Anatolia at the invitation of King Nicomedes of Bithynia who wanted them to fight in his war with the Seleucid (Syrian) King Antiochus I, who controlled most of Anatolia. The Celts who crossed to Anatolia were made up of three peoples, the Tolistobogii, the Tectosages and the Trocmi. They were led by Leonorios and Lutorios, who had separated from the main Celtic force in Greece the previous year. Antiochus defeated the Celts in 275 BC but they subsequently allied with Mithridates I of Pontus who settled them in Phrygia. Phrygia was not Mithridates' to give, it belonged to Seleucia, but the Celts could not be dislodged, and for many years they raided the rich cities of the Mediterranean coast lands. Their practice of sacrificing prisoners gained them an unenviable reputation for atrocity. The area settled by the Celts came to be known as Galatia, after Galatoi, the Greek name for them. The Galatians were somewhat tamed after Attalus of Pergamon defeated them in 240 BC but occasional raids continued. After another defeat in 189 BC, this time by the Romans, the Galatians turned their attentions east to Pontus and Cappadocia. Relations between the Galatians and the Romans gradually became closer: Galatia was permitted to expand and in 64 BC became a client kingdom until it was annexed peacefully by Rome in 25 BC.

The Galatians had a loose tribal organization, with each tribe divided into four clans. The tribes sent 'senators' to an annual assembly which met at an unidentified location called *Drunemeton*. This name is associated with Druidism in Britain and Gaul but there is no other evidence of Celtic

Under the wealthy Attalid dynasty (282–133 BC) Pergamon (right) became a major power in Anatolia, but it was only with difficulty that it contained the threat of the Galatians. Pergamon had several monuments commemorating victories over the Galatians, including this marble plaque (above) picturing captured Celtic weapons.

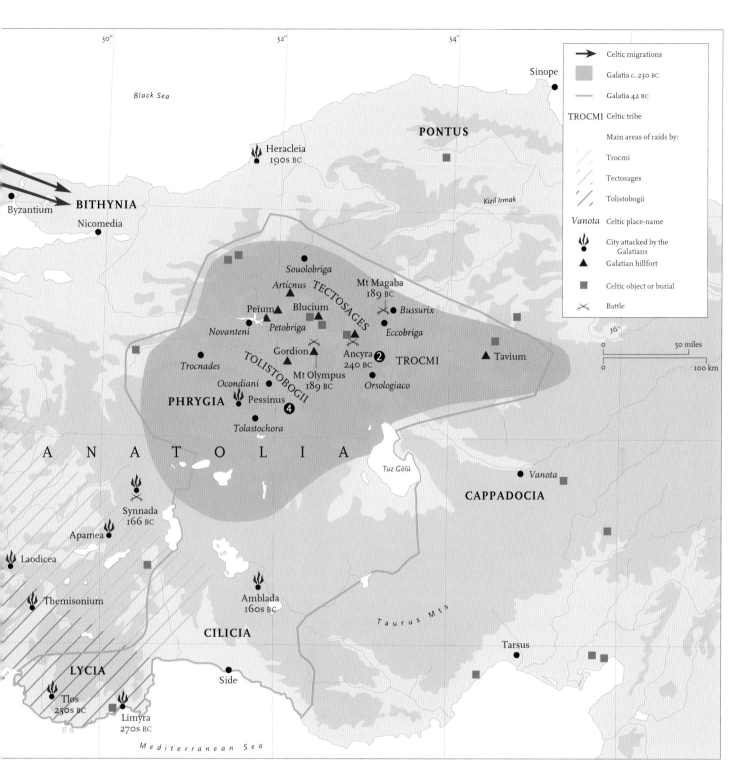

Black Sea

30° 32° 34°

Sinope

PONTUS

Heracleia
190s BC

Kizil Irmak

BITHYNIA

Byzantium

Nicomedia

Souolobriga

Articnus

TECTOSAGES

Mt Magaba
189 BC

Peïum Blucium

Bussurix

Novanteni Petobriga

Eccobriga

Gordion

Ancyra ❷
240 BC

TROCMI

Tavium

TOLISTOBOGII

Trocnades

Mt Olympus
189 BC

Ocondiani

Orsologiaco

PHRYGIA

Pessinus ❹

Tolastochora

A N A T O L I A

Tuz Gölü

Vanota

CAPPADOCIA

36°

0   50 miles

0   100 km

Synnada
166 BC

Apamea

Laodicea

Amblada
160s BC

Themisonium

Taurus Mts

Tarsus

CILICIA

LYCIA

Side

Tlos
250s BC

Limyra
270s BC

Mediterranean Sea

Legend

→ Celtic migrations

Galatia c. 230 BC

Galatia 42 BC

TROCMI Celtic tribe

Main areas of raids by:

Trocmi

Tectosages

Tolistobogii

Vanota Celtic place-name

City attacked by the Galatians

▲ Galatian hillfort

■ Celtic object or burial

✕ Battle

religious practices. After Mithridates VI of Pontus treacherously massacred their aristocracy in 88 BC, the Galatians adopted monarchical government.

There is very little archaeological evidence of the Celtic presence in Anatolia. This may be because it has not yet been looked for systematically but, alternatively, it may be a sign that the Galatians very quickly adopted the material culture of the native peoples, among whom they were certainly a minority. However, the Galatians long preserved the most important aspect of their Celtic identity, their language. Even as late as the 4th century AD, St Jerome would remark that the Galatians spoke the same language as the Gauls. How long after that they continued to do so is unknown but the name Galatia fell out of use in the 8th century.

MAP NOTES

❶ *Each Galatian tribe had its own agreed area of western Anatolia for plundering raids.*

❷ *The Galatians did not become urbanized but they built hillforts. Ancyra, modern Ankara, the capital of Turkey, originated as a Celtic hillfort.*

❸ *The Aigosages were recruited as mercenaries by the Bithynians: they were wiped out near Abydos after they turned against their employers.*

❹ *The native shrine of the Great Mother at Pessinus became an important religious centre for the Galatians.*

The Celts in Italy

Around 400 BC Celtic tribes, known to Roman writers as Gauls, crossed the Alpine passes and descended on the Etruscan cities of the Po Valley and Tuscany. Rome became involved in 390 (or possibly 387) BC when it sent ambassadors to the Etruscan city of Clusium (Chiusi) to mediate between it and a Gaulish tribe, the Senones. After the ambassadors broke the rules of diplomacy by fighting on the side of the Etruscans, the Celts launched a devastating retaliatory raid on Rome, withdrawing only after they had been paid a huge ransom.

THE GAULS SETTLED IN large numbers in the Po Valley, which became known after them as Cisalpine Gaul (Gaul this side of the Alps), and along the northern Adriatic coast. Some groups of Gauls travelled as far south as Apulia where they served as mercenaries for Greek rulers such as Dionysius of Syracuse (405–367 BC). In the north, tribes such as the Cenomani preserved an essentially La Tène material culture. The culture of more southerly tribes like the Boii and Senones was influenced by their Etruscan neighbours. Burial practices, for example, reflected both La Tène and Etruscan customs. Unlike Celts elsewhere in Europe at the time, many Cisalpine Gauls lived in towns. Northern Italy was already urbanized when the Gauls invaded and Etruscan cities such as Felsina (Bologna) became major centres of Gaulish population.

These invaders were not the first Celtic-speakers to live in Italy. Inscriptions dating back to the 6th century BC show that a distinctive form of Celtic, known as Lepontic, was already spoken in northwestern Italy at the time of the invasions. The Lepontic area coincides roughly with that of the Golasecca culture which originated *c*. 1000 BC. The Golaseccans may have been Celtic-speaking from the beginning or may have been gradually Celticized as a result of their close trade contacts with Celtic areas north of the Alps. The

(Above right) A cavalryman confronts a naked Celtic warrior on this Etruscan grave stela from Bologna, Italy. Despite Etruscan resistance, Bologna became a major Celtic settlement.

(Right) A bilingual Celtic-Latin inscription from Todi, Italy (2nd century BC). Evidence of literacy among Celtic-speaking peoples in Italy is found as early as the 6th century BC. (Below) Terrified Celtic raiders drop the spoils of a looted temple as they flee. Terracotta relief, Civitalba, Italy (2nd century BC).

Golaseccan culture is today tentatively associated with the Insubres, one of the main Celtic peoples of the Po Valley in Roman times.

Rome soon recovered from its sacking by the Gauls, though the Etruscan civilization never did so fully. Nevertheless, the Romans had learned to fear the Gauls and never felt secure until the last of them had been brought under their rule. The Senones were the first of the Gauls to be conquered by Rome, in 283 BC. After destroying a major Celtic army at the battle of Telamon in 225 BC, the Romans began to extend their control over the Po Valley. The Gauls supported Hannibal's Carthaginian army when he invaded Italy in 218 BC but to no avail: Celtic resistance to Roman rule was effectively ended by 191 BC. The Romans methodically consolidated their conquests by planting colonies of Roman citizens and reliable Italian allies among the defeated Gauls. The Romanization of Cisalpine Gaul proceeded rapidly and by 49 BC the whole area had been granted Roman citizenship.

MAP NOTES

❶ *The defeat of the Senones and their Etruscan, Umbrian and Sabine allies at Sentinum was followed by the Roman conquest of the Ager Gallicus.*

❷ *The Roman victory over the Boii and Insubres at Telamon broke Celtic power in Italy.*

❸ *The first Celtic-speakers in Italy were the people of the Golasecca culture: the Insubres were probably their descendants.*

❹ *Etruscan art was a formative influence on La Tène art, but Celtic raids sent the civilization into decline.*

❺ *Many tribal names of the Cisalpine Gauls, such as the Boii, Lingones, Senones and Cenomani, have equivalents north of the Alps, possibly indicating their origin.*

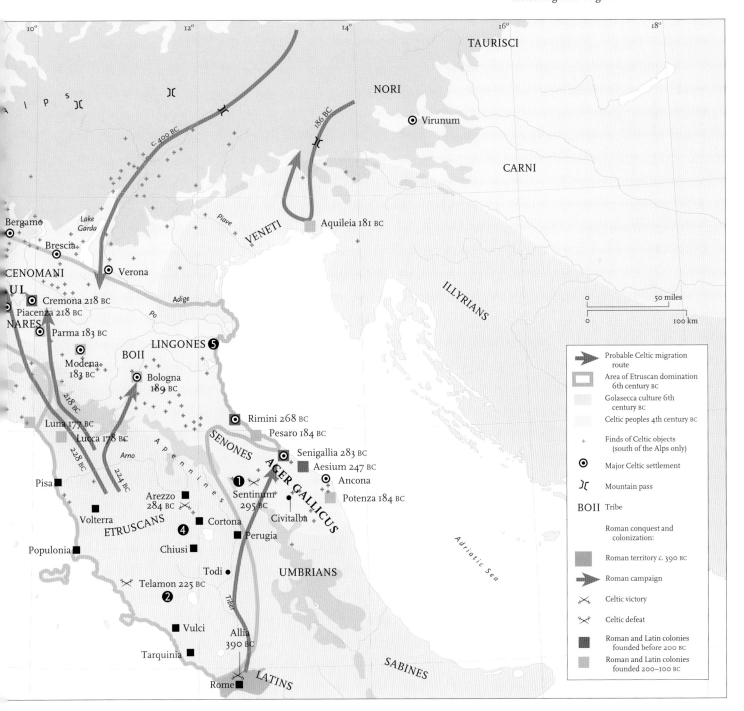

The Celtiberians

600 – 19 BC

Celtic-speaking peoples migrated into the Iberian peninsula in the course of the 7th or 6th century BC. Here they assimilated with the indigenous peoples to produce a culture which was linguistically Celtic but which in its material culture differed considerably from the Hallstatt and La Tène cultures north of the Pyrenees.

ACCORDING TO HERODOTUS, Celtic-speaking peoples were already established in the Iberian peninsula by 500 BC. These peoples called themselves Celtiberes and Celtici, Galli and Gallaeci. Linguistic evidence from the distribution of typical Celtic place-name elements, such as *-briga* ('fortified hill') and *Seg-* ('victory') and family names from inscriptions, such as Celtius, indicate that Celtic influence extended across most of central and western Iberia but not to the Mediterranean coast.

The Celtiberians built strongly fortified hilltop settlements – *castros* – the major concentration being in the upper Douro Valley. Most fell out of use *c.* 400 BC, but those that survived became increasingly urban in character as a result of contacts with the Iberians. By the time it was captured by the Romans in 133 BC, Numantia had a planned street pattern. The distribution of circular houses has often been taken as evidence of Celtic influence but, while the Celts built circular houses in some areas (e.g. Britain) in others, such as Gaul, they built rectangular houses, so nothing certain can be concluded from this.

The influence of the Hallstatt and La Tène cultures extended south of the Pyrenees but their practices were not slavishly adopted by the Celtiberians. La Tène-style brooches, e.g. horsemen fibulae, were popular but had Iberian rather than Celtic-style fastenings. Similarly torcs, although a typical La Tène object, were decorated in distinctive Celtiberian styles. Cremation burials were normal rather than the inhumations of La Tène culture.

MAP NOTES

❶ *Unable to defeat him in the field, the Romans ended Viriathus' Lusitanian revolt by bribing his retainers to murder him in 139 BC.*

❷ *Iberian dress, weapons and sculptures show Celtic influence. At Ullastret and elsewhere there is evidence of the adoption of the Celtic cult of the severed head.*

❸ *In 133 BC the Romans surrounded Numantia with 60,000 troops, 7 siege camps and 10 km (6.25 miles) of ramparts.*

❹ *The Meseta was the most Celticized part of Iberia: many aspects of Celtic material culture and social structure were not adopted further west.*

❺ *Celtiberians fought for both Carthage and Rome at Ilipa: after the Roman victory they resumed their independence.*

(Above) A Celtiberian warrior on a stone relief from Osuna, Andalucia. He is carrying a typical La Tène shield, but also has a falcata, a distinctive single-bladed thrusting sword adopted from the Iberians.

The advanced urban character of the Celtiberian castro of Numantia is evident in this aerial view showing its dense housing and orderly street plan. Castros fulfilled the same functions in Iberia as Celtic oppida did in western and central Europe.

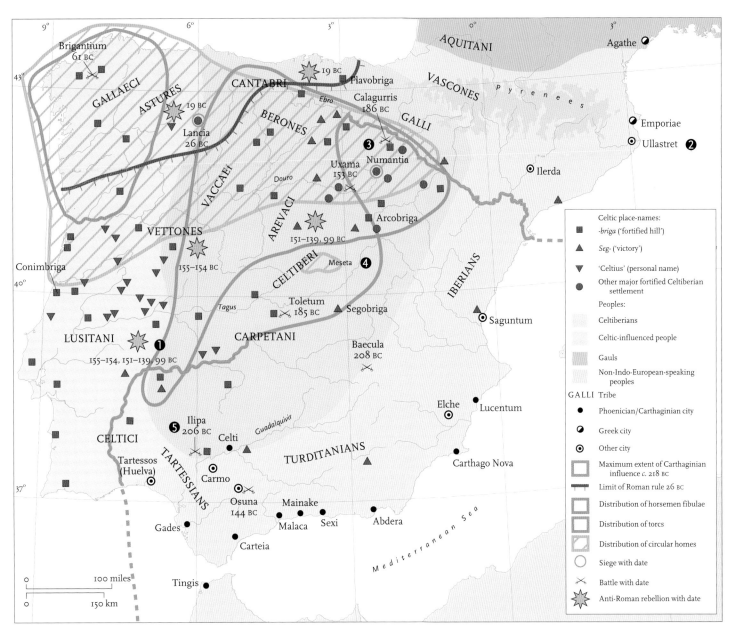

A pottery model of a wolf's head, shaped like the mouth of a carynx, the Celtic war horn, from Numantia (2nd–1st century BC). Such horns were widely used by the Celts in battle.

Though they adopted a version of the Iberian alphabet for use on memorials, the Celtiberians remained relatively isolated from the Mediterranean world until 237 BC, when Carthage began to build a territorial empire in Spain. The region south of the River Guadalquivir was brought under direct Carthaginian rule, but elsewhere in the peninsula Carthaginian influence was maintained through a series of alliances with Celtiberian chiefs. Large numbers of Celtiberians were recruited into Carthaginian armies in the Second Punic War (219–201 BC) with Rome. After Carthage's defeat, the Celtiberians resumed full independence while the entire Mediterranean coast came under Roman rule. Over the next 200 years, the Romans gradually extended their rule over the Celtiberians. The crucial years were between 151 and 133 BC, during which the Romans defeated a 12-year rebellion by the Lusitanians under Viriathus and captured the key Celtiberian stronghold of Numantia after an 11-year-long siege, but it was not until 19 BC that the last resistance to their rule, by the Gallaeci and Astures, was crushed. Under Roman rule Iberia became peaceful: Celtic speech survived into the 1st century AD but had died out by the end of Roman rule in the 5th century.

Hillforts and Oppida

The most visible monuments of the ancient Celts are their hillforts – tribal refuges and chieftains' residences – which are still prominent features of the European landscape. As the Celts advanced towards statehood in the late Iron Age, many hillforts were abandoned in favour of proto-urban tribal centres on lower ground called *oppida*.

THE FIRST HILLFORTS were built in the Bronze Age but their heyday was in the Iron Age, particularly the period from the 7th through to the 1st centuries BC. The distribution of hillforts across Celtic Europe is not even and is not related to the availability of suitable hills. Some areas with plenty of suitable sites, such as northern England, in fact have very low numbers of forts. In other areas, such as the Rhône Valley in the 2nd century BC, most of the population appears to have lived in small hillforts. Some hillforts seem never to have been permanently inhabited and may have served mainly as tribal refuges in times of war. Still others were high-status sites, either the strongholds of chieftains or religious sanctuaries. Studies of the Iron Age landscape of Hampshire in southern England have shown how the hillfort of Danebury lay at the centre of a system of fields and outlying dependent villages.

In their simplest form, hillforts could consist of nothing more than a ditch backed by an earth rampart and wooden palisade surrounding a suitable hill top. Over time defences became more sophisticated as extra circuits of ditches and ramparts were added and more complex gateways were designed. More sophisticated construction techniques were also introduced,

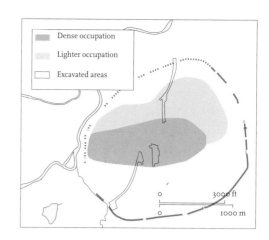

Dense occupation

Lighter occupation

Excavated areas

3000 ft

1000 m

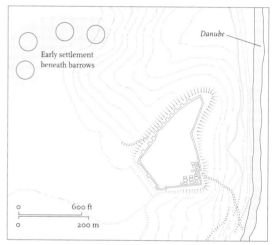

Danube

Early settlement beneath barrows

600 ft

200 m

(Top right) The oppidum of Manching, near Ingolstadt in Bavaria (3rd–1st century BC), covered an area of 380 ha (940 acres), surrounded by a timber-laced rampart 7 km (4.3 miles) long. The centre was densely occupied with houses laid out in an orderly manner, but there was also room within the ramparts for pasturing animals.

(Centre) The hillfort of Heuneburg, Baden-Württemberg, Germany. In the late 6th century BC the fort was given a circuit of Greek-style mud-brick walls with bastion towers, possibly indicating the presence of a Greek architect: they were soon rebuilt in materials more suited to the northern climate.

(Right) Runderberg near Urach, Baden-Württemberg, Germany: a well-positioned Iron Age hillfort which takes full advantage of natural defences.

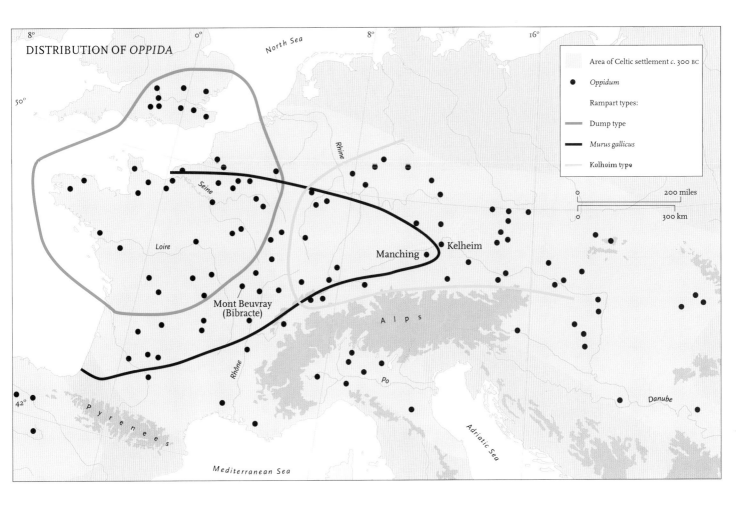

Area of Celtic settlement *c.* 300 BC
● *Oppidum*
Rampart types:
—— Dump type
—— *Murus gallicus*
—— Kelheim type

North Sea

Rhine

Seine

Loire

Kelheim

Manching

Mont Beuvray
(Bibracte)

Alps

Rhône

Po

Danube

Adriatic Sea

Pyrenees

Mediterranean Sea

including many different methods of timber-lacing. These techniques enabled vertical walls to be built of earth or stone rubble. Though they were resistant to being undermined or battered, and harder to scale than sloping earth ramparts, timber-laced ramparts could be set on fire. Several forts are known in Scotland where burning vitrified the surrounding stonework.

By the 1st century BC, hillforts had been abandoned in much of Celtic Europe in favour of more convenient and less restrictive sites on lower ground called *oppida*. The sites of *oppida* were often chosen with defence in mind – Kelheim in Germany, for instance, was built at the confluence of two rivers, giving it natural defences on two sides – and they were often strongly fortified. But *oppida* were larger and more complex settlements than hillforts, with well-planned street layouts. *Oppida* were centres for trade, industry and tribal government. Coins, often inscribed with the name of the tribe, were minted in many *oppida* and used as an everyday medium of exchange. Thus some *oppida* were fully developed towns, a sign of the social and economic sophistication achieved by the Celts on the eve of the Roman conquest.

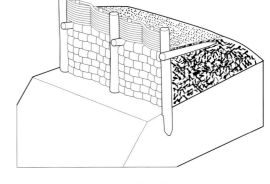

(Above) An example of a Kelheim-type rampart. An earth rampart was revetted with a timber frame and faced with stone. The horizontal timbers were used to anchor the wall into the rampart behind and stop it collapsing outwards under the weight of the earth.

Reconstruction of the walls of the oppidum of Bibracte (Mont Beuvray, France). An example of a murus gallicus (Gaulish wall), built of earth, stone rubble, masonry and thousands of wooden beams nailed together into a strong framework which was highly resistant to attack with a battering ram.

Villages and Farms

Most Celts lived not in hillforts or *oppida* but in dispersed farms or small villages of a few households, close to the fields and pastures where they worked. House-building traditions varied according to local customs and available materials.

CELTIC HOUSES CONFORMED to two main types: in most of continental Europe they had a roughly rectangular ground plan, in Britain, Ireland and parts of Spain they were circular. In most of Celtic Europe, timber was the normal building material. Though in some cases timber buildings were built on stone foundations to protect them from damp, usually timbers were set directly in the ground. All traces of the above-ground structures of wooden Celtic houses have long since decayed, but archaeologists can recover their ground plans by plotting the post-holes left in the ground by the main structural timbers. By the Iron Age, Europe had already experienced considerable deforestation for agriculture, so timber was used economically. Most buildings, whether round or rectangular, had timber frames, while non-load-bearing parts of the wall were simply filled in with wattle-and-daub (a lattice of thin branches sealed with mud). Roofs were thickly thatched. In Spain, Brittany and upland areas of the British Isles and elsewhere unmortared stone was used for walls. In Italy the Celts seem to have abandoned their own building traditions and adopted those of the native peoples.

The interiors of Celtic houses were dark, but they were warm and weatherproof. Smoke holes in the roofs would have created draughts and let rain in, so smoke from the fire was left to escape through the thatch and under the eaves. Being dry, deficient in oxygen and insect free, the smoky areas under the roof were ideal for hanging and preserving

Bronze figurine from Trier, Germany, of a Gallic peasant in a short hooded cloak. The position of his hands suggests he is a ploughman.

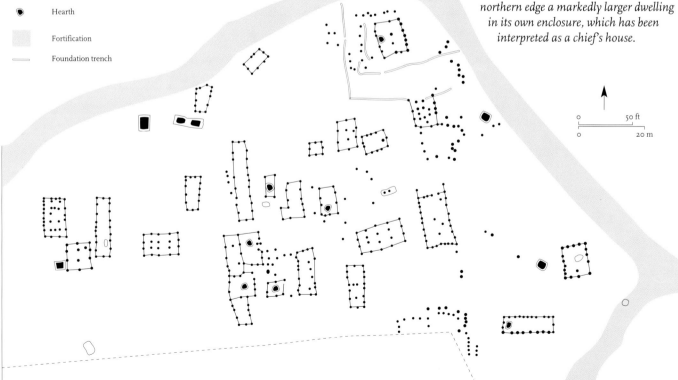

Plan of the Goldberg, near Stuttgart, Germany, a defended settlement of the late 6th–5th centuries BC. The settlement consists of a number of similar-sized family dwellings, each with its own range of byres and stores, and at the northern edge a markedly larger dwelling in its own enclosure, which has been interpreted as a chief's house.

- •   Post-hole
- ◉   Hearth
- ▪   Fortification
- —   Foundation trench

50 ft
20 m

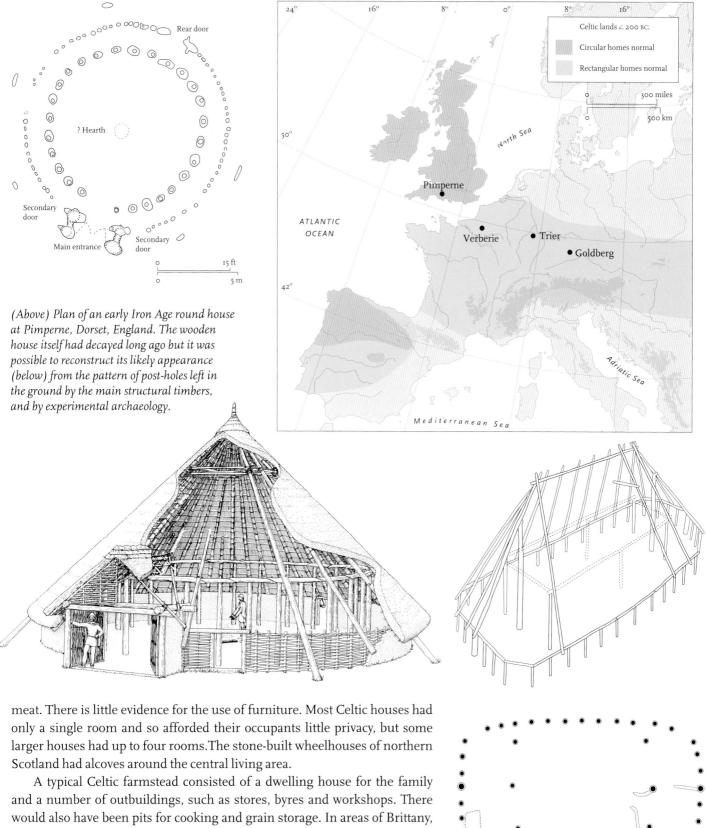

(Above) Plan of an early Iron Age round house at Pimperne, Dorset, England. The wooden house itself had decayed long ago but it was possible to reconstruct its likely appearance (below) from the pattern of post-holes left in the ground by the main structural timbers, and by experimental archaeology.

Rear door

? Hearth

Secondary door

Main entrance

Secondary door

15 ft

5 m

Celtic lands c. 200 BC:

Circular homes normal

Rectangular homes normal

300 miles

500 km

North Sea

ATLANTIC OCEAN

Pimperne

Verberie

Trier

Goldberg

Adriatic Sea

Mediterranean Sea

meat. There is little evidence for the use of furniture. Most Celtic houses had only a single room and so afforded their occupants little privacy, but some larger houses had up to four rooms. The stone-built wheelhouses of northern Scotland had alcoves around the central living area.

A typical Celtic farmstead consisted of a dwelling house for the family and a number of outbuildings, such as stores, byres and workshops. There would also have been pits for cooking and grain storage. In areas of Brittany, Ireland and Scotland, underground storage chambers called souterrains are found, which were probably used for keeping dairy products cool. Farmyards were often surrounded by a bank and ditch, not so much for defence as to keep livestock in or out. Villages were simply a group of farmsteads. Some have produced evidence of hierarchical social structures, such as the presence of large 'manor houses' and planned layouts, as well as communal buildings.

15 ft

5 m

Plan (above) and reconstruction (top) of a house with load bearing walls from Verberie, Oise, France.

Trade Routes of Celtic Europe

Trade and exchange in Celtic Europe were not motivated primarily by economic considerations, such as the need to acquire essential raw materials. Instead, they served a social function, providing social elites with the exotic luxury goods they needed to display their status, power and influence.

FOR MOST OF THE IRON AGE, the economy of Celtic Europe was based on subsistence farming. Most peasant families were self-sufficient in the production of the majority of their everyday necessities, such as food, clothing and pottery. It was, therefore, the needs of the social elites – who controlled the surplus production of the common people – which was the main stimulus to trade and exchange. The display of material wealth, such as jewelry, fine weapons and armour, and the conspicuous consumption of luxuries were essential ways for the Celtic elite to demonstrate and underpin their superior social status. Thus they needed to obtain both raw materials for native craftsmen to work in and exotic finished goods. The most important of exotic imports was wine from the Mediterranean lands. Wine-drinking conferred such prestige that the Celtic elite were also keen to acquire the tableware associated with wine-drinking in the Mediterranean, such as Etruscan bronze wine jugs and Greek pottery drinking cups, so that they would be clearly seen to be drinking wine. The Celtic elite of Germany, Gaul and southern Britain had, through imports such as these, begun to adopt a Romanized way of life even before the Roman conquest.

The main centres for trade and exchange were the hillforts of chieftains and, later, the tribal *oppida*. The presence of the social elite made them centres of demand, drawing in imports from a wide area. Thus the fortunes of trade routes were intimately linked to the centres that gave rise to them. In the early Iron Age the main centres of demand were the western Hallstatt chiefdoms, which had flourishing connections with Marseille via the River Rhône. With the decline of these chiefdoms *c.* 500 BC and the rise of the La Tène chiefdoms to the north and east, there was a shift in trade to the trans-Alpine routes to and from Italy. Long-distance trade was usually conducted through several intermediaries. For instance, in the 1st century BC Italian wine imported into Britain had passed through the hands of several Roman and Celtic merchants by the time it arrived there.

The intensification of contacts with the Mediterranean world in the late Iron Age led to the widespread adoption of coinage as a means of exchange and a move towards a market economy. The Roman conquest disrupted traditional trade routes: for example the main trade route to Britain shifted from the Atlantic to the southern North Sea, but there was a general increase in prosperity in the Celtic lands under Roman rule.

Barrels, more durable and capacious than the pottery amphorae used to transport liquids in the Mediterranean world, were a Celtic invention, first used in central Europe. This example from Roman times was found in the Rhineland.

Gold model of a boat from Broighter in Northern Ireland, 1st century BC. The Celts were the first peoples of northern Europe to use sailing ships, though this ship also has seven pairs of oars.

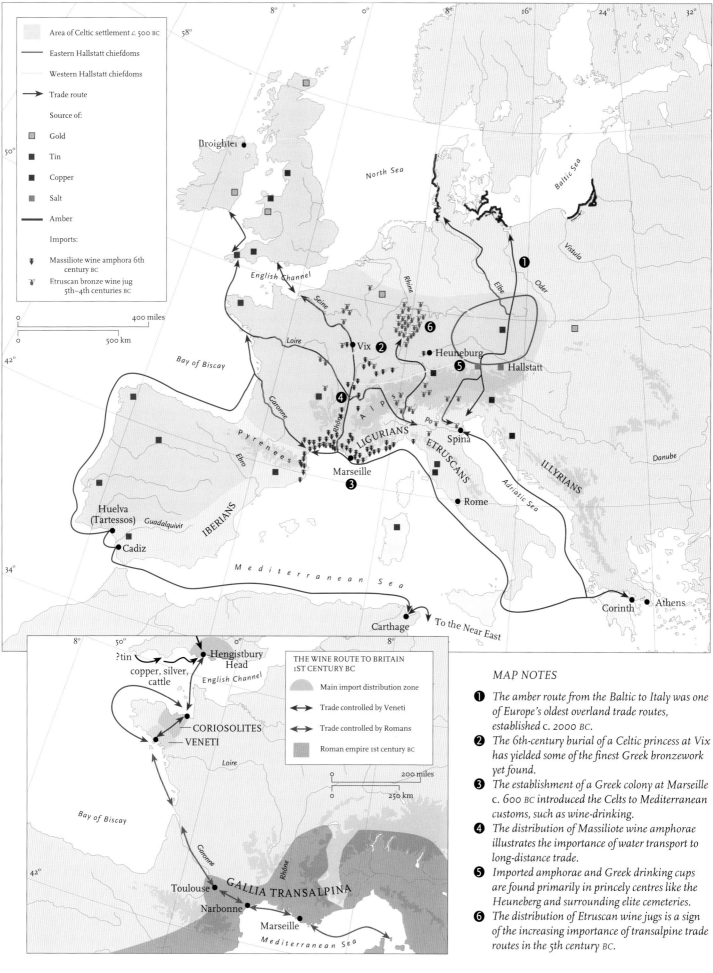

Legend

Area of Celtic settlement c. 500 BC

Eastern Hallstatt chiefdoms

Western Hallstatt chiefdoms

→ Trade route

Source of:
- ☐ Gold
- ■ Tin
- ■ Copper
- ☐ Salt

━━ Amber

Imports:
- ▼ Massiliote wine amphora 6th century BC
- ▽ Etruscan bronze wine jug 5th–4th centuries BC

400 miles

500 km

Main map labels

North Sea
Baltic Sea
Vistula
Droighter
English Channel
Bay of Biscay
Seine
Loire
Rhine
Elbe
Oder
Vix ❷
Heuneburg
❺ Hallstatt
❻
Garonne
Rhône
A l p s
LIGURIANS
Po
Spina
ETRUSCANS
ILLYRIANS
Danube
Adriatic Sea
Ebro
Pyrenees
Marseille ❸
❹
Guadalquivir
Huelva (Tartessos)
Cadiz
IBERIANS
Rome
Mediterranean Sea
Carthage
To the Near East
Corinth
Athens

Inset map: The Wine Route to Britain

THE WINE ROUTE TO BRITAIN
1ST CENTURY BC

Main import distribution zone

↔ Trade controlled by Veneti

↔ Trade controlled by Romans

Roman empire 1st century BC

200 miles

250 km

?tin
copper, silver, cattle
Hengistbury Head
English Channel
CORIOSOLITES
VENETI
Loire
Bay of Biscay
Garonne
Rhône
GALLIA TRANSALPINA
Toulouse
Narbonne
Marseille
Mediterranean Sea

MAP NOTES

❶ The amber route from the Baltic to Italy was one of Europe's oldest overland trade routes, established c. 2000 BC.

❷ The 6th-century burial of a Celtic princess at Vix has yielded some of the finest Greek bronzework yet found.

❸ The establishment of a Greek colony at Marseille c. 600 BC introduced the Celts to Mediterranean customs, such as wine-drinking.

❹ The distribution of Massiliote wine amphorae illustrates the importance of water transport to long-distance trade.

❺ Imported amphorae and Greek drinking cups are found primarily in princely centres like the Heuneberg and surrounding elite cemeteries.

❻ The distribution of Etruscan wine jugs is a sign of the increasing importance of transalpine trade routes in the 5th century BC.

At the time of Caesar's conquest, the Romans considered Gaul to be divided into two broad regions. In the south was the Romanized, and therefore civilized, Provincia Romana; to its north was what the Romans dismissively called Gallia Comata, barbaric 'long-haired Gaul'. In reality Gallia Comata had a prosperous farming economy and chiefdoms were beginning to give way to tribal states. The emergence of a fully developed Gallic urban civilization was prevented only by the Roman conquest.

CELTIC-SPEAKING PEOPLES were established in Gaul in very early times, but it was only with the foundation of cities such as Massalia (Marseille; Roman Massilia) by Greek colonists c. 600 BC that they were drawn into close contact with the Mediterranean civilizations. Massalia traded up the Rhône with the Hallstatt chiefdoms of central Gaul, exchanging Greek luxuries such as wine and drinking vessels for slaves and British tin. The Greeks exerted a strong influence over the Celtic and Celto-Ligurian tribes of the Mediterranean coast. The farming economy of southern Gaul became typically Mediterranean, as native peoples adopted Greek crops such as vines and olives so that they could become self-sufficient in wine and oil. In the 2nd century BC the Saluvian *oppidum* of Entremont developed into a Greek-style planned town with masonry defences modelled on those of the Greek coastal cities. Planned villages became common. The Saluvii and others also adopted the art of stone sculpture and the Greek and, later, Latin, alphabets. This area was conquered by the Romans in the 2nd century BC and became known simply as 'The Province' (*provincia*), from which the region's modern name Provence is derived.

Contacts with the Mediterranean world played little part in the emergence of states in inland Gaul, however. Here state formation was the result of an increasing population and prosperous agriculture stimulating local trade and the growth of *oppida*. Except in Brittany, where dispersed settlement remained normal, the countryside became thickly dotted with hamlets and villages and the population density was comparable with modern-day rural France. The process of state formation was most advanced in the area south of the Loire. By the 1st century BC, major tribal *oppida* in this region, such as Bibracte and Alesia, had become centres for tax gathering, craft production and long-distance trade. The Gaulish states developed political institutions, such as elected magistracies, which paralleled, and were to some extent modelled on, those of the Roman Republic. As in Rome, competition for power frequently caused political instability. The administration of these states was sophisticated enough to collect taxes, manage collective food stores, issue coinage and even conduct population censuses. These were not territorial states but were based on the tribe and kinship groups. States could therefore move if necessary. The rise of states was accompanied by religious changes. The appearance of temples in the 1st century BC, as at Ribemont, indicates that religion was becoming more formalized while at the same time formal burial of the dead ceased except in the Belgic area of the north.

Statue of an aristocratic Gaulish warrior from Vachères, southern France, wearing a torc and a chain-mail shirt (late 1st century BC).

MAP NOTES

❶ *Expanding Germanic tribes began to settle the west bank of the Rhine in the 1st century BC.*

❷ *The establishment of the Roman province began with the conquest of the Saluvii in 124 BC.*

❸ *The Aedui were ruled by an elected magistrate called a vergobret. The constitution prevented any one family controlling the office. He governed from Bibracte.*

❹ *The king of the Nervii was advised by a 'senate' of the 300 leading noblemen.*

❺ *Celtic states were mobile: the Helvetii had lived northeast of the Rhine until c. 100 BC, in 58 BC they attempted to move again, into the land of the Arverni.*

A dedication in Greek letters from Orgon in southern France to the thunder-god Taranis, one of the gods to whom human sacrifices were made.

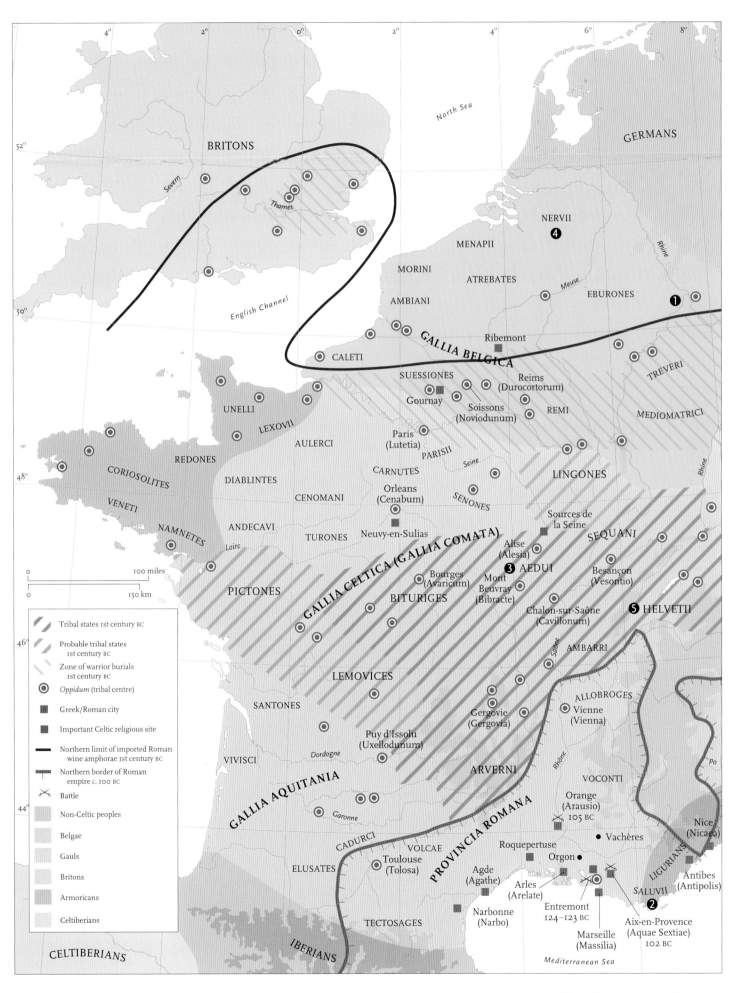

North Sea

52°

BRITONS

Severn

Thames

English Channel

50°

GERMANS

Rhine

NERVII
❹

MENAPII

MORINI

ATREBATES

AMBIANI

Meuse

EBURONES

❶

CALETI

GALLIA BELGICA

Ribemont

TREVERI

SUESSIONES

Reims
(Durocortorum)

MEDIOMATRICI

Gournay

Soissons
(Noviodunum)

REMI

UNELLI

LEXOVII

Paris
(Lutetia)

PARISII

Seine

AULERCI

CARNUTES

LINGONES

REDONES

48°

CORIOSOLITES

DIABLINTES

CENOMANI

Orleans
(Cenabum)

SENONES

Sources de
la Seine

SEQUANI

VENETI

Neuvy-en-Sulias

Alise
(Alesia)

Besançon
(Vesontio)

NAMNETES

Loire

TURONES

GALLIA CELTICA (GALLIA COMATA)

❸ AEDUI

Mont
Beuvray
(Bibracte)

o   100 miles

o   150 km

PICTONES

BITURIGES

Bourges
(Avaricum)

Chalon-sur-Saône
(Cavillonum)

❺ HELVETII

46°

LEMOVICES

Saône

AMBARRI

SANTONES

Gergovie
(Gergovia)

ALLOBROGES

Vienne
(Vienna)

Puy d'Issolu
(Uxellodunum)

ARVERNI

VOCONTI

Dordogne

Rhône

Po

VIVISCI

GALLIA AQUITANIA

Orange
(Arausio)

Nice
(Nicaea)

44°

Garonne

CADURCI

PROVINCIA ROMANA

105 BC

Vachères

LIGURIANS

Antibes
(Antipolis)

VOLCAE

Toulouse
(Tolosa)

Roquepertuse

Orgon

ELUSATES

Agde
(Agathe)

Arles
(Arelate)

Entremont
124–123 BC

SALUVII

❷

TECTOSAGES

Narbonne
(Narbo)

Marseille
(Massilia)

Aix-en-Provence
(Aquae Sextiae)
102 BC

CELTIBERIANS

IBERIANS

Mediterranean Sea

Tribal states 1st century BC

Probable tribal states
1st century BC

Zone of warrior burials
1st century BC

Oppidum (tribal centre)

Greek/Roman city

Important Celtic religious site

Northern limit of imported Roman
wine amphorae 1st century BC

Northern border of Roman
empire c. 100 BC

Battle

Non-Celtic peoples

Belgae

Gauls

Britons

Armoricans

Celtiberians

The Roman Conquest of Gaul I

58 – 55 BC

The Gallic sack of Rome in 390 BC assumed mythic proportions in the Romans' historical traditions and left them with a lasting fear of invasion by the northern barbarians. This deep-seated insecurity made it easy for the ambitious Roman general Julius Caesar to claim that his essentially unprovoked conquest of Gaul was necessary to protect Rome from a ferocious enemy.

BY THE 1ST CENTURY BC it was becoming increasingly likely that Gaul would fall victim to Roman expansionism. The development of states, towns and a wealthy agricultural economy meant that Gaul was becoming very similar to the Mediterranean world already dominated by Rome. Thus the conquest of Gaul would be profitable and its absorption into the empire would be straightforward. The 1st century BC was a time of unparalleled political turbulence in Rome as the republican system of government began to collapse in the face of competition for power between ambitious aristocrats. The surest way to power was success in war as this brought prestige, the support of the army and wealth from plunder and slaves: the relentless expansion of the empire was driven by internal Roman politics rather than by an imperial master plan.

It was therefore to further his political career that Julius Caesar, newly appointed governor of Gallia Transalpina, sought a pretext to conquer Gaul. This was provided by the Helvetii, a powerful tribe in modern Switzerland, who, in 58 BC, tried to migrate west and conquer new lands near the Bay of Biscay. This threatened to destabilize Gaul and interrupt Roman trade with the region and Caesar quickly drove them back by force. At this point, the Aedui, long-standing allies of Rome, and other Gallic tribes appealed to Caesar against the Suebi, a Germanic tribe which had recently crossed the Rhine under its king Ariovistus. Caesar defeated them and drove them back across the Rhine, but did not withdraw his troops, probably now having determined on the complete conquest of Gaul. The following year, Caesar campaigned against the Belgic tribes of the northeast, whom he defeated in several pitched battles. After this the Gauls tried to avoid battle and the war became one of sieges and scorched earth. In 56 BC Caesar extended his operations to Armorica and Aquitania and by 55 BC he felt secure enough to mount expeditions against the Germans and Britons to discourage them from interfering in Gaul.

It may be that Caesar's strategy in these years had commercial interests in mind. The economically and politically advanced heart of Gaul was avoided, perhaps because it was such an important market for Roman merchants, while Caesar's campaigns on the Channel coast and against the Veneti may have been designed to gain control of trade with Britain.

Vanquished Gauls appear in chains on the Roman triumphal arch at Carpentras, Vaucluse, France (1st century AD).

MAP NOTES

❶ According to Caesar, of 386,000 Helvetii who began the migration, only one-third survived to return to their homeland.

❷ The Remi were Rome's most reliable allies in Gaul, remaining loyal throughout Caesar's campaigns.

❸ The Nervii suffered a major defeat after ambushing the Roman army as it crossed the River Sambre, supposedly losing 60,000 men.

❹ Caesar spent ten days building a bridge across the Rhine as part of a punitive campaign against the Germans.

❺ In the earliest recorded naval battle in northern waters, Roman galleys defeated the sailing ships of the Veneti.

Mont Beuvray, Saône-et-Loire, France, site of the oppidum of Bibracte, the capital of the Aedui at the time of Caesar's invasion of Gaul.

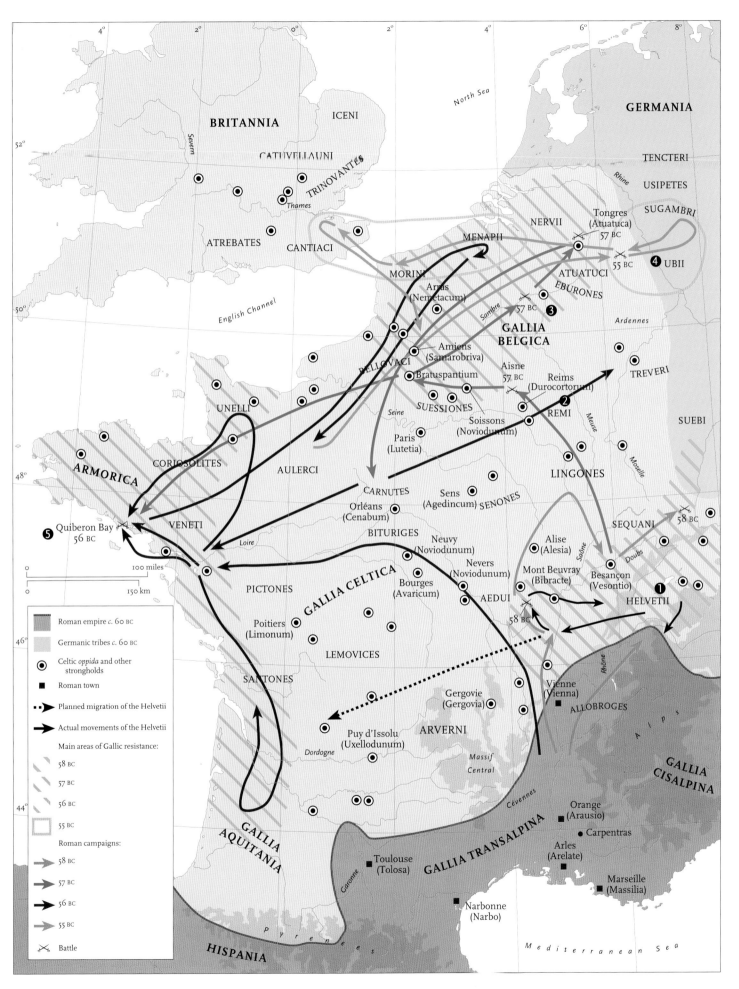

BRITANNIA

ICENI

Severn

CATUVELLAUNI

TRINOVANTES

Thames

ATREBATES

CANTIACI

North Sea

GERMANIA

TENCTERI

USIPETES

Rhine

SUGAMBRI

NERVII

Tongres
(Atuatuca)
57 BC

MENAPII

MORINI

Arras
(Nemetacum)

Sambre

57 BC 3

ATUATUCI

EBURONES

Ardennes

55 BC 4 UBII

GALLIA
BELGICA

English Channel

Amiens
(Samarobriva)

BELLOVACI

Bratuspantium

Seine

SUESSIONES

Paris
(Lutetia)

Aisne
57 BC

Reims
(Durocortorum)

2

Soissons
(Noviodunum)

REMI

Meuse

Moselle

TREVERI

SUEBI

LINGONES

UNELLI

ARMORICA

CORIOSOLITES

AULERCI

CARNUTES

Orléans
(Cenabum)

Sens
(Agedincum)

SENONES

Alise
(Alesia)

Saône

Doubs

SEQUANI

58 BC

Quiberon Bay
56 BC

5

VENETI

Loire

BITURIGES

Neuvy
(Noviodunum)

Nevers
(Noviodunum)

AEDUI

Mont Beuvray
(Bibracte)

Besançon
(Vesontio)

58 BC

HELVETII

1

PICTONES

GALLIA CELTICA

Bourges
(Avaricum)

Poitiers
(Limonum)

LEMOVICES

SANTONES

Puy d'Issolu
(Uxellodunum)

Dordogne

Gergovie
(Gergovia)

ARVERNI

Massif
Central

Vienne
(Vienna)

ALLOBROGES

Rhône

Alps

GALLIA
CISALPINA

GALLIA
AQUITANIA

Cévennes

Orange
(Arausio)

Carpentras

Arles
(Arelate)

GALLIA
TRANSALPINA

Toulouse
(Tolosa)

Garonne

Marseille
(Massilia)

HISPANIA

Pyrenees

Narbonne
(Narbo)

Mediterranean Sea

Roman empire c. 60 BC

Germanic tribes c. 60 BC

Celtic *oppida* and other
strongholds

Roman town

Planned migration of the Helvetii

Actual movements of the Helvetii

Main areas of Gallic resistance:

58 BC

57 BC

56 BC

55 BC

Roman campaigns:

58 BC

57 BC

56 BC

55 BC

Battle

100 miles

150 km

The Roman Conquest of Gaul II

By the beginning of 54 BC Caesar believed that he had broken Gallic resistance and decided to launch a second invasion of Britain. Though it was an impressive undertaking, Caesar's expedition achieved little and, far worse, while he was away, the discontented Gauls plotted rebellion.

BEFORE THE YEAR WAS OUT the Belgae had begun an uprising during which their skilful war leader, Ambiorix, trapped and annihilated a Roman force one-and-a-half legions strong at Atuatuca (Tongres). Caesar successfully crushed the Belgae in 53 BC, but their resistance inspired a massive rebellion in central Gaul under Vercingetorix, a chieftain of the Arverni. The area had seen little fighting and, believing it to have been pacified, Caesar had left his legions concentrated in the north against the Belgae, while he returned to Italy for administrative reasons.

Vercingetorix tried to take advantage of the situation by invading the Roman province late in 53 BC, hoping that this would tie Caesar down in the south while the isolated legions in the north could be destroyed. Caesar reacted with lightning speed, first driving Vercingetorix out of the province, then making an unexpected crossing of the snow-covered Cévennes in January 52 BC to attack the Arverni (so pinning Vercingetorix down in the south) before rushing north to join his legions at Sens.

The next few months were decisive. Caesar sought to draw the Gauls into open battle by besieging their *oppida*, massacring or enslaving entire populations when they fell. Vercingetorix countered with a scorched earth policy designed to force the Romans to withdraw for lack of supplies. A Gallic victory seemed close when the allied tribe of the Aedui rebelled, forcing the Romans to lift their siege of Gergovia, but within weeks Caesar had regained the initiative with a victory over Vercingetorix's cavalry on the Vingeanne river. Vercingetorix retreated to the *oppidum* of Alesia, where Caesar closely besieged him. Despite heroic efforts to break the siege, both from within and by a relief army outside the Roman lines, Vercingetorix was forced to surrender in October 52 BC and Gallic resistance collapsed. By the end of 51 BC Gaul had been completely pacified.

Although the Gauls had generally outnumbered Caesar's legions and had fought with desperate bravery, their resistance had in the end been overcome. Roman soldiers were certainly better led, better disciplined and much better equipped than Gallic warriors, but the decisive factor in the Roman victory was the uncoordinated nature of Gallic resistance: the Romans never had to face their united strength. The Gauls simply did not see themselves as a single people and traditional tribal rivalries often overrode their common interest in resisting Roman rule. Even a charismatic leader like Vercingetorix failed to unite all the Gauls against Rome at the same time.

A gold coin of the Arverni, depicting the Gallic war leader Vercingetorix. Captured at Alesia in 52 BC, Vercingetorix was executed as part of the celebrations of Caesar's triumph in 44 BC.

MAP NOTES

❶ *The leader of the Belgic revolt in 53 BC, Ambiorix was a chieftain of the Eburones, one of the last tribes to submit to Rome.*
❷ *Vercingetorix's revolt began with a massacre of Roman merchants at Cenabum.*
❸ *The Romans massacred all but 800 of Avaricum's population of 40,000 when this oppidum fell in 52 BC.*
❹ *Caesar surrounded Alesia with 22.5 km (14 miles) of ramparts, one circuit facing in to prevent the defenders escaping, one facing out to fend off the Gallic relief army.*
❺ *The last major Gallic stronghold to fall: those who had taken part in its defence had their hands cut off.*

The hilltop oppidum *of Alesia: though sporadic resistance continued for a further year, the fall of Alesia to Caesar in 52 BC was the decisive event of the Gallic war.*

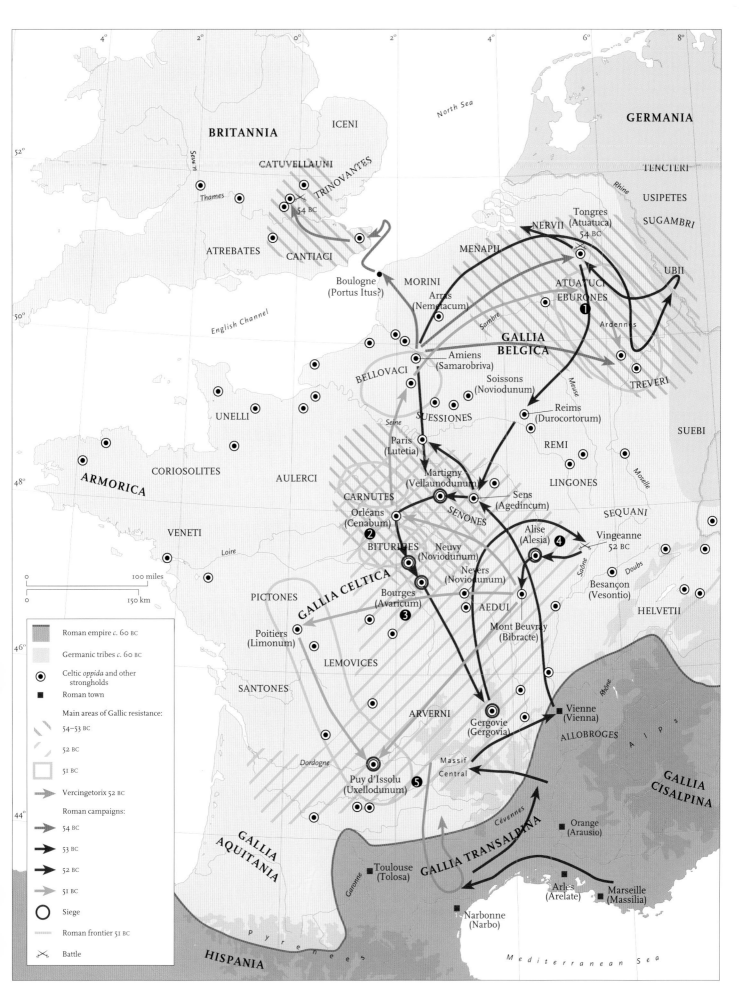

BRITANNIA

ICENI

CATUVELLAUNI

Thames

TRINOVANTES

54 BC

ATREBATES

CANTIACI

English Channel

UNELLI

ARMORICA

CORIOSOLITES

AULERCI

VENETI

Loire

PICTONES

Poitiers
(Limonum)

SANTONES

Dordogne

GALLIA
AQUITANIA

Toulouse
(Tolosa)

Garonne

Pyrenees

HISPANIA

North Sea

GERMANIA

TENCTERI

Rhine

USIPETES

SUGAMBRI

Boulogne
(Portus Itus?)

MORINI

Arras
(Nemetacum)

Amiens
(Samarobriva)

BELLOVACI

Seine

SUESSIONES

Paris
(Lutetia)

CARNUTES

Orléans
(Cenabum) ②

BITURIGES

Bourges
(Avaricum) ③

GALLIA CELTICA

ARVERNI

Gergovie
(Gergovia)

Massif
Central

Cévennes

GALLIA TRANSALPINA

Arles
(Arelate)

Narbonne
(Narbo)

Mediterranean Sea

MENAPII

NERVII

Tongres
(Atuatuca)
54 BC

ATUATUCI

EBURONES ①

Sambre

GALLIA
BELGICA

Soissons
(Noviodunum)

Meuse

Reims
(Durocortorum)

REMI

Martigny
(Vellaunodunum)

SENONES

Sens
(Agedincum)

LINGONES

Neuvy
(Noviodunum)

Nevers
(Noviodunum)

AEDUI

Mont Beuvray
(Bibracte)

Alise
(Alesia) ④

Vingeanne
52 BC

Saône

Doubs

Besançon
(Vesontio)

Vienne
(Vienna)

ALLOBROGES

Rhône

Orange
(Arausio)

Marseille
(Massilia)

UBII

TREVERI

Ardennes

SUEBI

Moselle

SEQUANI

HELVETII

A l p s

GALLIA
CISALPINA

LEMOVICES

Puy d'Issolu
(Uxellodunum) ⑤

Legend:

Roman empire *c.* 60 BC

Germanic tribes *c.* 60 BC

⊙ Celtic *oppida* and other
   strongholds

■ Roman town

Main areas of Gallic resistance:

54–53 BC

52 BC

51 BC

→ Vercingetorix 52 BC

Roman campaigns:

→ 54 BC

→ 53 BC

→ 52 BC

→ 51 BC

○ Siege

Roman frontier 51 BC

✕ Battle

0   100 miles

0   150 km

52°

50°

48°

46°

44°

4°   2°   0°   2°   4°   6°   8°

The Gauls under Roman Rule

Roman rule brought many economic and social changes to Gaul. The Gauls themselves, especially the aristocracy, adopted a Romanized way of life and, increasingly, the Latin language, but they retained much of their native culture and beliefs, resulting in the development of a distinctive Gallo-Roman identity.

GAUL HAD SUFFERED terrible destruction during the Roman conquest and pacification proceeded rapidly. In 27 BC the territories conquered by Caesar were divided into three provinces, Belgica, Lugdunensis and Aquitania, known as Tres Gallia, the Three Gauls (in the 1st century AD parts of Belgica and Lugdunensis were detached to form the provinces of Germania Superior and Germania Inferior). Unlike the southern province of Narbonensis, which had been under Roman rule since the 2nd century BC, the Three Gauls never became completely Romanized. As a result of a number of rebellions in the 1st century AD, none of which actually won widespread support, the Romans remained wary of the Gauls and this became a barrier to their complete assimilation.

The Three Gauls were divided into local government areas called *civitates*, which were based on the former tribal territories, and elective magistracies and other Roman civic institutions were introduced. Members of the native aristocracy who held public office were rewarded with Roman citizenship. As a result, Roman Gaul was governed largely by Gauls. The capitals of the *civitates* were usually tribal *oppida*, though if the site of an *oppidum* was unsuitable, because it was on a confined hilltop for example, a new town would be founded nearby. To promote Romanization, the *civitas* capitals were equipped with the amenities of Roman civilization, such as theatres and amphitheatres, metalled roads, aqueducts and baths. Gauls could also gain Roman citizenship through military service, a popular option as it was a substitute for inter-tribal warfare as a way to win prestige. By the time they were discharged, Gallic recruits had become thoroughly accustomed to Roman ways and language. Under the emperor Claudius (AD 41–54), Gallic aristocrats became

MAP NOTES

❶ *The Batavian chief Julius Civilis rebelled in AD 69 in an attempt to create an independent 'Empire of the Gauls'.*
❷ *Aeduan aristocrats were the first Gauls to become members of the Roman Senate, during the reign of Claudius (41–54).*
❸ *Ribemont was one of many Celtic religious sites which show continuity of use from the Iron Age through the Roman period.*
❹ *The Altar of the Gauls at Lugdunum was the chief centre in Gaul for the worship of the imperial cults which symbolized loyalty to the empire.*
❺ *It was under Roman rule that the Bordeaux region was established as a major wine producer.*

An altar to the Matronae Aufaniae, *a triad of mother goddesses known only in the Rhineland. The quality of the carving and the prominence of the name of Quettius Severus, a magistrate from Cologne, demonstrates the reverence shown to Celtic cults by the aristocracy under Roman rule.*

Part of a fragmentary bronze calendar from Coligny, France, 1st century BC–1st century AD. The calendar, reckoned by nights rather than days, lists propitious and ill-omened days for different important activities. Though the calendar is written in Roman letters, the language is Gaulish.

BRITANNIA

Legend:
- The Three Gauls
- ⊙ Provincial capitals
- ▪ *Civitas* capitals of the Gauls and Germanies
- ■ Legionary base
- ▲ Celtic religious site
- ✦ Rebellion with date
- ▬▬ Border of the Roman empire
- ── Provincial border
- ── Major road

Scale: 0 — 100 miles / 0 — 150 km

1. Arras (Nemetacum)
2. Mainz (Moguntiacum)
3. Worms (Borbetomagus)
4. Amiens (Samarobriva)
5. Beauvais (Caesaromagus)
6. Soissons (Augusta Suessionum)
7. Reims (Durocortorum)
8. Brumath (Brocomagus)
9. Strasbourg (Argentorate)
10. Sources de la Seine (Fontes Sequanae)
11. Langres (Andematunnum)
12. Augst (Augusta Rauricorum)
13. Chalon-sur-Saône (Cavillonum)
14. Clermont-Ferrand (Augustonemetum)
15. Feurs (Forum Segusiavorum)
16. Lyon (Lugdunum)

A. ALPES GRAIAE ET POENINAE
B. ALPES COTTIAE
C. ALPES MARITIMAE

Map labels: Caerleon (Isca); Thames; London (Londinium); Dover (Dubris); Boulogne (Gesoriacum); English Channel; Cassel (Castellum Menapiorum); Thérouanne (Tarvanna); MENAPII; ATREBATES; NERVII; MORINI; Bavay (Bagacum); TUNGRI; Nijmegen (Noviomagus); Xanten (Vetera); Neuss (Novaesium); Cologne (Colonia Agrippina); Tongres (Atuatuca); Bonn (Bonna); UBII; BATAVI; GERMANIA INFERIOR; AD 69–70; Trier (Augusta Treverorum); TREVERI; VANGIONES; Metz (Divodurum); MEDIOMATRICI; LEUCI; Toul (Tollum); TRIBOCI; GERMANIA SUPERIOR; AD 21, 69–70; Lillebonne (Iuliobona); Lisieux (Noviomagus); CALETI; VELIOCASSES; Rouen (Rotomagus); Coutances (Cosedia); UNELLI; LEXOVII; Bayeux (Augustodurum); Avranches (Legedia); Corseul (Fanum Martis); BAIOCASSES; ESUVII; PARISII; Paris (Lutetia); Gournay; AMBIANI; GALLIA BELGICA; BELLOVACI; SUESSIONES; REMI; Ribemont; OSISMII; Carhaix (Vorgium); CORIOSOLITES; ABRINCATES; Sées (Sagii); CARNUTES; Chartres (Autricum); GALLIA LUGDUNENSIS; TRICASSES; Troyes (Augustobona); Sens (Agedincum); Rennes (Condate Redonum); CENOMANI; Fleury (Floriacum); Mont Auxois; LINGONES; SEQUANI; VENETI; REDONES; ANDECAVI; Le Mans (Suindinum); Orléans (Cenabum); SENONES; AD 21, 68; AD 68; Vannes (Darioritum); NAMNETES; Angers (Iuliomagus); Tours (Caesarodunum); AEDUI; Autun (Augustodunum); Besançon (Vesontio); RAURACI; Nantes (Portus Namnetum); TURONES; BITURIGES; Bourges (Avaricum); Beaune; Avenches (Aventicum); HELVETII; PICTONES; Poitiers (Limonum); ARVERNI; Coligny; ALLOBROGES; Alps; SANTONES; LEMOVICES; AD 68; SEGUSIAVI; Saintes (Mediolanum); Limoges (Augustoritum); Chamalières; Vienne (Vienna); HELVII; VOCONTI; Aime (Aixima); Bordeaux (Burdigala); PETROCORII; Périgueux (Vesunna); Dordogne; Cévennes; St Remy (Glanum); Susa (Segusio); VIVISCI; NITOBRIGES; CADURCI; RUTENI; Rodez (Segodunum); Cimiez (Cemenelum); Eauze (Elusa); Agen (Aginnum); Cahors (Divona); VOLCAE; Auch (Elimberris); NARBONENSIS; Nîmes (Nemausus); Marseille (Massilia); Aix-en-Provence (Aquae Sextiae); SALUVII; Dax (Aquae Tarbellicae); ELUSATES; AUSCI; TECTOSAGES; Toulouse (Tolosa); St-Bertrand-de-Comminges (Lugdunum Convenarum); Narbonne (Narbo); Arles (Arelate); TARBELLI; CONVENAE; HISPANIA; Pyrenees; Bay of Biscay; Caronne; Rhône; Jura; Rhine; Meuse; Seine; Mediterranean Sea

---

eligible to become senators, though in practice few were actually appointed. The aristocracy soon adopted the Latin language and the Roman gods (though often assimilated with local cults), but Celtic beliefs, customs and language long survived among the peasantry. Traditional Celtic temples and sanctuaries continued to be built, though using Roman techniques.

Gaul prospered under Roman rule, the presence of the legionary armies on the Rhine frontier providing a great stimulus to both agriculture and industry. By the 2nd century Gaul had probably overtaken Italy in wealth. Intensive grain production changed the landscape of northern Gaul and many landowners were able to build comfortable villas on the proceeds. Peasant farmers, the majority of the population, continued to live in conditions that differed little from pre-conquest times, however.

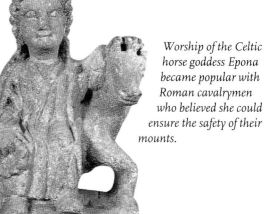

Worship of the Celtic horse goddess Epona became popular with Roman cavalrymen who believed she could ensure the safety of their mounts.

Celts, Romans and Germans in Central Europe

200 – 9 BC

In the last centuries BC, the old Celtic heartland of southern Germany and the Alps saw the growth of states and the introduction of coinage and literacy. But, as in Gaul, this development towards a Celtic urban civilization was arrested when central Europe was conquered by three expansionist powers: the Romans, Dacians and Germans.

THE MOST POWERFUL Celtic state to emerge in central Europe was the kingdom of Noricum in modern-day Austria. The kingdom developed in the early 2nd century BC from a coalition of tribes led by the Nori and became a Roman ally in 186 BC. The kingdom controlled several Alpine passes and exported iron and steel to the Roman empire. In the early 1st century BC a native coinage was introduced. The royal centre of Noricum was the alpine *oppidum* of Virunum. Below the hilltop native settlement, a permanent colony of Roman merchants was established in the 1st century BC, complete with forum and other Roman urban amenities. Under the colony's influence, the native elite adopted an increasingly Romanized lifestyle.

The first threat to the Celts of central Europe came from their eastern neighbours, the Dacians, who began to expand northwest across the Carpathians into Transylvania in the 170s BC, absorbing the local Celtic population. In the early 1st century BC Dacia emerged as a powerful and expansionist kingdom under King Burebişta. Around 60 BC Burebişta attacked the Celtic Scordisci, Taurisci and Boii, adding what is now northern Hungary and Slovakia to his kingdom. The Boii abandoned this region and fled through Noricum to take refuge with the Helvetii. The Boii supported their hosts in their attempt to migrate into Gaul, so helping to give Caesar the excuse he needed to begin its conquest.

The Germanic threat was manifested spectacularly in 120 BC when the Cimbri and Teutones migrated from Jutland into the Celtic lands of central Europe and Gaul, where they went on a seemingly aimless but terrifying

MAP NOTES

❶ In the 2nd century BC, Manching became one of the largest oppida north of the Alps. It was destroyed c. 120 BC and completely rebuilt with massive defences 7 km (4.4 miles) in length.

❷ Staré Hradisko flourished from its position on the amber route between the Baltic Sea and the Adriatic.

❸ After its conquest by the Dacians c. 60 BC this region became depopulated and was known as the 'desert of the Boii'.

❹ The abandonment of the oppidum of Závist after its destruction by fire c. 25–20 BC probably marks the Germanic occupation of Bohemia.

❺ A permanent colony of Roman merchants, established outside the native oppidum of Virunum c. 90 BC, was a powerful agent of Romanization in Noricum.

❻ A gold rush in the territory of the Taurisci in the 140s–130s BC attracted miners from as far away as Italy.

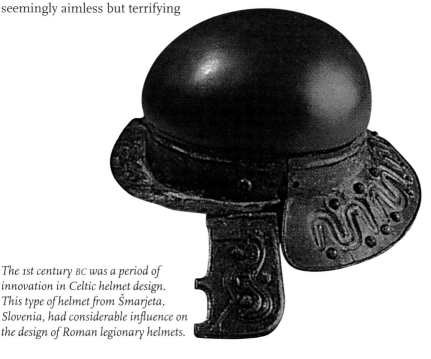

The 1st century BC was a period of innovation in Celtic helmet design. This type of helmet from Šmarjeta, Slovenia, had considerable influence on the design of Roman legionary helmets.

rampage for several years until they were defeated and dispersed by the Romans in 102–101 BC. After this, the Celts were constantly under pressure as the Germanic tribes moved steadily south, reaching the Danube in 16–8 BC. The Germans were not seen as a threat by all Celts: the Sequani, Arverni and Nori all at different times formed alliances with the Germanic Suebi against their tribal enemies.

Rome showed little interest in expansion north of the Alps until the reign of Augustus (27 BC–AD 14). In 15 BC the Romans conquered the Vindelici and Raeti; Noricum was peacefully annexed around the same time. Another major campaign conquered Pannonia and Illyricum in 12–9 BC. In only six years, all the Celts south of the Danube had been brought under Roman rule. As in Gaul, the civilization of these tribes had proved their undoing: their centralized political structures, hierarchical social structures and advanced economies made conquest both attractive and viable and their assimilation into the Roman system as contented provincials was swift.

The Celts of central Europe developed high-quality gold and silver coinage inspired by Hellenistic models. This silver horseman coin of the Boii was minted at the oppidum *at Bratislava, Slovakia, in the 1st century BC.*

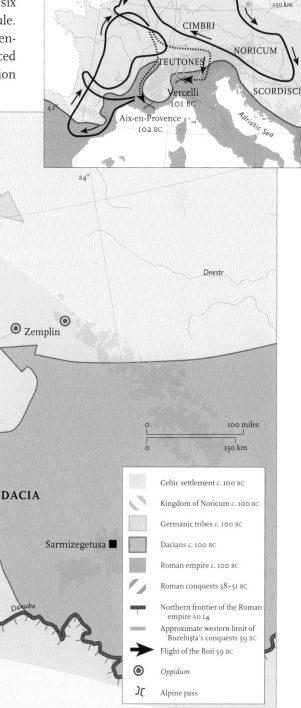

Celtic lands *c.* 120 BC
Roman empire *c.* 120 BC
Migration route of the Cimbri and Teutones 120–101 BC

150 miles
250 km

CIMBRI
NORICUM
TEUTONES
SCORDISCI
Vercelli 101 BC
Aix-en-Provence 102 BC
Adriatic Sea

GERMANIA
MARCOMANNI
Dnestr

❹
Závist
Stradonice
BOII
Staré Hradisko ❷
Regensburg
Vltava
BOII ❸
Zemplin
Passau
RAETI
Linz
Vienna
Bratislava
Tisza
❻ TAURISCI
Hallstatt
ERAVISCI
Dürrnberg
Velem-Szent-Vid
NORI
PANNONIA
DACIA
AMBIDRAVI
❺
Neumarkt (Noreia)
CARNI
Zollfeld (Virunum)
SCORDISCI
Sarmizegetusa ■
Aquileia
Drava
Šmarjeta
DARDANI
Sara
ILLYRICUM
Danube
Belgrade
Adriatic Sea
ILLYRIANS

100 miles
150 km

Celtic settlement *c.* 100 BC
Kingdom of Noricum *c.* 100 BC
Germanic tribes *c.* 100 BC
Dacians *c.* 100 BC
Roman empire *c.* 100 BC
Roman conquests 58–51 BC
Northern frontier of the Roman empire AD 14
Approximate western limit of Burebiṣta's conquests 59 BC
Flight of the Boii 59 BC
Oppidum
Alpine pass

The End of Celtic Gaul

The emperor Caracalla's decree of 212 extending Roman citizenship to all free inhabitants of the empire marks at one level the final integration of Gaul into the empire, but it did not mark the end of Gallic identity. If anything the 3rd century saw a resurgence of Gallic self-confidence.

THE 3RD CENTURY was one of the most difficult in the history of the Roman empire. The German tribes were becoming stronger and better organized, and in the later 2nd century they began to exert constant pressure on the borders of the empire. The Germans were held at bay, but the political and economic cost was so high that in the 3rd century the empire collapsed into political anarchy. As rivals for the imperial throne fought one another, the border defences were neglected and the Germans were quick to take advantage, raiding Gaul repeatedly. Despairing of help from the centre, in 260 the Gauls set up their own independent 'Gallic Empire' under the general Postumus, which in addition included Spain and Britain. Postumus won popularity for his effective defence of the Rhine frontier. After Postumus was assassinated in 268, Spain returned to allegiance to Rome and his successor Victorinus lost the lands east of the Rhône to Claudius II *c.* 269. The rest of the Gallic Empire was reabsorbed by Rome after the defeat of its last emperor Tetricus in 274.

Gaul achieved its greatest importance in the 4th century when Trier became one of the capitals of the Roman empire. In the 5th century a Gallo-Roman, Avitus, even briefly became emperor. Aristocratic Gallo-Romans were proud of their contribution to the empire, proud to be steeped in Classical culture and tradition but also still proud to be Gauls. The positive loyalty to the empire of the aristocracy was not shared by the peasantry. The cost of defending the empire was high and fell mainly on the peasantry, which became desperately impoverished. Many, known as *bagaudae*, resorted to brigandage. When the German tribes again overran the Roman frontiers in the 5th century, there was little popular resistance. Relieved of the burden of imperial taxation most of the people of Gaul found that they were better off under their new German rulers.

Though it had retained a distinct identity throughout the period of Roman rule, by this time most of Gaul had ceased to be in

(Below) The insecurity of the 3rd century led many Gallic towns to build defensive walls. Often rebuilt and strengthened, as here at Carcassonne, Aude, these frequently continued in use right through the Middle Ages.

(Opposite below) 'Marcus Paionius Victorinus, tribune of the praetorian guard, restored this at his own expense': mosaic floor from a house in Trier owned by the Gallic emperor Victorinus.

(Left) Sword hilt and scabbard, richly decorated with gold and garnets, from the grave of the early Frankish king Childeric (d. 482) at Tournai, Belgium.

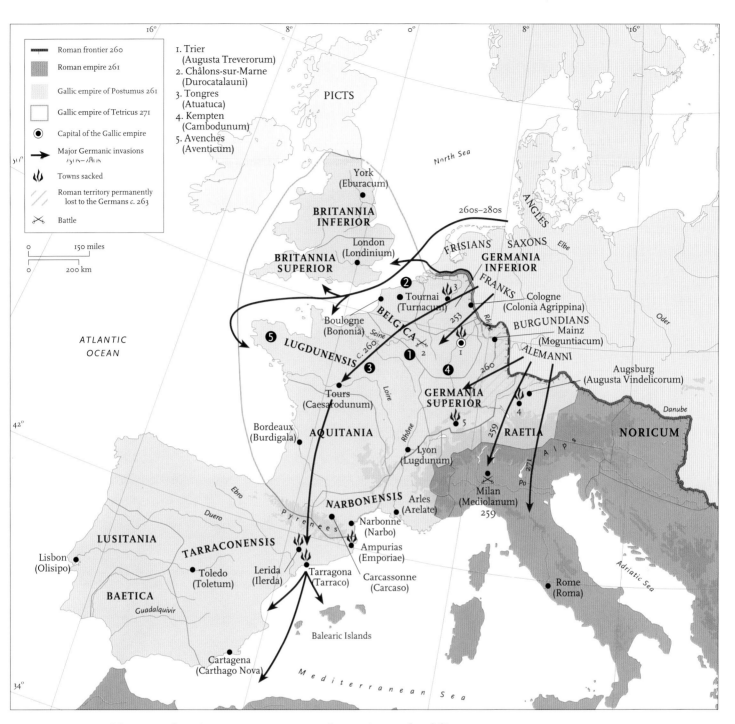

Map legend:

- Roman frontier 260
- Roman empire 261
- Gallic empire of Postumus 261
- Gallic empire of Tetricus 271
- ⊙ Capital of the Gallic empire
- → Major Germanic invasions 250s–280s
- ♨ Towns sacked
- ⁄⁄ Roman territory permanently lost to the Germans *c.* 263
- ✕ Battle

1. Trier (Augusta Treverorum)
2. Châlons-sur-Marne (Durocatalauni)
3. Tongres (Atuatuca)
4. Kempten (Cambodunum)
5. Avenches (Aventicum)

Scale:
0 — 150 miles
0 — 200 km

any meaningful sense Celtic. Except in Armorica (modern Brittany), local dialects of Latin – the precursors of the modern French language – had been adopted even by the peasantry, and Christianity had replaced Celtic religion by *c.* 400. The term Gaul continued to be used for several centuries but eventually gave way to a name derived from its Germanic conquerors, *Francia*.

MAP NOTES

❶ *The last Gallic emperor Tetricus surrendered to Aurelian after defeat at Châlons.*

❷ *Britain and northern Gaul again became independent under the Menapian admiral Carausius in 286 until recaptured 293–96.*

❸ *From the 280s Lugdunensis was affected by peasant brigands called* bagaudae.

❹ *Gaul was seriously affected by invasions and economic and political disruption in the 3rd century: of 87 known* vici *(large villages) in Gallia Belgica, 31 failed to survive the century.*

❺ *Armorica was the least Romanized part of Gaul: Celtic language and beliefs survived there until the end of Roman rule in the 5th century.*

Celtic Religion: Druids, Sanctuaries, Temples and Tombs

In their religious beliefs, the ancient Celts were very similar to their Greek, Roman and German neighbours. Among the most distinctive aspects of Celtic religion were the Druids, a specialized priestly and intellectual class, and a cult of the severed human head.

LIKE THE OTHER PAGAN PEOPLES of Europe, the Celts were polytheists, though unlike the Greeks and Romans they had no well-ordered pantheon of universal gods. Most gods were associated only with a particular tribe or place. Also like their neighbours, the Celts recognized the divinity of natural features, such as rivers and springs. There must have been thousands of such local gods, the equivalent of the Roman *genius loci*. Some gods, however, were worshipped more widely: Lugh (probably a sun god) was worshipped in Ireland, Gaul and Iberia. The gods were propitiated with offerings of valuable metalwork and animal and human sacrifices. The Celts had no concept of Heaven and Hell and apparently believed that the afterlife would be much like this one as they buried their dead with grave offerings appropriate to their status. In Hallstatt times barrow burial was widespread for the elite, but this practice ceased in most areas in the 5th century BC and interment in flat cemeteries became normal for all. Cremation was becoming more usual by the 2nd century.

The Celts had both priests and priestesses, most important among whom were the Druids. Druids served a rigorous 20-year apprenticeship during which time they had to master an enormous body of orally transmitted verse, comprising religious lore, law, magic, history and astronomy. Druids are said to have conducted worship in sacred groves, the locations of some of which may be identified by the place-name element *nemeton* ('sanctuary') and its derivatives.

From *c.* 150 BC evidence for burials becomes scarcer, although one cannot necessarily conclude that there was a major change in funerary customs or

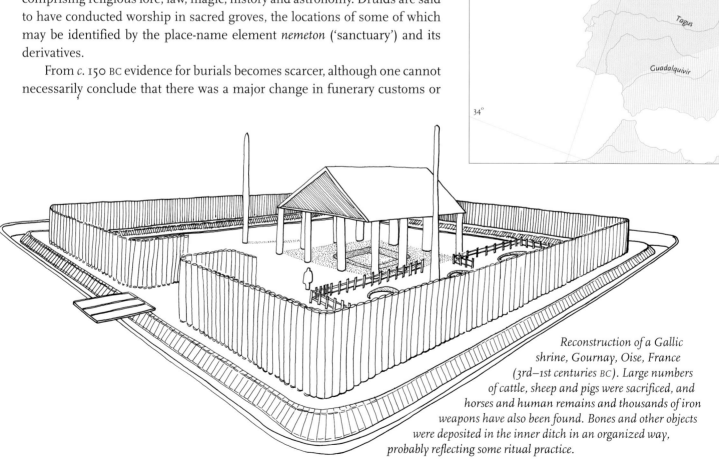

Reconstruction of a Gallic shrine, Gournay, Oise, France (3rd–1st centuries BC). Large numbers of cattle, sheep and pigs were sacrificed, and horses and human remains and thousands of iron weapons have also been found. Bones and other objects were deposited in the inner ditch in an organized way, probably reflecting some ritual practice.

Navan
Crúachain
Tara
Dún Ailinne

❸ Taw Valley *nemeto-, nymet* and *nymp-* place-names

ATLANTIC OCEAN

Nemetobriga

Tagus

Guadalquivir

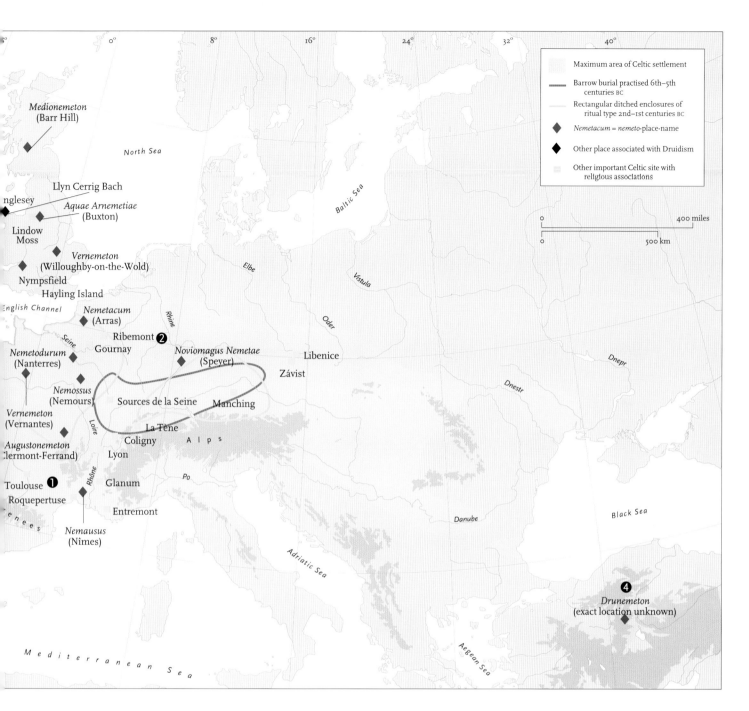

Legend:

Maximum area of Celtic settlement

Barrow burial practised 6th–5th centuries BC

Rectangular ditched enclosures of ritual type 2nd–1st centuries BC

◆ *Nemetacum = nemeto*-place-name

◆ Other place associated with Druidism

Other important Celtic site with religious associations

0   400 miles
0   500 km

religious beliefs. Temples and sacred enclosures became common, indicating a shift to more formal forms of worship comparable to those of the Classical world. In southern Gaul, these show Classical influences in their stone architecture and sculpture, though retaining distinctive Celtic features, such as skull niches. Further north, an indigenous form of rectangular ditched enclosure appeared, often containing wooden ritual structures and sacrificial pits.

With the exception of human sacrifice, which was suppressed, Celtic religion was easily accommodated within the religious diversity of the Roman empire. The Romans saw many of the Celtic gods as equivalents of their own gods. A well-known example is the Celtic goddess Sul, worshipped at Bath in England, who was equated with Minerva, the goddess of wisdom. Some Romans adopted Celtic cults, such as that of the horse goddess Epona, which was popular among cavalrymen, and many Celts adopted Mediterranean cults including, in time, Christianity.

MAP NOTES

❶ *After capturing Toulouse in 107 BC, the Romans claimed to have looted over 50 tonnes of gold and as much silver from a temple and its sacred lakes.*

❷ *Excavations of the sanctuary of Ribemont recovered the decapitated and dismembered bodies of at least 1000 men and women.*

❸ *The Taw Valley in Devon contains around 20 place-names derived from* nemeton *('sanctuary'), including King's Nympton, Nymet Bridge, East Nymph and a Roman fort which was called* Nemetostatio.

❹ *Drunemeton ('sacred oak grove'), the meeting place of the Galatians, is evidence that Druids may have been found even in the farthest corners of the Celtic world.*

The Origins of Brittany

AD 300 – 700

Archaeological evidence suggests that Brittany, then known as Armorica, suffered severely during the 3rd-century crisis of the Roman empire. The economy collapsed, settlements were abandoned and the population declined. Then around 300, newcomers began infiltrating the region and reoccupying sites abandoned in the previous century. Fragments of southern British pottery at these sites suggest that the newcomers were Britons.

No CONTEMPORARY WRITER noticed the arrival of these earliest British immigrants, though traditions recorded by Geoffrey of Monmouth in the 12th century tell the story of the British leader Conan Meriadec who founded a dynasty in Gaul in the late 4th century. The early 6th-century British writer Gildas tells us that the Britons who settled in Armorica were fleeing from the Anglo-Saxon invasions of Britain. Other traditions about the settlement are preserved in the *vitae* (religious biographies) of early Breton saints, most of whom like Mawes (Maudez), Samson and Winwaloe (Guénolé) were born in Cornwall or South Wales, but on the whole these date from some centuries after the period they describe. The earliest monastic foundations associated with these saints tend to be along the north coast of the peninsula. These British churchmen brought with them practices typical of the insular Celtic church, including the observance of Easter.

The main source of evidence for the British settlement comes from place-names. The similarity of Welsh and Cornish to Breton place-names is obvious. *Plou-* (from Latin *plebs*, Welsh *plwyf* = 'people') is common. Associated with *plou-* names are *gui-* and *guic-* names (from Latin *vicus*, 'settlement'). Other common elements of British origin include *lan* (Welsh *Llan*, 'church'), *tré-* (Welsh *tref*, subdivision of a parish), *coët* (Welsh *coed*, 'wood') and *ker* (Welsh *caer*, 'hamlet'). The main distribution of British place-name elements is in the north and west. In the southeast the place-name elements *-ac*, *-é* and *-y*, derived from the Gallo-Roman suffix *-acum* ('place'), are common, indicating that British settlement was less dense here. An enclave of Romance-speakers long survived around Quimper.

The political organization of early Brittany is very unclear, though the Britons seem to have settled under several chiefs. One leader, Riothamus, is described as a

Many prehistoric monuments, like this octagonal Iron Age stela at Lampaul-Ploudalmézeau (Finistère), were christianized following the conversion of Brittany.

Legend:

- Eastern limit of the Breton language *c.* 800
- Main concentration of *plou-*, *guic-*, *tré-* and *lan-* place-name elements
- Main concentration of place-name suffix *-ac* and related names
- Romance-speaking enclave until 11th century
- ✠ 5th/6th-century monastic foundations and associated saint
- ■ Late Roman forts
- ⊙ Other archaeological site

MAP NOTES

❶ *Roman coastal forts were built to protect the region against Saxon and Frankish pirate raids, not British migrants.*

❷ *Mid-4th-century cemetery contains skeletal types resembling those of southwest Wales and southwest England.*

❸ *The Loire Valley was the scene of fighting in 469–70 between the British king Riothamus and the Visigoths.*

❹ *Many early monasteries were founded on islands for reasons of security and seclusion.*

❺ *St Samson's foundation at Dol became Brittany's leading ecclesiastical centre.*

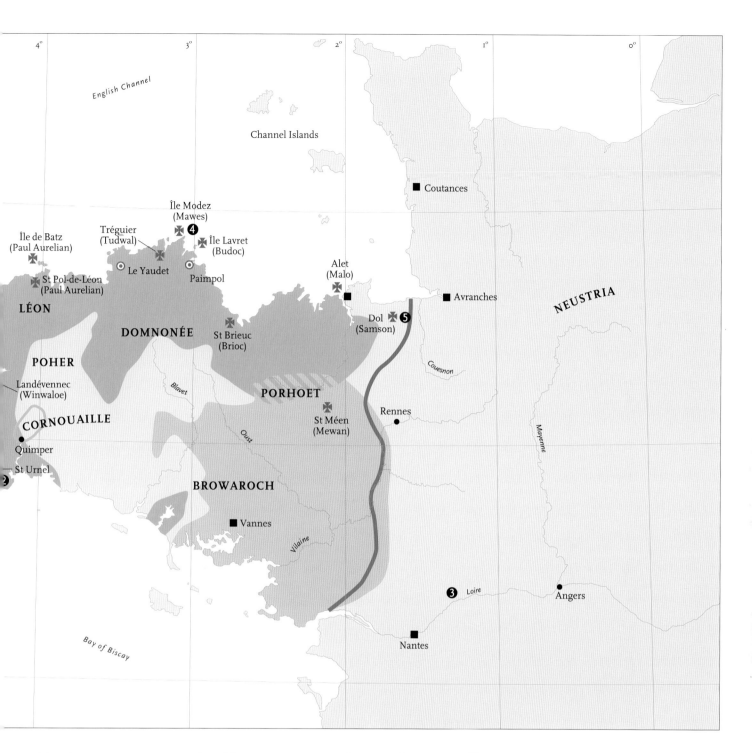

Channel Islands

Coutances ■

Île Modez
(Mawes) ✠ ➍

Île de Batz
(Paul Aurelian) ✠

Tréguier
(Tudwal) ✠ Île Lavret
(Budoc) ✠

St Pol-de-Léon
(Paul Aurelian) ✠

⊙ Le Yaudet   ⊙ Paimpol

Alet ✠
(Malo) ■

Avranches ■

NEUSTRIA

LÉON

DOMNONÉE

St Brieuc
(Brioc) ✠

Dol ✠ ➎
(Samson)

POHER

Landévennec
(Winwaloe)

PORHOET ✠

St Méen
(Mewan)

Rennes ●

Blavet

CORNOUAILLE

Oust

Quimper ●
St Urnel

➋

BROWAROCH

Vannes ■

Vilaine

Couesnon

Mayenne

➌ Loire

Angers ●

Bay of Biscay

Nantes ■

king by a contemporary writer. The Romans retained nominal authority until the 460s, but by the end of the century the Franks had laid claim to the region. By the mid-6th century three main regional powers had emerged, Cornouaille (Cornovia) in the west, about which virtually nothing is known; Domnonée (Dumnonia), along the north coast, where a royal dynasty emerged in the 7th century; and Browaroch in the south, founded by Waroc, a chieftain from Vannes, some time after 560. The Bretons came under pressure from the Franks in the 7th century and in 635 King Judicael of Domnonée was forced to accept a subordinate relationship to the Merovingian king Dagobert I. By 691 the Bretons enjoyed full independence again, thanks to the decline of the Merovingian dynasty.

Armorican coin of the late Iron Age. Armorica was the only region of Gaul where Celtic speech still survived in the 5th century. Invigorated by the arrival of British settlers, Armorican contributed to the development of the Breton language.

Until the middle of the 8th century almost nothing is known of political developments in Brittany. The Bretons themselves were not politically unified and unity when it came was imposed from outside. By 778 the Franks had established a military frontier zone, the Breton March, based on the counties of Rennes, Vannes and Nantes – its count was the French hero Roland who was killed at Roncesvalles. Under Charlemagne (768–814) and his son Louis the Pious (814–40) the Franks tried several times to conquer Brittany but always apparent success was followed by rebellions in which the Bretons used guerrilla tactics to great effect.

IN 831, LOUIS TRIED a different approach and appointed a native Breton noble, Nomenoë, as *missus imperatoris* for Brittany. This entailed Nomenoë becoming an imperial vassal, for which he was rewarded with Vannes. It was a mutually advantageous arrangement: Nomenoë became the pre-eminent Breton leader, while Louis gained title to lands which he did not really control. Brittany as a united political entity was their joint creation. A dispute over the county of Nantes led Nomenoë to rebel against the Frankish king Charles the Bald in 845, whom he defeated at Ballon near Redon. In 849 Nomenoë expelled the Frankish bishops of Alet, Dol, Quimper, St Pol-de-Léon and Vannes and replaced them with native Breton-speakers. Military campaigns expanded Nomenoë's territories as far east as the River Mayenne.

Following Nomenoë's death in 851, Charles invaded Brittany, but Nomenoë's son Erispoë defeated him in a decisive battle at Jengland-Beslé. The disaster forced Charles to grant Erispoë regal status as a vassal king within the Frankish empire: Brittany had become a kingdom. Erispoë was murdered in 857 by his successor Salomon (857–74) who became the most successful of Breton rulers.

An important factor in the rise of Brittany had been the Vikings. Although Brittany suffered numerous coastal raids, the Vikings found the rich Frankish lands much more attractive. Distracted also by dynastic problems, Charles the Bald was usually unable to concentrate on Brittany. On occasion the Bretons even allied with the Vikings, as in 866 when together

Legend (map key):

- Brittany c. 778
- Territory acquired by Nomenoë 831–51
- Territory acquired by Salomon 863
- Territory acquired by Salomon 867
- Approximate western border of the Frankish Breton March c. 778
- Approximate eastern limit of Viking occupation 914–37
- Alain Barbetorte's reconquest of Brittany 936–39
- Archbishopric
- Bishopric
- Monastery or other church sacked or abandoned 836–939
- Viking fort/camp
- Viking ship burial
- Breton victory
- Breton defeat

ATLANTIC OCEAN

0 — 20 miles
0 — 30 km

(Far left) Beginning of St Mark's Gospel from the 9th century Evangeliary of Landévennec. St Mark is usually represented by a lion, the Breton custom of representing him with a horse is a pun on the Old Breton word marc'h, *'horse'.*

(Left) A gold bangle from the 10th-century pagan Viking ship burial on Île de Groix, one of the few tangible reminders of the Viking occupation of Brittany.

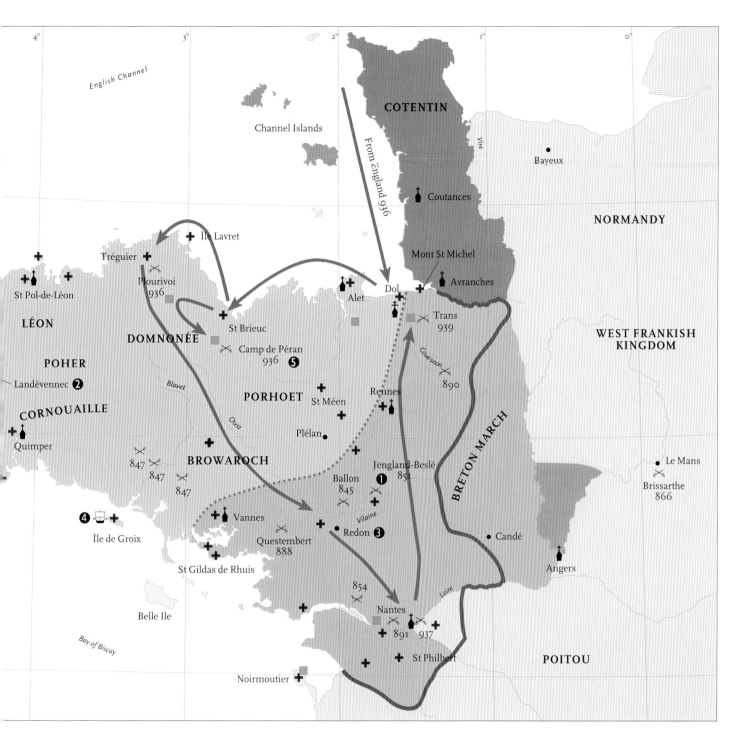

English Channel

4°   3°   2°   1°   0°

Channel Islands

COTENTIN

Vire

Bayeux

Coutances

NORMANDY

Île Lavret

Tréguier

Plourivoi
936

St Pol-de-Léon

LÉON

DOMNONÉE

St Brieuc

Mont St Michel

Dol

Alet

Avranches

Trans
939

**WEST FRANKISH
KINGDOM**

Coesnon

Camp de Péran
936 ⑤

POHER

Landévennec ②

Blavet

PORHOET

St Méen

Rennes

890

BRETON MARCH

CORNOUAILLE

Quimper

Oust

Plélan

847   847

847

BROWAROCH

Ballon
845

Jengland-Beslé
851 ①

Le Mans

Brissarthe
866

④ 🚢

Île de Groix

Vannes

Questembert
888

Redon ③

Vilaine

Candé

St Gildas de Rhuis

854

Loire

Angers

Belle Ile

Bay of Biscay

Nantes

891   937

St Philbert

POITOU

Noirmoutier

From England 936

they defeated the Franks at Brissarthe, forcing Charles to cede the Cotentin peninsula to Salomon in 867 and make him the symbolic gift of a crown. This was the apogée for early medieval Brittany. But although Brittany was independent, the influence of the Carolingian Renaissance was steadily undermining the Celtic character of Breton culture.

The Vikings became more of a problem to the Bretons after the settlement of Rollo in Normandy in 911 closed the Seine to them. In 913 Landévennec was sacked and there was a general flight of monks to the greater security of Francia. In 919 Breton resistance collapsed and by 921 Nantes was the capital of a Viking kingdom. Alain Barbetorte ('twistbeard') led a successful reconquest in 936–39, but the effect on Breton independence had been disastrous. Alain was unable to impose his authority on the Breton aristocracy and ruled only as a duke, not a king.

MAP NOTES

① *Erispoë's victory over the Franks at Jengland-Beslé established Brittany as a kingdom.*

② *Landévennec was an important centre for book production in the later 9th century.*

③ *Breton monks spent years wandering after fleeing the Vikings in 913. Those of Redon moved first to Plélan, then Angers, Candé, Auxerre (Yonne) before finding refuge in Poitou.*

④ *A 10th-century Viking chief was cremated in his longship with a human sacrifice, weapons, jewelry, tools and gaming pieces.*

⑤ *Excavations of a Viking fort show it was destroyed by fire in the 930s, perhaps by Alain Barbetorte.*

The Decline of
Celtic Brittany

AD 939 – 1532

In the two centuries after the expulsion of the Vikings, Brittany developed into a decentralized feudal society, dominated by local castellans, which owed little to its Celtic roots. Virtually the only sign of ducal authority was the success of the policy of Alain Barbetorte and his successors to encourage the restoration of monastic life. The church in general fell under the control of the aristocracy: bishops ran in family dynasties. Church reform was eventually carried out by the papacy, aided by the spread of the Cistercian monastic movement in the 12th century and the friars in the 13th century.

BRITTANY WAS AFFECTED by developments in the powerful neighbouring principalities of Normandy and Anjou. From the 990s Brittany drifted into the Norman orbit until Henry of Anjou became king of England in 1156, when it became an Angevin satellite. In 1204 Brittany came under the influence of Capetian France. With the connivance of King Philip Augustus, Pope Innocent III ended the independence of the Breton church by suppressing the archbishopric of Dol.

A steady stream of emigration from Brittany (which has continued to the present day) began in the second half of the 11th century. For those of the poorer classes the main destination was France, especially Paris, where they were mocked for their inability to speak French. For members of the knightly class, careers beckoned in Normandy and England and the Norman principalities in southern Italy. After 1066 up to 20 per cent of land in England was held by Bretons who had accompanied William the Conqueror. Commercial relations with England became important in the later Middle Ages.

A disputed succession to the duchy in 1341 dragged Brittany into the early stages of the Hundred Years War. When Philip VI of France nominated Charles of Blois to succeed, Edward III of England supported his rival Jean de Montfort and civil war broke out. Though de Montfort benefited in Breton

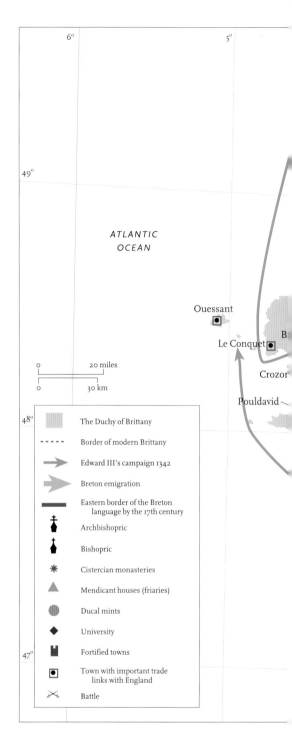

(Left) Wayside calvaries, monuments carved with scenes from the Passion of Christ, were a prominent feature of the Breton countryside in the later Middle Ages. Notre Dame de Tronoën, Finistère, c. 1450–70.

(Right) A collection of charters and other acts spanning the late 8th to the 12th centuries, the Cartulary of Redon is a uniquely detailed source of information about the economic and social structure of medieval Brittany.

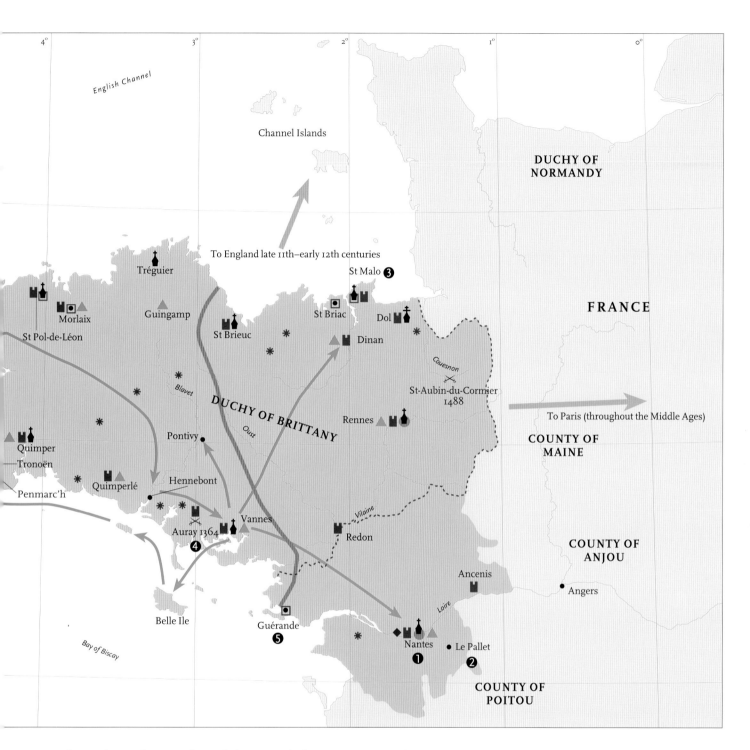

To England late 11th–early 12th centuries

Channel Islands

English Channel

DUCHY OF NORMANDY

FRANCE

To Paris (throughout the Middle Ages)

COUNTY OF MAINE

COUNTY OF ANJOU

COUNTY OF POITOU

Tréguier

Morlaix

St Pol-de-Léon

Guingamp

St Brieuc

St Briac

St Malo ❸

Dol

Dinan

DUCHY OF BRITTANY

Coesnon

St-Aubin-du-Cormier 1488

Rennes

Blavet

Oust

Pontivy

Quimper

Tronoën

Penmarc'h

Quimperlé

Hennebont

Vannes

Auray 1364 ❹

Vilaine

Redon

Ancenis

Angers

Belle Ile

Guérande ❺

Loire

Nantes ❶

Le Pallet ❷

Bay of Biscay

eyes by not being the French candidate, it took direct intervention by Edward III in 1342 to save his cause, and it was only in 1365 that France finally recognized his son, Jean IV, as duke. The final defeat of England by France in 1454 changed the balance against Brittany. After crushing the Bretons at St-Aubin-du-Cormier in 1488, France gained effective control. In 1491 the heiress to Brittany, Anne, was married to King Charles VIII and formal incorporation of the duchy into France took place in 1532. Though the Breton parliament survived until the French Revolution, its powers were gradually undermined by the centralizing French monarchy – despite sometimes violent resistance.

Ironically, after Brittany's absorption into France Breton developed as a literary language, with poetry, drama and prose written for ordinary people. Despite this Breton began to lose ground to French, though French governments actively discriminated against the language only after the Revolution.

MAP NOTES

❶ Nantes was the most important political and cultural centre of ducal Brittany.

❷ Many Bretons moved to Paris to study, the most famous of whom was the philosopher Peter Abelard, born at Le Pallet in 1079.

❸ Founded in the 13th century on the island of Alet, St Malo quickly became Brittany's premier port.

❹ The Montfort victory over Charles of Blois at Auray in 1364 ended the Breton civil war.

❺ Sea salt, produced from salines around Guérande, became a Breton export in the 15th century.

The Celts of Britain and Ireland were different. So far as we know, none of the Celtic-speaking inhabitants of those islands ever used the word Celt to describe themselves before modern times. Though Roman writers recognized similarities of language and culture between the British Celts and the Gauls, they regarded them as a separate people, as, indeed, the Britons seem to have regarded themselves.

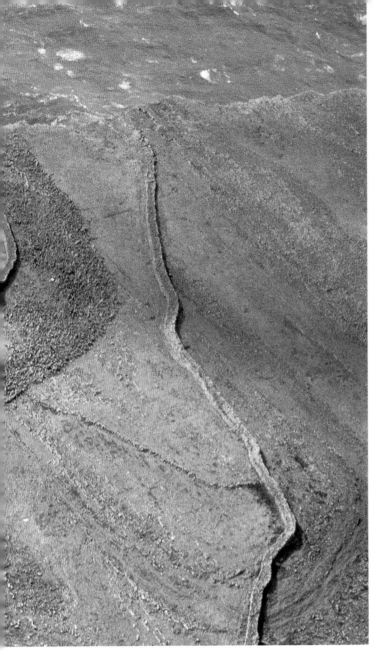

PART 2

The great Iron Age cliff-top fort of Dun Aengus on the island of Inishmore, Co. Galway, Ireland. Three circuits of stone walls and a barrier of chevaux de frise *meant that the fort was strongly defended, but the raised platform at its centre suggests that it may also have served a ritual function.*

WHILE THE CONTINENTAL CELTS were conquered and assimilated by Rome, some of the Atlantic Celts always preserved their independence, and even those who did not were never completely Romanized. Once the power of Rome waned, the Atlantic Celts triumphantly reasserted themselves.

Britain and Ireland in Late Prehistory

Britain and Ireland were known to the Mediterranean civilizations from at least the 6th century BC, probably earlier, but it is not until Julius Caesar's Roman invasions of 55–54 BC that we have any reliable eyewitness reports of their inhabitants. At this time, Britain was occupied by two different Celtic peoples, the Britons, who occupied the whole island south of the Forth-Clyde isthmus, and the Caledonians to its north. The Britons spoke Brithonic, a form of p-Celtic related to Gaulish and ancestral to modern Welsh. Little is known about the Caledonian language but it was

THE ATLANTIC CELTS

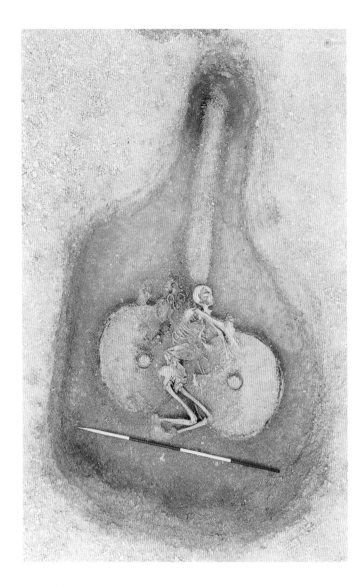

launched their full-scale conquest of Britain in AD 43, these differences exerted a decisive influence on events.

Britain – at least the south – had close links with Gaul. Caesar tells us that earlier in the 1st century Diviciacus, a king of the Belgic Suessiones, had actually ruled part of Britain. He also records that the Belgae had raided Britain and some had settled. In 50 BC, another Gaul, Commius, became king of the Atrebates. Archaeology and literary sources both attest to trade links, especially with the Veneti of Brittany. It was no doubt through contacts such as these that the continental Hallstatt and La Tène art styles reached Britain and, eventually, Ireland. These, and other, continental influences were never adopted slavishly but were always adapted to local needs. Contacts are one thing, but there is no convincing evidence for major migrations of Continental Celtic peoples to Britain in the Iron Age, or indeed for a long time before. Settlement patterns and the archaeology of daily life indicate a high degree of cultural and ethnic continuity in Britain and Ireland stretching back into the Bronze Age and even the Neolithic. This raises questions, unanswerable at present, as to when and how the peoples of the British Isles became Celtic-speaking.

As had been the case with Gaul, the Romans conquered and pacified the economically and politically advanced southeast of Britain with relative ease, but the further west and north they advanced, the harder they found it to pacify the local tribes. And while the settled farmers of the southeast could be profitably assimilated within the Roman economic system, the seasonally mobile pastoralists of the north and west could not. In the end, the Romans abandoned the complete conquest of Britain and settled for a frontier within the island (for most of the time based on the Solway-Tyne isthmus). North of the frontier the Celtic Iron Age continued, as it did in Ireland, which remained almost completely unaffected by the Roman presence across the Irish Sea. The Roman general Agricola contemplated the conquest of Ireland, but its social and economic development was similar to northern Britain's and it would have proved just as difficult and unprofitable to subdue.

Britain never became as highly Romanized as Gaul. Some craftsmen continued to use traditional Celtic decorative styles, Celtic pagan religion was still flourishing in the late 4th century and most of the population remained Celtic-speaking throughout. In the mountainous north and west of the Roman province, which remained under military government, even the old tribal identities survived. After Roman rule ended in AD 410, much of Britain quickly returned to its Celtic roots: the most long-lasting conse-

probably similar to Brithonic. Ireland was inhabited by peoples known to the Romans as Hiberni: these spoke a form of q-Celtic ancestral to Gaelic.

Compared to their Continental cousins, the Atlantic Celts were somewhat backward. The southeast was experiencing the first stirrings of urbanization and state formation, a process accelerated by Caesar's conquest of Gaul, which exposed the southeast to the powerful Romanizing influences of trade and diplomacy. By the 1st century AD there were several powerful kingdoms in the southeast, while in much of the rest of Britain hillforts were still the most important settlements. Some of these were the large and impressive strongholds of powerful chiefs, but less centralized forms of society prevailed elsewhere, especially in the far north. Ireland too had its hillforts, and some of the royal sites of early medieval Ireland were already occupied.

There were also major economic differences between the southeast and the rest of Britain. The southeast had a prosperous mixed farming economy, trade was an important source of wealth and coinage was becoming widely used as a medium of exchange. In the north, the west and in Ireland, a pastoralist economy prevailed. When the Romans

quence of Roman rule was the introduction of Christianity, which had spread throughout Celtic Britain and Ireland by the 6th century. Even this developed its own distinctive Celtic style, however.

The Britons and the Anglo-Saxon Invasions

The two centuries which followed the end of Roman rule are the most poorly documented of British history. The unity which Roman rule had imposed on the Britons broke down as local aristocrats seized power and founded independent dynastic kingdoms. In the less Romanized north and west some of these at least were based on the Iron Age tribes. It is less clear what happened in the southeast because by the end of the 5th century it had been overrun by the Anglo-Saxons, Germanic tribes from the North Sea coast of Germany and Denmark. These peoples seem to have been invited in to defend the Britons against their Celtic neighbours, the Picts and Scots, but they subsequently rebelled and began to seize territory for themselves. The struggle between the Britons and the Anglo-Saxons, or the English, as they came to call themselves, continued for centuries, but by c. 700 the British territories had been divided into three enclaves, Cornwall, Wales and Strathclyde.

How was it possible for the Anglo-Saxon barbarians to overrun the wealthiest and most populous part of Britain so quickly? Being the most Romanized part of Britain, the bonds of traditional Celtic tribal society were perhaps weakest here. It was probably also here that the Roman administration, and its tax collectors, had been most effective. In the late Roman empire the tax burden fell most heavily on the peasantry, undermining positive loyalty to the empire. Nowhere in the collapsing Roman world did the invading Germanic barbarians face much popular resistance and, as they were not efficient tax collectors, most peasants were better off without the empire. The Romano-British elite in the southeast probably tried to maintain a Romanized government – it was the only model of government they knew – but this enthusiasm would not have been shared by the peasants who were expected to pay for it. Without the bonds of tribal solidarity, resistance to the Anglo-Saxons probably collapsed very quickly. The peasants remained on the land, eventually becoming assimilated to the culture and language of the conquerors: most modern English will have ancient Britons among their ancestors.

The British enclaves in Cornwall and Strathclyde did not last – the first was conquered by the English in the 8th century, the second by the Scots in the 11th. Wales proved resilient. This was partly due to its mountainous terrain, but this also worked against the Welsh because the difficult communications prevented co-ordinated resistance and were an obstacle to political unity. Wales never became a single nation, but remained divided into separate kingdoms, none of which could maintain supremacy over the others for long: English intervention frequently saw to this. Wales was finally conquered by England in the 13th century, but there was a last flare-up of resistance under Owain Glyndŵr in 1400 which was suppressed only with great difficulty. In 1536–42 Wales officially became part of England, but the Welsh language and identity survived. The Protestant Reformation took root in Wales and the Bible was translated into

Reconstructed crannog at Craggaunown, Co. Clare, Ireland. Crannogs were artificial islands, usually just large enough for one homestead and a defensive palisade. Widespread in Ireland and Scotland, most date to the Iron Age and early Middle Ages.

Welsh in 1567–88. Although it had no place in administration, law and state education, Welsh thus became the language of religious instruction and so remained central to Welsh culture and identity. Despite its early conquest, Cornwall never became completely anglicized and today remains perhaps the only part of England where the inhabitants will not automatically describe themselves as English.

Harlech Castle, Gwynedd, Wales. Harlech was one of several state-of-the-art castles begun by Edward I to consolidate his conquest of Wales in 1282–83. The castle was not impregnable – it was taken by the Welsh in 1404 during Owain Glyndŵr's rebellion.

Kings and High Kings

Roman contacts with Ireland were limited and it is only with its conversion to Christianity in the 5th century that it comes fully into the light of history. In Ireland, Christianity met the La Tène Iron Age face to face: the surprisingly harmonious fusion of the two produced one of the most creative and original civilizations of early medieval Europe. The influence of this largely monastic-based society extended far beyond Ireland, but claims that the Irish saved European civilization are taking justified national pride a bit too far.

Early Christian Ireland was still a very decentralized society, with half a dozen high kingdoms and dozens of sub-kingdoms and local dynasties. The kings of Tara enjoyed a clear but undefined superiority over other Irish kings and by the 9th century, under the Uí Néill (O'Neill) kings, this came to be seen as a mark of the supreme kingship of Ireland. The high kings could exercise authority outside their ancestral lands only through the intermediary of tributary kings who were always ready to withdraw their allegiance if they thought they could get away with it. Even Brian Boru, the greatest of early Irish kings, had to work within these constraints and they proved his undoing in the end.

Celtic Ireland faced its first major external challenge at the end of the 8th century with the beginning of Viking pirate raids. The Vikings ranged across Ireland seemingly at will (though never with impunity) and there is no doubt that they caused great damage and suffering. Yet, in striking contrast with England, the Vikings never succeeded in settling outside a few fortified coastal enclaves. Ireland's extreme decentralization made it difficult to organize a co-ordinated response to Viking raids, but it also made it impossible for the Vikings to conquer and hold territory securely. It was possible to negotiate with the relatively centralized Anglo-Saxon kingdoms, or even take them over completely, but in Ireland there was a never-ending succession of kings to fight.

Ireland and the English

Ireland's decentralization also proved to be a major obstacle to Anglo-Norman ambitions after 1169. Ireland's reputation for rebellion discouraged English settlers: those who did come were, like the Vikings before them, largely confined to the security of fortified towns and had a distressing tendency (from the English government's point of view) to 'go native'. This applied even to the Anglo-Norman aristocracy, which envied the unconstrained powers of Irish kings. The Reformation proved to be a turning point in English policy towards Ireland. Protestantism was rejected both by the Irish and the 'Old English' settlers. Fearful that the hostile Catholic powers of Europe might use Ireland as a base to attack England, the English government for the first time made the subjugation of the Irish a priority. After the defeat of the last great Irish potentate, Hugh O'Neill, the earl of Tyrone, in 1603, the English government planned to overwhelm the Catholic Irish by encouraging mass settlement of Lowland Scots and English Protestants. But the new English colonies in North America were more attractive prospects for settlement than eternally troublesome Ireland, and the plans were only partly fulfilled. At the end of the 17th century the large majority of the population of Ireland was still Gaelic-speaking and Catholic, though all but 14 per cent of the land was in the hands of a new English-speaking Protestant elite.

The Birth of Scotland

Though never conquered, the Caledonians of northern Britain were profoundly affected by Rome. Roman invasions started a process whereby the tribes gradually amalgamated into larger units. By the end of the 3rd century a common Pictish identity had emerged. Though much feared by the Romans and Britons, the Picts did not survive into the modern age. In the 4th and 5th centuries Irish pirates called Scotti began raiding western Britain. Irish settlements followed in the Isle of Man, Wales and in Argyll, where the northern Irish Dál Riata dynasty founded a small kingdom. In the 9th century Kenneth MacAlpin, the king of Dál Riata, conquered the Picts and took over their institutions of kingship, so creating a kingdom which became known as Alba, from the Irish Gaelic word for Britain, or Scotia – Scotland. The Picts were assimilated with the Scots in little more than a century; their language died out, replaced by Gaelic. Since the Middle Ages, Scottish consciousness of Irish origins has declined and in recent years the Picts have been restored to a prominent place in Scottish national mythology.

With the annexation in the 10th–11th centuries of the British kingdom of Strathclyde and the northern English province of Lothian, Scotland reached approximately its modern extent. This process is usually described as the unification of Scotland – a parallel development to the unification of England under the Wessex dynasty – but this is not strictly true. While a common English identity preceded the creation of a unified English kingdom, there was still no sense of the Scots as a distinct people at this time. Scotland

was simply the area ruled by the king of the Scots, who still thought of themselves as being Irish. Scotland long remained a multi-ethnic kingdom of Gaelic, English and Welsh speakers. Even after the Wars of Independence with England consolidated a common Scottish national identity, the kingdom remained divided between the English-speaking Lowlands and the Gaelic-speaking Highlands – in effect a half-Celtic hybrid.

The Suppression of the Gaels

During the 12th and 13th centuries, Scotland's Celtic monarchy gradually became anglicized as a result of Anglo-Norman influence, but Gaelic lords retained their power, influence and prestige. Several bloody Highland interventions in Lowland politics in the 16th and 17th centuries made the government more determined to impose its authority effectively in the Highlands. This was finally achieved by the suppression of the 1745 Jacobite Rising, which was followed by the destruction of the last traditional Celtic society. Although often presented today as a Scottish rising against English rule it was not even a rising of all the Highlands, and then not against England but the Hanoverian dynasty, which most Scots continued to support. In its indiscriminate repression of the Highlanders after Culloden, the British government enjoyed the full support of Lowland Scots.

Carved Pictish stone from Aberlemno, Tayside, Scotland. The stone is thought to commemorate the victory of King Bridei mac Bili over the Northumbrians (shown here wearing helmets with noseguards) in the battle of Nechtansmere near Dunnichen Moss in 685.

Prehistoric Celtic Britain and Ireland

Iron Age Britain and Ireland had much in common with Celtic Europe, but there were also important differences. Before the late 20th century, archaeologists concentrated on the similarities and concluded that Celtic language and culture were introduced to Britain by invaders from the European continent. More recently, archaeologists have focused on the differences and concluded that these prove that there were no major Celtic invasions. Britain and Ireland are now regarded by some archaeologists as part of the zone where the Celtic languages originally developed.

ALTHOUGH THERE MAY HAVE been no major invasions, the British Isles were open to continental influences, such as the Hallstatt and La Tène art styles, through trade and political contacts. The British Isles were not culturally uniform and large areas in the west and north were relatively unaffected by continental influences.

The most obvious physical remains of the Iron Age are fortifications, which are frequent in much of Britain though rather less so in Ireland. Hillforts are the most common type of fortification south of the Grampian Mountains, with the largest forts concentrated in the Welsh borderlands and central-southern England, and an isolated group in southeast Ireland. North and west of the Grampians stone brochs and duns (small round forts) were built. Small defensive enclosures, known as raths or rounds, are also found in southwest Wales and southwest England. Raths are also very common in Ireland but, though some are probably prehistoric, most date from early Christian times. Hillforts had different functions. Many, such as Danebury, were the permanently occupied strongholds of chieftains. Ingleborough, on a 724-m (2375-ft) high hilltop, was probably an emergency refuge. Some major Irish sites, like the Navan, were primarily ritual centres.

By the time of Caesar's punitive expeditions in 55–54 BC, hillforts were developing into proto-urban *oppida* in southeastern Britain and some were being abandoned in favour of less restrictive open sites on lower ground. The approaches to the *oppida* at Colchester and Selsey were defended by linear earthworks, a sign of the presence of powerful rulers. Another indication of the beginning of state formation in the southeast is the development of a native coinage. Extensive linear earthworks in northern Ireland point to the emergence of a powerful kingdom there.

Evidence of religious practices comes from votive deposits of precious metalwork discovered in bogs, lakes, rivers and sacrificial pits. Finds of preserved bodies in bogs and skeletons in pits show that human sacrifice was not unknown. Burial practices are uncertain. Most people probably received no formal burial at all, but cremation was practised in southeast Britain and inhumation in the north and west. Both customs were practised in Ireland. Princely burials are known, such as the Welwyn group in the southeast and the east Yorkshire Arras group, which shows the influence of La Tène customs.

The Turoe Stone, Loughrea, Co. Galway, Ireland, 1st century BC–1st century AD. Carved from granite with swirling La Tène patterns, it presumably served some unknown ritual function.

MAP NOTES

❶ *Southern Britain had close links with the Belgae of Gaul, some of whom may have settled there c. 100 BC.*

❷ *Linear earthworks may have been border defences for the kingdom of Ulaid, known to have dominated northern Ireland in early historical times.*

❸ *Over 150 weapons and other items of prestige metalwork were deposited in this lake 1st century BC–1st century AD.*

❹ *One of the few excavated raths, this protected a community of six households 3rd century BC–3rd century AD.*

❺ *Promontory forts were built on easily defended headlands: one of the best preserved, this was protected by ramparts and a stone blockhouse.*

❻ *1st-century BC Welwyn-type burials included imported metalwork, pottery, glass and wine amphorae.*

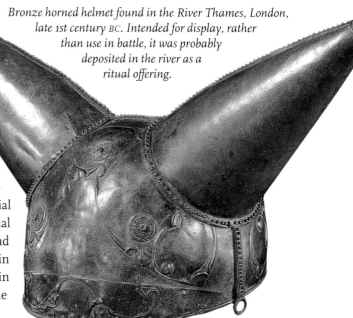

Bronze horned helmet found in the River Thames, London, late 1st century BC. Intended for display, rather than use in battle, it was probably deposited in the river as a ritual offering.

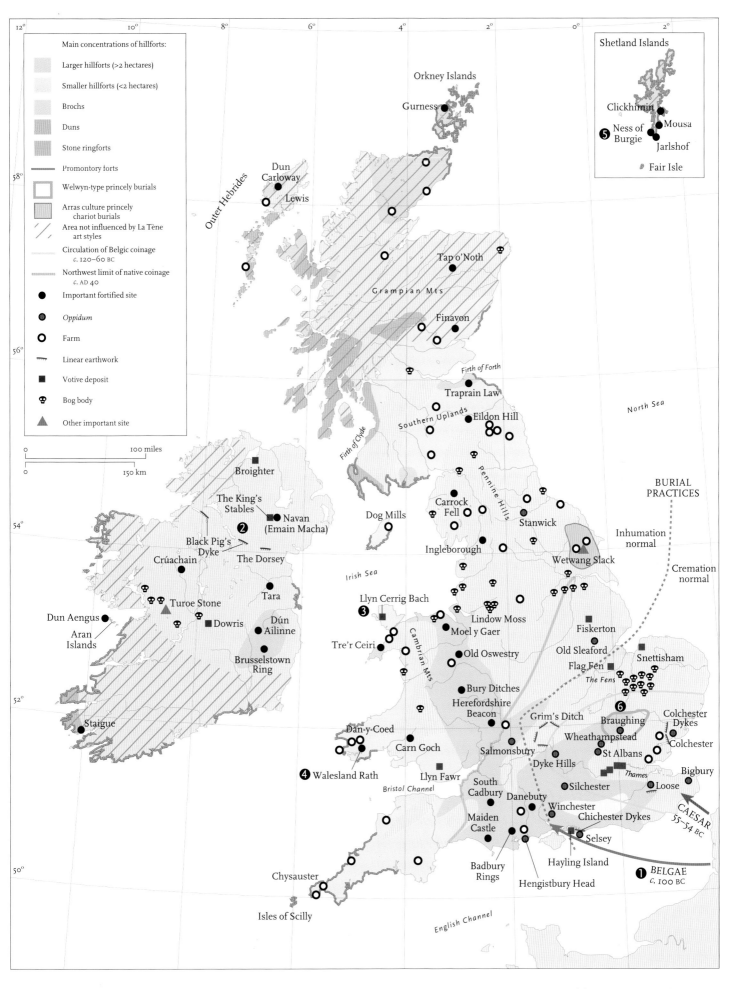

Main concentrations of hillforts:

Larger hillforts (>2 hectares)

Smaller hillforts (<2 hectares)

Brochs

Duns

Stone ringforts

Promontory forts

Welwyn-type princely burials

Arras culture princely chariot burials

Area not influenced by La Tène art styles

Circulation of Belgic coinage *c.* 120–60 BC

Northwest limit of native coinage *c.* AD 40

● Important fortified site

◑ *Oppidum*

○ Farm

〰 Linear earthwork

■ Votive deposit

⚉ Bog body

▲ Other important site

Shetland Islands

Clickhimin

Ness of Burgie ❺

Mousa

Jarlshof

Fair Isle

Orkney Islands

Gurness

Dun Carloway

Lewis

Outer Hebrides

Grampian Mts

Tap o'Noth

Finavon

Firth of Forth

Firth of Clyde

Traprain Law

Southern Uplands

Eildon Hill

North Sea

Broighter

The King's Stables

❷ Navan (Emain Macha)

Black Pig's Dyke

The Dorsey

Dog Mills

Carrock Fell

Pennine Hills

Stanwick

BURIAL PRACTICES

Inhumation normal

Cremation normal

Crúachain

Turoe Stone

Dowris

Tara

Dún Ailinne

Ingleborough

Wetwang Slack

Irish Sea

Dun Aengus

Aran Islands

Brusselstown Ring

❸ Llyn Cerrig Bach

Lindow Moss

Fiskerton

Old Sleaford

Snettisham

Tre'r Ceiri

Moel y Gaer

Old Oswestry

Flag Fen

The Fens

Staigue

Cambrian Mts

Bury Ditches

Herefordshire Beacon

Grim's Ditch

Braughing

❻

Colchester Dykes

Dan-y-Coed

Carn Goch

Salmonsbury

Wheathampstead

St Albans

Colchester

❹ Walesland Rath

Llyn Fawr

South Cadbury

Danebury

Dyke Hills

Silchester

Thames

Loose

Bigbury

Bristol Channel

Maiden Castle

Winchester

Chichester Dykes

CAESAR 55–54 BC

Chysauster

Badbury Rings

Hengistbury Head

Hayling Island

Selsey

❶ BELGAE *c.* 100 BC

Isles of Scilly

English Channel

0   100 miles

0   150 km

Brochs and Duns

c. 500 BC – AD 200

War was a pervasive feature of Celtic society and fortifications were common, nowhere more so than in northern and western Scotland, Orkney and Shetland, where hundreds of small stone forts called duns and stone towers called brochs were built in the late Iron Age.

BROCHS, IN PARTICULAR, are often attributed to the Picts but they long predate them – the earliest were built in the 6th century BC and their main period of use was from the 2nd century BC to the 2nd century AD. Brochs predominate in the far northeast of Scotland and in the Orkney and Shetland islands, while duns predominate on the west coast. Few of either are found south of the Forth-Clyde isthmus, which in the 1st century AD was the border between the Caledonian tribes to the north and the Britons to the south, and they are virtually absent from the coast lands between the Moray Firth and the Firth of Tay.

Duns are simply circuits of drystone walls, up to 3 m (10 ft) high and 15–40 m (50–130 ft) in diameter. Entrances often had guard chambers and walls had galleries and internal stairs. Brochs are much more sophisticated structures: massive drystone round towers 12–25 m (40–80 ft) in diameter and 9–13 m (30–42 ft) tall. Walls could be up to 5 m (16 1/2 ft) thick at the base but higher up were hollow. This allowed taller walls to be built without putting too much weight on the foundations and provided useful storage space. Brochs were built to house a single family. Interiors were divided into a central communal space with a hearth and a water tank (for cooking), surrounded by small alcoves or sleeping compartments. Some became the nuclei for villages, as at Gurness in Orkney. Brochs may have been a development of the dun or of an earlier type of Iron Age fortification, the blockhouse.

The proliferation of small fortifications implies that a very decentralized society prevailed in much of late Iron Age Scotland with no large-scale political units able to enforce peaceful conditions over a wide area. Each broch and dun may have been the stronghold of a petty chieftain ruling over no more than a few families. By the mid-2nd century AD, the perceived need for defence declined and most were abandoned. A few brochs remained occupied in the Pictish period, reduced in height and converted into houses, while many duns were reoccupied in the early Middle Ages. The abandonment of fortifications may be linked to changes in the early centuries AD which saw the numerous Caledonian tribes replaced by the Picts.

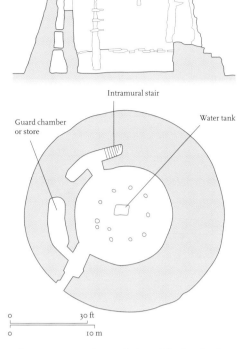

Intramural stair

Guard chamber or store

Water tank

0   30 ft
0   10 m

(Above) Cross-section and plan of the broch of Dun Troddan, Inverness. (Below) Reconstruction of the broch of Clickhimin, Shetland, as it may have appeared around the end of the 1st century BC.

Clickhimin broch, Lerwick, Shetland. Sometime after the broch fell into disuse in the 2nd or 3rd century AD, its height was reduced and its interior was converted into a house.

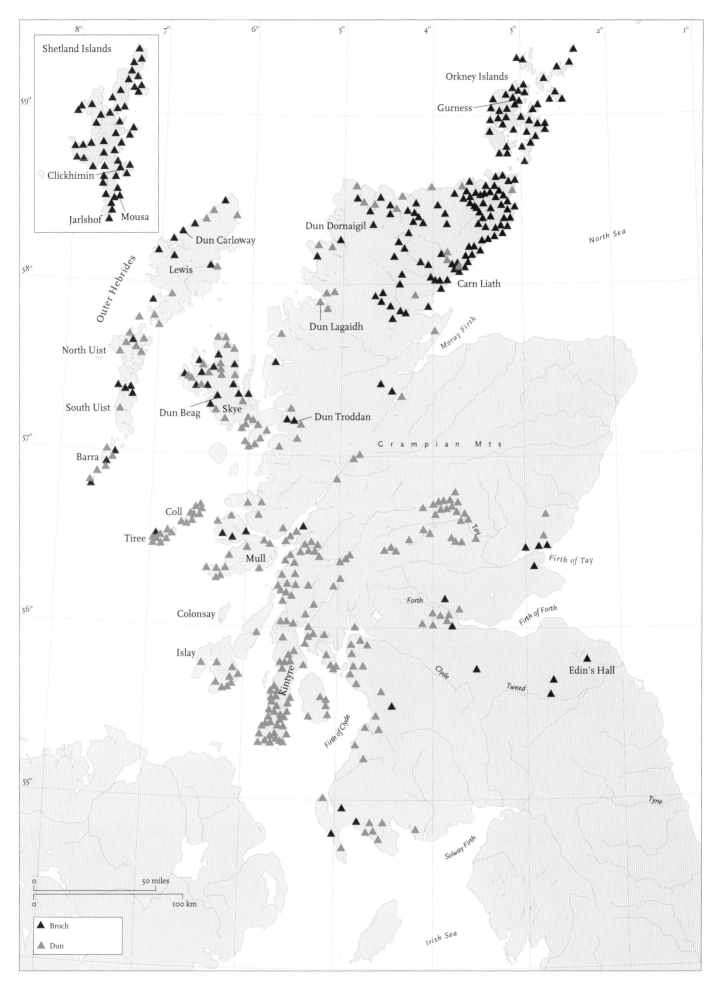

Shetland Islands

59°

Clickhimin

Jarlshof — Mousa

Dun Carloway

Lewis

58°

Outer Hebrides

North Uist

South Uist

Dun Beag — Skye

57°

Barra

Coll

Tiree

Mull

Colonsay

56°

Islay

Kintyre

55°

Orkney Islands

Gurness

North Sea

Dun Dornaigil

Carn Liath

Dun Lagaidh

Moray Firth

Dun Troddan

Grampian Mts

Tay

Firth of Tay

Forth

Firth of Forth

Clyde

Tweed

Edin's Hall

Firth of Clyde

Tyne

Solway Firth

Irish Sea

50 miles

100 km

▲ Broch
▲ Dun

The Roman Conquest of Britain

55 BC – AD 84

Before the 1st century BC Britain was of interest to the Romans only as a source of tin. Little was known about the island for certain and it remained a shadowy, almost mythical place until Caesar launched his invasions in 55–54 BC to punish the Britons for aiding the Gauls.

CAESAR'S EXPEDITIONS achieved little, but his conquest of Gaul opened south-eastern Britain to strong Romanizing influences through trade and diplomacy. The process of state formation accelerated and powerful tribal kingdoms emerged, most important among them being the Atrebates, Catuvellauni and Trinovantes. Romanizing influences are apparent in an increase in luxury imports, especially wine, and a Roman-style coinage with inscriptions in the Latin alphabet. British kings actively sought Roman support and some even travelled to Rome itself.

Colchester became a major port of entry for Roman goods and the Trinovantes and Catuvellauni both competed to control it. Around AD 10 the two peoples were united by Cunobelinus, who subsequently dominated the southeast. On his death in the early 40s, Cunobelinus' kingdom was inherited by his sons Caratacus and Togodumnus. Aggressive rulers, they attacked the Atrebates and expelled the tribe's ruler, a Roman ally.

This gave the new emperor, Claudius – who needed a military success to establish his credibility with the army – a perfect justification to order the invasion of Britain in late spring 43. Colchester was captured about two months after the initial landings: Togodumnus was killed but Caratacus escaped and caused trouble later. Several British rulers submitted to Rome and were rewarded with client status. By 47 the Romans had conquered most of Britain south of a line from the Bristol Channel to the Humber. This was the most politically and economically advanced part of the country and so was the region that could most easily and profitably be absorbed within the Roman system. It is possible that the Romans intended to establish a permanent frontier along this line. If so, events drew them on to attempt the conquest of the whole island.

Caratacus persuaded the Silures to attack the Romans, who launched an invasion of Wales. Caratacus was captured in 51 but the final conquest was delayed by the rebellion in 60 of Boudica, queen of the Iceni. A rebellion by Venutius, husband of Cartimandua, the client-queen of the Brigantes, led to a further move north to the Solway-Tyne isthmus in the 70s. It was left to Agricola to complete the conquest of Britain: between 78 and 83 he conquered the northern British tribes and campaigned up to the Moray Firth against the Caledonians. After his victory at *Mons Graupius*, Agricola established a frontier zone along the 'Highland Line', but he was recalled to Rome and the offensive was never resumed. His frontier proved undefendable and the Romans gradually pulled back to the Solway. The high tide of Roman conquest had passed.

MAP NOTES

❶ A luxury villa at Fishbourne, built c. 70, was possibly a reward for the elderly client king Cogidubnus' loyalty.

❷ Fragments of a monument, erected by the Romans to commemorate their invasion, have been found at Richborough.

❸ Colchester was the first Roman capital of Britain. London became the capital after Boudica's revolt.

❹ Inchtuthil was built in 83 as a legionary fortress to control the Caledonians but was abandoned less than four years later.

❺ The identity of Mons Graupius is unknown but was probably Bennachie above Durno camp.

❻ Agricola believed Ireland could be conquered with one legion and a few auxiliaries, but this was never put to the test.

Maiden Castle, near Dorchester, Dorset, England. The hillfort's complex earthwork defences proved no obstacle to the Romans who captured it in around AD 44. A mass burial of Britons slain in the assault has been excavated at the fort.

Allegorical sculpture from Aphrodisias, Turkey, showing the emperor Claudius defeating a personification of Britannia, dating from the 1st century AD.

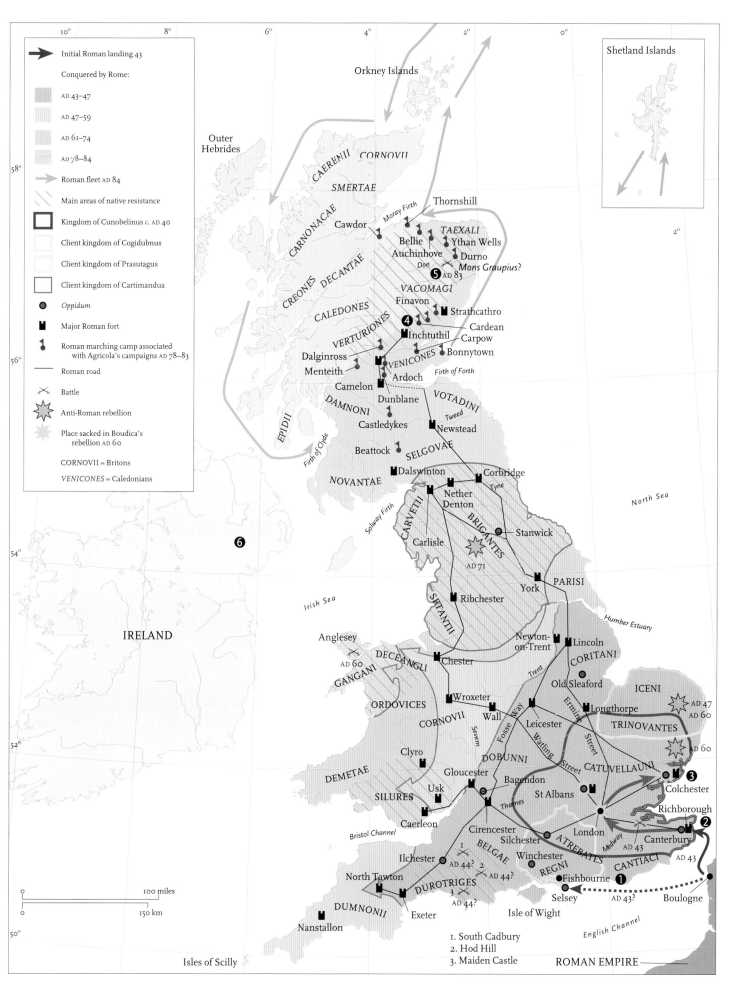

Legend:

Initial Roman landing 43

Conquered by Rome:

AD 43–47

AD 47–59

AD 61–74

AD 78–84

Roman fleet AD 84

Main areas of native resistance

Kingdom of Cunobelinus *c.* AD 40

Client kingdom of Cogidubnus

Client kingdom of Prasutagus

Client kingdom of Cartimandua

Oppidum

Major Roman fort

Roman marching camp associated with Agricola's campaigns AD 78–83

Roman road

Battle

Anti-Roman rebellion

Place sacked in Boudica's rebellion AD 60

CORNOVII = Britons

VENICONES = Caledonians

Map labels:

Orkney Islands

Shetland Islands

Outer Hebrides

CAERENII CORNOVII

SMERTAE

CARNONACAE

Cawdor

Thornshill

Moray Firth

TAEXALI

Bellie Ythan Wells

Auchinhove

CREONES DECANTAE

Durno

Don *Mons Graupius?*

❺ AD 83

VACOMAGI

Finavon

CALEDONES

Strathcathro

VERTURIONES

❹ Inchtuthil

Cardean

Dalginross

Carpow

Menteith

VENICONES

Bonnytown

Camelon

Ardoch

Firth of Forth

Dunblane

VOTADINI

Castledykes

Tweed

DAMNONI

EPIDII

Firth of Clyde

Beattock

SELGOVAE

Newstead

Dalswinton

NOVANTAE

Corbridge

Tyne

North Sea

CARVETII

Nether Denton

Solway Firth

BRIGANTES

Carlisle

Stanwick

AD 71

SETANTII

York

PARISI

Ribchester

Irish Sea

Humber Estuary

IRELAND

Anglesey

DECEANGLI

Newton-on-Trent Lincoln

AD 60

Chester

CORITANI

GANGANI

Old Sleaford

ICENI

ORDOVICES

Wroxeter

Wall

AD 47

AD 60

Trent

CORNOVII

Leicester

TRINOVANTES

Severn

Fosse Way

Watling Street

AD 60

Clyro

DOBUNNI

Ermine Street

CATUVELLAUNI

❸

DEMETAE

Gloucester

Bagendon

St Albans

Colchester

Usk

Richborough

SILURES

Cirencester

London

❷

Caerleon

Silchester

ATREBATES

Canterbury

Thames

Medway AD 43

Bristol Channel

BELGAE

REGNI

CANTIACI

AD 43

Ilchester

Winchester

Fishbourne

1 AD 44?

North Tawton

2 AD 44?

Selsey AD 43?

Boulogne

DUROTRIGES

3

Isle of Wight

DUMNONII

AD 44?

Exeter

English Channel

Nanstallon

ROMAN EMPIRE

Isles of Scilly

1. South Cadbury
2. Hod Hill
3. Maiden Castle

❻

Scale:

0   100 miles

0   150 km

The Celts and Roman Britain

The Roman conquest brought major political, economic and cultural changes to Britain, but it remained one of the least Romanized of the empire's provinces. Despite a veneer of Latin, the everyday speech of the majority of its inhabitants continued to be Celtic, and many aspects of Celtic culture and religion survived.

THE ROMANS introduced a system of government to Britain similar to the one operating in Gaul. The area under Roman control became the province of Britannia, ruled by a governor in London. Most of Britain was subdivided into *civitates* – local self-government areas based on the Iron Age tribal territories.

Roman rule brought a rapid increase in urbanization. To promote Romanization, colonies (*coloniae*) of Roman citizens were founded. Some *oppida* such as Silchester were adopted as *civitas* capitals; in other cases new towns were founded. The native aristocracy was easily accommodated within the administrative hierarchy of province and *civitas*, and their lifestyle became Romanized. British town-dwellers enjoyed most of the amenities associated with Roman urban life, including hot baths, amphitheatres and aqueducts. Classical sculpture, wall painting and mosaics were introduced, but La Tène decorations remained popular for personal ornaments. Change was much less dramatic in the countryside, where 95 per cent of the population lived. The economically advanced southeast saw the growth of large farming estates and villas, especially in the 4th century, but in the west and north, farming and building techniques continued relatively unchanged.

The Romans introduced the imperial cults to Britain and suppressed the Druids because they practised human sacrifice and were politically disruptive, but native Celtic cults continued to flourish. Celtic deities were often linked with a Roman deity with similar attributes and worshipped in Classical temples, although Gallic-type temples are also known. Springs and other natural sites continued to be revered. In the 3rd century eastern cults, such as Mithraism and Christianity, were introduced to Britain.

In the 2nd century the northern frontier of Britannia stabilized on a system based on Hadrian's Wall. The British tribes immediately to the north were supervised by agents and kept friendly with subsidies. In the far north, the Roman invasion had caused the tribes to coalesce into two federations by *c.* 200: the Caledones and the Maeatae. Despite periodic hostilities, there was considerable trade between the Roman province and northern Britain: Roman goods even reached the Shetland Islands.

Ireland preserved a vigorous late La Tène culture. Literary sources record trade between Roman Britain and Ireland but few Roman objects have been found there. Reports from merchants gave Roman geographers the first reasonably accurate descriptions of the island and its peoples. A few sites known to have been important for kingship rituals in early Christian times can be recognized, though – surprisingly – not Tara.

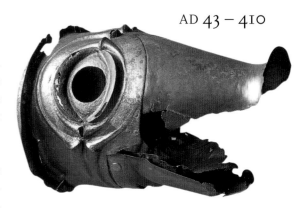

The mouth of a bronze carnyx (war trumpet) in the shape of a boar from Deskford, Grampian region, Scotland, 1st century AD. Loud, raucous noise was an important part of Celtic warfare.

MAP NOTES

❶ *Excavations of a very large promontory fort here have produced evidence of frequent contacts with the Roman world.*

❷ *Built in 122, Hadrian's Wall was the main element of the northern frontier system for most of the next 300 years.*

❸ *Built in c. 142, the Antonine Wall was permanently abandoned only 21 years later.*

❹ *Pilgrims to the temple of the healing god Nodens at Lydney made offerings of model dogs, a symbol of healing in Celtic religion.*

❺ *Maiden Castle hillfort was evacuated for Dorchester after the Roman conquest, but it remained in use as a religious sanctuary.*

❻ *Romano-British style cremation burial may be of the wife of a British trader living in Ireland.*

This enamelled bronze brooch probably from northern England (late 1st century AD) illustrates the tenacity of Celtic decorative traditions under the Romans. This type of brooch was still made in Roman Britain in the 3rd century.

Celtic craftsmen adapted Classical themes, as in this striking head of Medusa from the temple of Sulis Minerva at Bath. Late 1st century AD.

Legend

Roman empire in 122

Roman territory abandoned 84–105

Territory reoccupied by Rome 138–54, 158–63

Main distribution of villas

■ Provincial capital

◉ *Civitas* capital

— *Civitas* borders

◉ *Colonia* of Roman citizens

▮ Legionary fortress

◉ Romano-Celtic temple

○ Other Celtic religious site

▲ Other important site

• Roman imports of 1st–3rd centuries (Ireland and north of the Antonine Wall only)

✴ Anti-Roman rebellion

100 miles

150 km

Shetland Islands

Orkney Islands

Outer Hebrides

North Sea

Deskford

CALEDONES

MAEATAE (VERTURIONES)

Dumyat

Antonine Wall ❸

Firth of Forth

Traprain Law

VOTADINI

Blackburn

Eckford

SELGOVAE

Locus (Maponi)

DAMNONI

Firth of Clyde

NOVANTAE

❷ Hadrian's Wall

Coventina's Well

Carlingwark

Carlisle (Luguvalium)

Solway Firth

CARVETII

Tyne

Aldborough (Isurium Brigantum)

York (Eburacum)

BRIGANTES

c. 154

PARISI

VENNICONII

ROBOGDI (DÁL RIATA)

Navan (Emain Macha) (Isamnion)

ERNAEI

DARINI (DÁL FIATACH)

NAGNATAE

VOLUNTI (ULAID)

Isle of Man

Brough (Petuaria)

Crúachain (Regia?)

EBDANI

Chester (Deva)

Buxton (Aquae Arnemetiae)

Lincoln (Lindum)

Tara

Drumanagh (Ebdana?) ❶

DECEANGLI

CORNOVII

CORITANI

CAUCI

Dún Ailinne (Dunon?)

Irish Sea

ORDOVICES

Wroxeter (Viroconium Cornoviorum)

Leicester (Ratae Coritanorum)

ICENI

AUTEINI

MANAPII

Norwich (Venta Icenorum)

USDIAE

Stonyford ❻

CORIONDI

BRIGANTES

DEMETAE

DOBUNNI

CATUVELLAUNI

TRINOVANTES

GANGANI

Carmarthen (Moridunum)

❹ Lydney

Gloucester (Glevum)

St Albans (Verulamium)

Gosbecks

❽ 8

VELLABORI

SILURES

3

Heathrow

Harlow

Chelmsford

IVERNI (ÉRAINN)

4 5

2

ATREBATES

6

Silchester (Calleva Atrebatum)

Springhead

7

Bristol Channel

1

BELGAE

REGNI

CANTIACI

Brean Down

Cannington

Lamyatt

Isle of Wight

Chichester (Noviomagus Regnensium)

Hayling Island

DUROTRIGES

DUMNONII

❺ Maiden Castle

Dorchester (Durnovaria)

Winchester (Venta Belgarum)

Exeter (Isca Dumnoniorum)

Isles of Scilly

English Channel

GAUL

1. Bath (Aquae Sulis)
2. Nettleton
3. Cirencester (Corinium Dobunnorum)
4. Caerleon (Isca)
5. Caerwent (Venta Silurum)
6. London (Londinium)
7. Canterbury (Durovernum Cantiacorum)
8. Colchester (Camulodunum)

The Origins of the Picts

AD 200 – 600

Alone among the Celtic peoples known to have lived in the British Isles in historical times, the Picts have vanished completely, their language, culture and identity destroyed by the Scots in the early Middle Ages. Their beautiful but enigmatic symbol stones, so obviously full of meaning to their makers but so impenetrable to the modern historian, have only heightened the sense of mystery that surrounds the Picts.

THE PICTS are first mentioned in Roman literature in 297. The name, meaning 'painted people', probably originated as a nickname among Roman frontier garrisons, perhaps because they decorated their bodies with tattoos. The Picts were not newcomers to Britain but were the descendants of the Iron Age Caledonian tribes. The Grampian Mountains divided the Picts into northern and southern groups, probably equivalent to the Caledones and the Maeatae. Concentrations of high-status sites and pre-Christian barrow cemeteries and burial cairns indicate that the heartlands of these two groupings were around the Moray Firth and Strathmore. Skeletal evidence from their burials disproves the story put about by medieval writers that the Picts were pygmies.

Few records of the Pictish language have survived: our knowledge is restricted mainly to personal and place-names. Some Pictish words have defied attempts at translation and may represent elements of a non-Celtic language which had survived from the time before the Celtic languages had evolved. Most Pictish words, however, show that the language was related to the Brithonic language of the Britons, particularly the Cumbric dialect spoken in what is now northern England and southern Scotland. The most distinctive Pictish place-name element is the prefix *pit-* (as in Pitlochry), from the Gallo-Brithonic word *pett*, meaning 'a piece of land'. The location of these seems to indicate that the densest Pictish settlement was east of the Grampians, but it is likely that *pit-* place-names have been lost in Caithness, Orkney and Shetland through the influence of Norse, and on the west coast as a result of the severe rural depopulation experienced in the 18th and 19th centuries.

Pictish silver plaque from Norrie's Law, Fife, with a version of the common double disc and Z-rod symbol (possibly 5th century). The plaques were originally enamelled in red.

MAP NOTES

❶ *Some of the earliest known Pictish symbols are incised on the walls of Covesea cave. Beheaded skeletons buried there are evidence that the Picts practised human sacrifice.*

❷ *Built c. 300, Burghead is the largest Pictish fort known. Inside the fort was a ritual well. The fort was destroyed, probably by Vikings, in the 9th century.*

❸ *Square barrow cemeteries, like Redcastle, were used from the 1st to 7th centuries AD.*

❹ *Find site of the only symbol stone to be found so far in a scientifically datable context (mid-6th century).*

❺ *Many Iron Age brochs, such as Gurness, were reoccupied by the Picts who converted them into dwellings or used them as stone quarries to build new houses.*

Pre-Christian Pictish symbol stone from Aberlemno, Tayside. The stone features three of the most common Pictish symbols: the snake; the double disc and Z-rod; and the mirror.

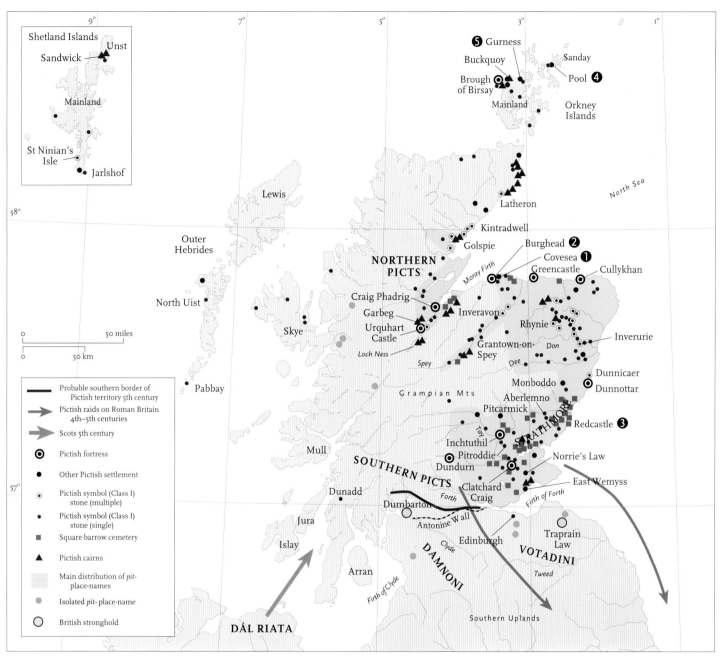

Shetland Islands

Sandwick · Unst
St Ninian's Isle · Jarlshof
Mainland

⑤ Gurness
Buckquoy
Brough of Birsay
Mainland
Sanday · Pool ④
Orkney Islands

Lewis

Outer Hebrides

North Uist

Skye

Pabbay

Mull

Jura

Islay

Arran

Latheron
Kintradwell
Golspie

NORTHERN PICTS

Craig Phadrig
Garbeg
Urquhart Castle
Loch Ness
Inveravon
Grantown-on-Spey
Spey

Burghead ②
Covesea ①
Greencastle
Cullykhan
Rhynie
Inverurie
Don
Dee
Grampian Mts
Monboddo
Dunnicaer
Dunnottar
Aberlemno
Pitcarmick
Redcastle ③
STRATHMORE
Inchtuthil
Pitroddie
Tay
Dundurn
Clatchard Craig
Norrie's Law
East Wemyss
Firth of Forth

SOUTHERN PICTS

Dunadd
Dumbarton
Forth
Antonine Wall
Edinburgh
Clyde
VOTADINI
Traprain Law
Tweed

DAMNONI
Firth of Clyde
Southern Uplands

DÁL RIATA

North Sea

Moray Firth

58°
57°

9° 7° 5° 3° 1°

Legend

— Probable southern border of Pictish territory 5th century
→ Pictish raids on Roman Britain 4th–5th centuries
→ Scots 5th century
◉ Pictish fortress
● Other Pictish settlement
◉ Pictish symbol (Class I) stone (multiple)
• Pictish symbol (Class I) stone (single)
■ Square barrow cemetery
▲ Pictish cairns
▨ Main distribution of *pit-* place-names
● Isolated *pit-* place-name
○ British stronghold

50 miles
50 km

The most famous Pictish artifacts are the symbol stones. The earliest known symbols appear on metalwork datable to the 4th century, but the first symbol stones were probably not erected until the 5th or, more likely, 6th century. About 40 to 50 different symbols are known: their meaning is not understood, yet the fact that they continued to be used after the conversion of the Picts to Christianity suggests that they did not have religious significance. Symbols were usually used in combinations of 2–4: the particular combination perhaps identifying an individual, family or tribe. Although the purpose of the stones is also not known for certain, several have been found in association with burials. Some at least, therefore, will have been tombstones, a custom adopted as a result of contacts with the Romans or early British Christians.

A sketch on slate of a man's head, from the Pictish settlement at Jarlshof in the Shetland Islands.

Britain and the Britons   AD 300 – 550

The popular image of the Britons after the end of Roman rule is that of the helpless and demoralized victims of rampaging Anglo-Saxons, Picts and Scots. But this picture of moral collapse was created by later ecclesiastical writers for their own didactic purposes; in reality, the Britons defended themselves with determination and enjoyed considerable success.

IN CONTRAST WITH the rest of the western Roman empire, much of the 4th century was a time of prosperity for Britain. Saxon and Pictish pirate raids were a problem, but Roman coastal defences saved Britain from any serious incursions until 368, when it was temporarily overrun by an alliance of Saxons, Picts and Irish. Order was restored, but the province's economy began to decline, and of the dozens of towns of Roman Britain few have produced evidence of continued occupation in the 5th century. The province was left increasingly exposed as troops were withdrawn to the continent and so, in 410, the Britons expelled the Roman administration and organized their own defence. Britain thus became the only province ever to leave the Roman empire voluntarily. Events of the 5th century are obscure. Leadership probably devolved on the local Romano-British aristocracy who established themselves as hereditary rulers. By the 6th century Britain was divided into several small kingdoms, at least some of which, like Dumnonia, were based on old tribal identities.

The Britons found themselves between two expansionist peoples, the Irish (Scotti) and the Anglo-Saxons. The distribution of ogam inscriptions indicates considerable Irish settlement in parts of western Britain, but their main success was against the Picts. The only British territory the Irish won permanent control of was the Isle of Man. Having raided Britain for over 100 years, the Anglo-Saxons began to settle in the south and east in the 5th century. Later traditions relate how the British king Vortigern invited them to settle in Britain in return for military service – a well-established Roman practice – but they subsequently rebelled and began to take over the country. British resistance was rallied by Ambrosius Aurelianus and after the battle of Mount Badon (location unknown) in *c.* 500, Anglo-Saxon expansion was halted for 70 years. The Britons also engaged in successful expansionism themselves, settling in Brittany in large numbers in the 5th century.

The 4th century saw Christianity become well established among the Britons. In the 5th century British missions began to convert the Picts and Irish, though the southeast reverted to paganism under the Anglo-Saxons. Political and, after the Anglo-Saxon takeover of the southeast, physical isolation from Rome allowed the British church to develop its own distinctive customs and practices, characterized as 'Celtic Christianity'. Isolation also produced a revival of Celtic art forms.

Early Welsh wheel cross from Margam Abbey, Glamorgan, South Wales.

MAP NOTES

❶ *The 'Saxon Shore' was a Roman coastal defence command against Anglo-Saxon pirates.*

❷ *Originally Brithonic-speaking, the population of the Isle of Man became Goidelic-speaking as a result of Irish settlement in the 5th century.*

❸ *The appearance of long cist cemeteries (cemeteries of stone-slab lined graves) is thought to mark the introduction of Christianity to the Picts and northern Britons.*

❹ *Kings and aristocrats favoured sites with strong natural defences for their residences, such as the rocky outcrop of Dinas Emrys, or they reoccupied Iron Age hillforts, including South Cadbury.*

❺ *Wroxeter provides evidence for the flourishing of urban life after the end of Roman rule, with major new building in the 5th century. It was finally abandoned c. 600.*

Dumbarton Rock commands the entrance to the River Clyde and has seen a succession of fortifications. In the early Middle Ages it was the main stronghold of the British kingdom of Strathclyde.

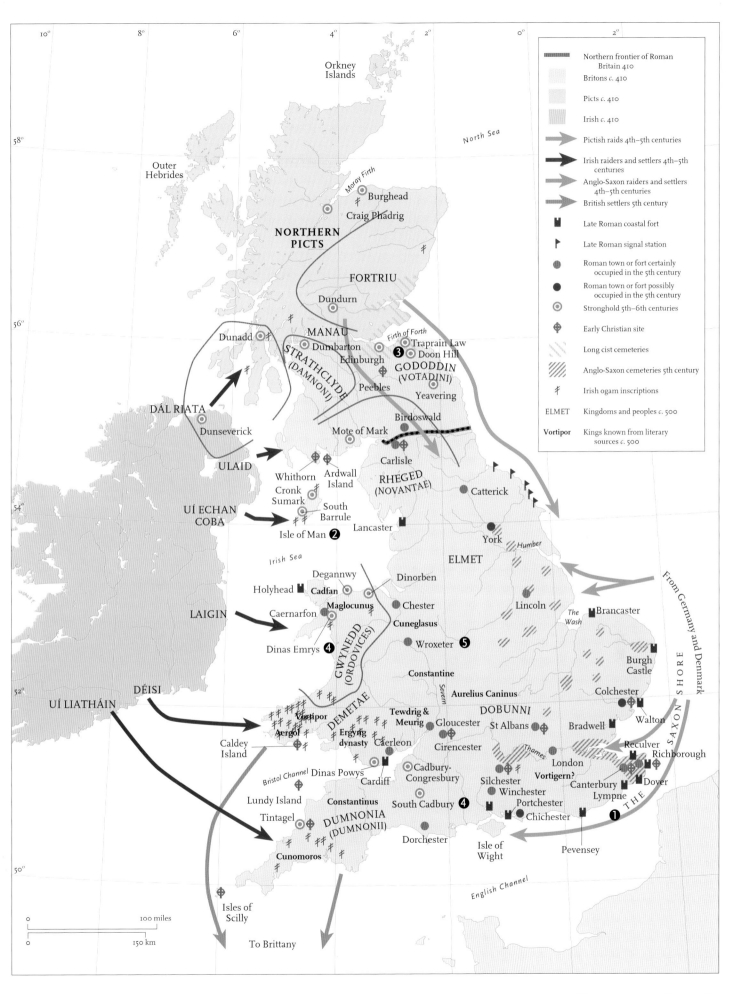

Map legend

- Northern frontier of Roman Britain 410
- Britons c. 410
- Picts c. 410
- Irish c. 410
- Pictish raids 4th–5th centuries
- Irish raiders and settlers 4th–5th centuries
- Anglo-Saxon raiders and settlers 4th–5th centuries
- British settlers 5th century
- Late Roman coastal fort
- Late Roman signal station
- Roman town or fort certainly occupied in the 5th century
- Roman town or fort possibly occupied in the 5th century
- Stronghold 5th–6th centuries
- Early Christian site
- Long cist cemeteries
- Anglo-Saxon cemeteries 5th century
- Irish ogam inscriptions
- ELMET Kingdoms and peoples c. 500
- Vortipor Kings known from literary sources c. 500

Map labels

Orkney Islands

Outer Hebrides

North Sea

NORTHERN PICTS

Moray Firth
Burghead
Craig Phadrig

FORTRIU

Dundurn

Dunadd

MANAU
Dumbarton
STRATHCLYDE (DAMNONI)
Edinburgh
Peebles

Firth of Forth
Traprain Law
❸ Doon Hill
GODODDIN (VOTADINI)
Yeavering

DÁL RIATA
Dunseverick

ULAID

Whithorn
Ardwall Island
Cronk
Sumark
UÍ ECHAN COBA
South Barrule
Isle of Man ❷

Birdoswald
Mote of Mark
Carlisle
RHEGED (NOVANTAE)
Catterick

Lancaster
York
Humber

ELMET

Irish Sea

Degannwy
Holyhead Cadfan
Maglocunus
Caernarfon
Dinas Emrys ❹
GWYNEDD (ORDOVICES)

LAIGIN

Dinorben
Chester
Cuneglasus
Wroxeter ❺
Constantine

Lincoln
The Wash
Brancaster
Burgh Castle
Colchester
Walton

DÉISI

UÍ LIATHÁIN

Caldey Island

DEMETAE
Vortipor
Aergol
Ergyng dynasty
Tewdrig & Meurig
Gloucester
Caerleon
Cirencester

Aurelius Caninus
DOBUNNI
St Albans
Bradwell
Reculver
Richborough

Severn
Thames
London
Vortigern?
Canterbury
Dover
Lympne
Pevensey
❶

Bristol Channel Dinas Powys
Cardiff

Lundy Island
Constantinus
Tintagel

Cadbury-Congresbury
South Cadbury ❹
Silchester
Winchester
Portchester
Chichester

DUMNONIA (DUMNONII)
Dorchester
Isle of Wight

THE SAXON SHORE

From Germany and Denmark

Cunomoros

Isles of Scilly

To Brittany

English Channel

100 miles
150 km

King Arthur

The period of British history from the 5th to the 8th centuries did not become known as the 'Dark Ages' for nothing: there is hardly any contemporary written evidence for the period. The figure who looms largest in this period is Arthur, usually thought of as a great Celtic war leader who triumphed over the invading Anglo-Saxons at the battle of Mount Badon in *c.* 500. However, it is likely that Arthur was originally a folkloric figure who was historicized when actual events became associated with his name.

THE MONK GILDAS, writing 40 years after Mount Badon, apparently attributes the victory to the leadership of Ambrosius Aurelianus and makes no mention at all of Arthur. In fact the earliest document to refer to Arthur as the victor of Mount Badon, the *History of the Britons,* dates to no earlier than the 9th century. This work includes much that is plainly legendary and should be regarded not so much as evidence that Arthur was a historical figure, as that by the time it was written he had come to be regarded as one.

Dozens of places in Britain have become associated with King Arthur. Not all of these associations are particularly ancient – the tradition that Arthur and his knights lie sleeping in the ancient copper mines in Alderley Edge, Cheshire, dates only from the 19th century, for example – but many can be proven to have been established long before the end of the Middle Ages. One such is Arthur's O'en (oven), a ruined Roman building near the Antonine Wall, which was first recorded in 1293. What is particularly noteworthy about the distribution of these sites is that almost all of them lie within the areas of Britain where the Britons longest retained their independence: southwest Scotland, Cumbria, Wales and Cornwall. This is not evidence, one way or the other, that Arthur was a real person, but it does emphasize the British origin of the stories. Emigrant Britons took the stories with them to Brittany, where there are also a number of Arthur-related sites.

The majority of sites associated with Arthur are prehistoric monuments, such as tumuli (Bwrdd Arthur), megalithic tombs (Coetan Arthur), hillforts (Moel Arthur) and henges (King Arthur's Round Table), built long before the times when Arthur is supposed to have lived. Other sites have become associated with the Arthurian stories on etymological grounds. Colchester was thought to have been Camelot because its Roman name was Camulodunum. Carmarthen in southwest Wales was said to derive from Kaermerdin, 'Merlin's fortress'. But not all Arthurian associations are entirely fanciful. Archaeological excavations have shown that Tintagel, South Cadbury, Dinas Emrys, Mote of Mark (i.e. King Mark of Cornwall, the rival of Arthur's father Uther Pendragon) and Dumbarton Rock were all important power centres of Dark Age Britain.

The antiquary John Leland first identified South Cadbury hillfort as Camelot in the 17th century, perhaps on the basis of local tradition but most likely on the dubious grounds that it overlooks the villages of Queen Camel and West Camel.

MAP NOTES

❶ *Monks at Glastonbury in the 12th century claimed to have discovered the coffins of King Arthur and Guinevere.*

❷ *Caer Gai is a Roman fort traditionally reputed to be the castle of Sir Kay, one of the Knights of the Round Table.*

❸ *Slaughterbridge over the River Camel is claimed to be the site of Arthur's last battle, Camlann.*

❹ *Geoffrey of Monmouth was the first to identify Bath as the site of the battle of Mt Badon.*

❺ *In local tradition the castle of Arthur's father Uther Pendragon, the castle dates only from the 14th century.*

❻ *Traditionally held to be the burial place of the magician Merlin.*

❼ *'King Arthur's Round Table' at Winchester Castle was actually made in the 13th century: English kings appropriated Arthurian legends to support their own claims to overlordship of Britain.*

'King Arthur's Round Table' in Winchester Castle, Hampshire, was made in the 13th century for Edward III. The painted decoration dates to the reign of the Tudor king Henry VIII who exploited Arthurian imagery because of his family's Welsh origins.

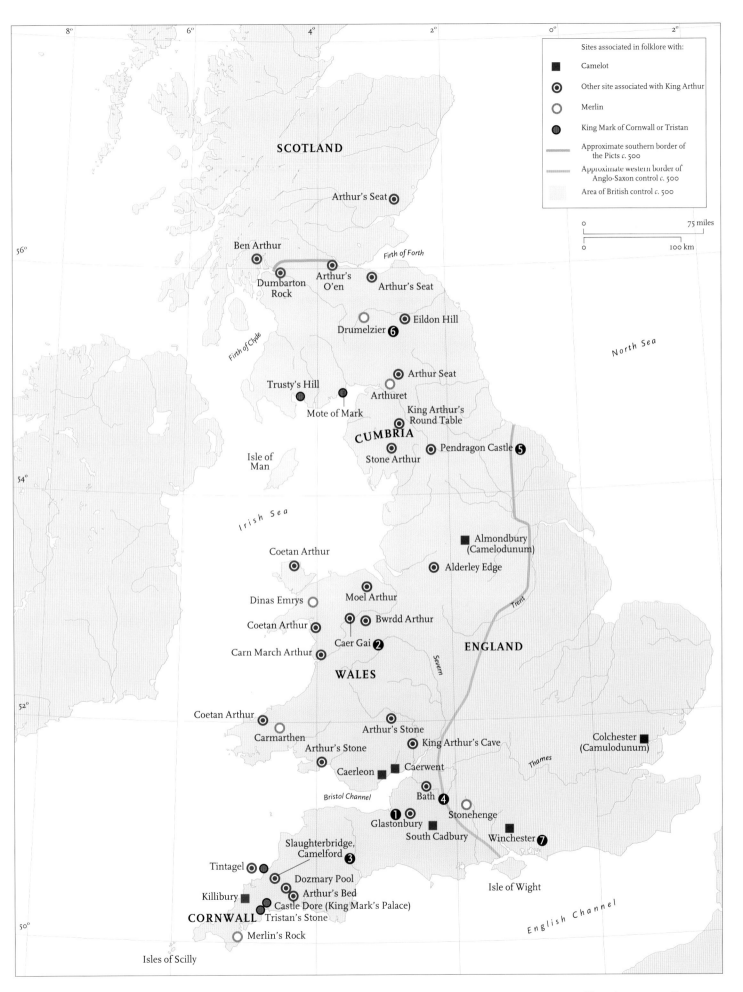

Sites associated in folklore with:

- ■ Camelot
- ◉ Other site associated with King Arthur
- ○ Merlin
- ◕ King Mark of Cornwall or Tristan
- ▬ Approximate southern border of the Picts *c.* 500
- ▬ Approximate western border of Anglo-Saxon control *c.* 500
- Area of British control *c.* 500

0   75 miles
0   100 km

SCOTLAND

Arthur's Seat ◉

Ben Arthur ◉

Firth of Forth

Dumbarton Rock ◉   Arthur's O'en ◉

Arthur's Seat ◉

Firth of Clyde

Drumelzier ○   Eildon Hill ◉ ❻

North Sea

Trusty's Hill ◕   Arthur Seat ◉

Mote of Mark ◕   Arthuret

King Arthur's Round Table ◉

CUMBRIA

Isle of Man

Stone Arthur ◉   Pendragon Castle ◉ ❺

Irish Sea

Coetan Arthur ◉

Almondbury (Camelodunum) ■

Alderley Edge ◉

Dinas Emrys ○   Moel Arthur ◉

Coetan Arthur ◉   Bwrdd Arthur ◉

Caer Gai ◉ ❷

Carn March Arthur ◉

WALES

Severn

ENGLAND

Trent

Coetan Arthur ◉

Carmarthen ○

Arthur's Stone ◉

Arthur's Stone ◉   King Arthur's Cave ◉

Colchester (Camulodunum) ■

Caerleon ■   Caerwent ■

Bristol Channel

Bath ◉ ❹

Thames

Glastonbury ❶ ◉   Stonehenge ○

South Cadbury ■   Winchester ■ ❼

Slaughterbridge, Camelford ❸

Isle of Wight

Tintagel ◕   Dozmary Pool ◉

Killibury ■   Arthur's Bed ◉

Castle Dore (King Mark's Palace) ◕

CORNWALL   Tristan's Stone ◕

English Channel

Merlin's Rock ○

Isles of Scilly

The Scots and the Picts   *c. AD 500 – 900*

In the 4th century Irish pirates began attacking Britain. They described themselves as 'Scotti', meaning simply 'raiders', but the name was soon applied to all the Irish, pirates or not. In the late 5th century the northern Irish Dál Riata dynasty established control of Argyll. Over the next several centuries, their descendants extended their rule over most of northern Britain to create the kingdom of Scotland.

ACCORDING TO EARLY Scottish traditions, the Irish settlement of Argyll was led by King Fergus MacErc (d. 501) who conquered Kintyre, while his brothers Loarn and Oengus conquered Lorn and Islay. The story may have been invented to explain the traditional division of Scottish Dál Riata (Argyll) into three tribes: Cenel Loairn, Cenel nOengusa and Cenel nGabrain (named after Fergus' grandson Gabran). Fergus and his successors ruled both Irish Dál Riata and Argyll until 637, when the two halves of the kingdom became independent of one another.

The Scots introduced a new language to Britain, Gaelic, and the Irish ogam writing system, which was adopted by the Picts. Irish monks followed the colonists and founded monasteries. St Columba's foundation on Iona became one of the most influential churches of the British Isles and the major centre for the conversion of the northern Picts and the Northumbrians in the late 6th to early 7th centuries. Conversion of the southern Picts had already been begun by the Britons in the 5th century. Christianity stimulated Pictish art, leading to the production of spectacular sculpted cross slabs combining native, Northumbrian and Irish decorative styles.

In 843 Kenneth MacAlpin (*c.* 840–58) of Scottish Dál Riata conquered Pictish Fortriu, creating a new kingdom known by *c.* 900 as Alba (from the Irish word for Britain) or Scotia. This was the culmination of a century of increasing Scottish influence over the Picts. From the early 8th century, many Pictish kings had had Scottish origins and it was the death in battle against the Vikings of one of these kings, Eoganan, in 839 that had given Kenneth his

MAP NOTES

❶ Over 6 m (19 ft) tall, Sueno's Stone is the largest, and perhaps last, of the Pictish cross slabs. It commemorates a victory over an unknown enemy in the 9th or 10th century.

❷ A Northumbrian attempt to conquer the Picts was decisively defeated by Bridei mac Bili at Nechtansmere near Dunnichen Moss in 685.

❸ Iona was the traditional burial ground for the kings of the Scots in the 9th to 11th centuries. Kenneth MacAlpin and Macbeth are among those buried there.

❹ In the 7th century kings of Fortriu became high kings of the Picts, exercising authority as far afield as Orkney.

❺ Often claimed to be the capital of Scottish Dál Riata, excavations of Dunadd have produced evidence of craftworking and international trade contacts compatible with a very high-status site.

(Below left) Carved stone from Rosemarkie, Ross-shire, combining Christian symbols with traditional Pictish symbols, the double disc with Z-rod and the crescent with V-rod (8th–9th century).

(Below right) Footprint-shaped depression carved in a slab of rock on the summit of Dunadd, the craggy stronghold of the Scots of Dál Riata. The footprint is thought to be associated with rites of kingship.

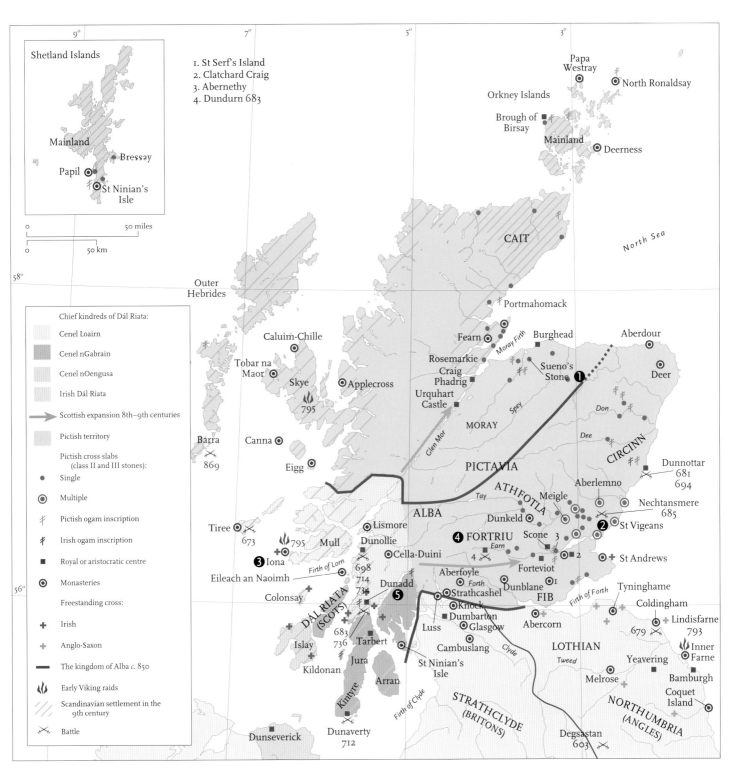

Map labels

Shetland Islands (inset)
Mainland
Bressay
Papil
St Ninian's Isle

50 miles
50 km

1. St Serf's Island
2. Clatchard Craig
3. Abernethy
4. Dundurn 683

Orkney Islands
Papa Westray
North Ronaldsay
Brough of Birsay
Mainland
Deerness

North Sea

CAIT

Outer Hebrides

Portmahomack
Fearn
Rosemarkie
Craig Phadrig
Urquhart Castle
Moray Firth
Burghead
Sueno's Stone ❶
Aberdour
Deer

Caluim-Chille
Tobar na Maor
Skye
795
Applecross

MORAY
Spey
Glen Mor
Don
Dee
CIRCINN

Barra 869
Canna
Eigg

PICTAVIA
Aberlemno
Dunnottar 681 694
ATHFOTLA
Tay
Meigle
Nechtansmere 685
Dunkeld
St Vigeans ❷
ALBA
Scone 3
FORTRIU ❹
Earn
1
4
2
St Andrews
Forteviot

Tiree 673
Mull 795
Lismore
Dunollie
Cella-Duini
❸ Iona
Eileach an Naoimh
698
714
734
Dunadd ❺
Aberfoyle
Forth
Dunblane
1
FIB
Firth of Forth
Tyninghame
Coldingham

Firth of Lorn
Colonsay
DÁL RIATA (SCOTS)
Strathcashel
Knock
Dumbarton
Luss
Glasgow
Abercorn
679
Lindisfarne 793
LOTHIAN
Yeavering
Inner Farne

Islay
683 736
Jura
Tarbert
Cambuslang
Clyde
Tweed
Melrose
Bamburgh
Coquet Island

Kildonan
Kintyre
Arran
St Ninian's Isle
Firth of Clyde
STRATHCLYDE (BRITONS)
NORTHUMBRIA (ANGLES)

Dunseverick
Dunaverty 712
Degsastan 603

Legend

Chief kindreds of Dál Riata:
Cenel Loairn
Cenel nGabrain
Cenel nOengusa
Irish Dál Riata

→ Scottish expansion 8th–9th centuries

Pictish territory

Pictish cross slabs (class II and III stones):
● Single
◉ Multiple
Pictish ogam inscription
Irish ogam inscription
■ Royal or aristocratic centre
◉ Monasteries

Freestanding cross:
✚ Irish
✚ Anglo-Saxon

━ The kingdom of Alba c. 850
Early Viking raids
Scandinavian settlement in the 9th century
✕ Battle

---

opportunity. A rival Scottish dynasty took advantage of the disruption caused by the Viking raids to capture Moray around the same time. The Scots, too, suffered from the Viking raiders and lost their west coast districts to them in the later 9th century. Viking settlement in Orkney, Shetland and Caithness in this period was so dense that the native Picts were completely assimilated with the newcomers. The fate of the Picts under Scottish rule was the same. The use of traditional Pictish symbols died out before the end of the 9th century and the last contemporary references to the Picts date to c. 900. The Pictish language became extinct soon after, replaced by Gaelic. No Pictish literature has survived: the Scots were unsympathetic to Pictish culture and may deliberately have suppressed it.

A richly decorated silver cone, probably a belt adjustor for a sword harness, from a hoard of Pictish silver discovered in the ruins of an early Christian church on St Ninian's Isle in Shetland. Dating to c. 800 the hoard was probably buried to hide it from Viking raiders.

The Origins of Wales
AD 500 – 900

By the 9th century, the main stronghold of independent Britons was a mountainous region of western Britain closely approximating to modern Wales. Though it lacked political unity, the region developed, through law, literature and language, a single cultural identity that is the basis of the modern Welsh national identity. The country's English name (in the Welsh language it is Cymru) derives from the Anglo-Saxon name for the Britons, *waelisc* or 'foreigners'.

THE BALANCE OF POWER which had existed in Britain since the British victory at Mount Badon began to shift in favour of the Anglo-Saxons around the mid-6th century. Their early advances had won the Anglo-Saxons control of the best farmlands in Britain and this probably gave them a long-term advantage over the Britons, enabling them to recover from a serious military reverse. By 600, the Anglo-Saxon advance had reached the west coast, dividing the Britons into three isolated territories: Strathclyde in modern Scotland, modern Wales and Dumnonia in the southwest (modern Devon and Cornwall or 'West Wales' to the Anglo-Saxons). Dumnonia was conquered piecemeal by the West Saxons in the 8th century but retained vassal kings until the late 9th century. Devon was already becoming anglicized in the 8th century, but Celtic speech survived in Cornwall into the 18th century.

Though politically disunited, the Britons of Wales maintained their independence and by 700 their dialect of Brithonic had developed into the Welsh language. By this time the Anglo-Saxons had advanced to a line along the foothills between the Cambrian Mountains that very roughly approximates to the modern Welsh-English border. The 240-km (185-mile) long rampart built by the Mercian king Offa *c.* 790 was probably an attempt to stabilize the frontier as much as to stop cross-border raiding by the Welsh. If so, 'Offa's Dyke' failed, as in some areas the English later advanced to its west and in the northeast the Welsh regained territories to its east. In the 9th century Gwynedd emerged as the strongest Welsh kingdom, but an attempt by its king Rhodri Mawr (d. 877) to impose political unity on Wales achieved only temporary success as his lands were divided between his sons after his death.

There was little cultural interaction between the Britons and the Anglo-Saxons (the Celtic influences in Anglo-Saxon civilization generally came from the Irish). The Britons apparently did not even try to convert the pagan Anglo-Saxons to Christianity. The British population of the areas conquered by the Anglo-Saxons was not exterminated but was assimilated by the newcomers by adopting their language and culture. A degree of intermarriage between the British and Anglo-Saxon aristocracy is hinted at in the British names of some of the early kings of the West Saxons, including Cerdic (d. 534), the founder of the kingdom that would one day unite England.

The Lichfield (or St Chad) Gospels, made c. 730, contain the earliest examples of written Welsh – records of monastic charters written in the margins of the Latin text in the 9th century.

MAP NOTES

❶ The West Saxon victory at Dyrham led to the fall of Gloucester, Cirencester and Bath.

❷ The early Welsh heroic poem The Gododdin records a failed attempt by the Britons to drive the Anglo-Saxons out of Catterick.

❸ A Celtic-speaking population still survived in the Fenlands as late as c. 700.

❹ British enclave until c. 700.

❺ Offa's Dyke was the longest of many linear earthwork defences built by both British and Anglo-Saxon rulers.

❻ The British names of these early Northumbrian kingdoms suggest that the Anglo-Saxons here took over existing British power structures.

Offa's Dyke at Spring Hill, Shropshire. The lack of gateways in the 8th-century rampart suggests that Offa saw the Welsh as a serious threat.

94 THE ATLANTIC CELTS

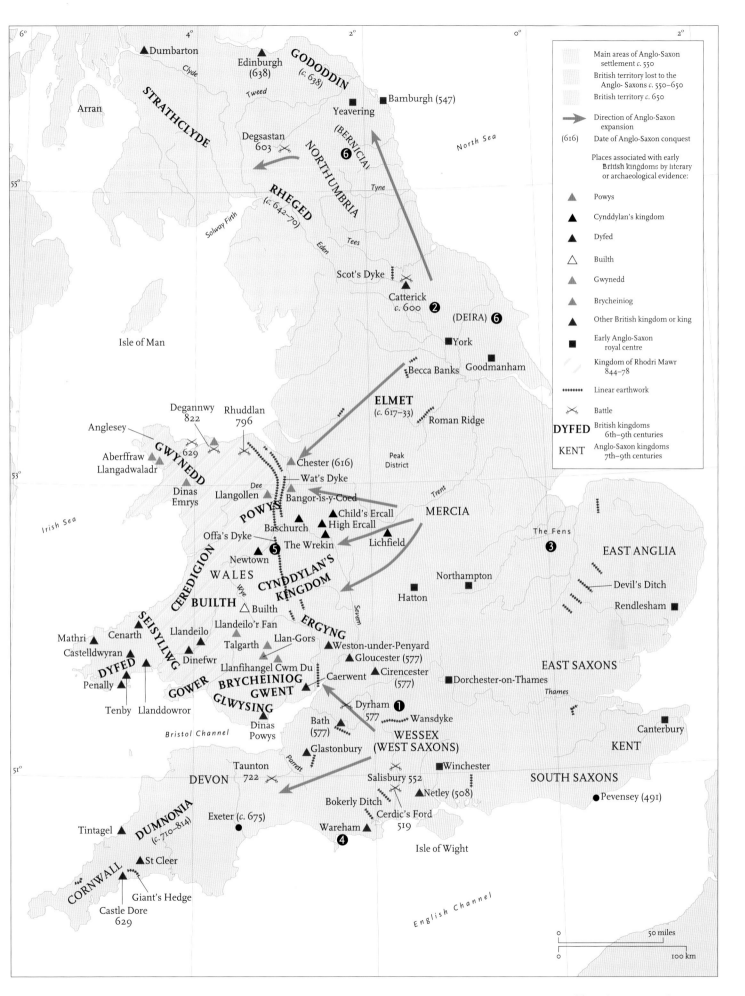

Map legend

Main areas of Anglo-Saxon settlement *c*. 550

British territory lost to the Anglo-Saxons *c*. 550–650

British territory *c*. 650

→ Direction of Anglo-Saxon expansion

(616) Date of Anglo-Saxon conquest

Places associated with early British kingdoms by literary or archaeological evidence:

▲ Powys

▲ Cynddylan's kingdom

▲ Dyfed

△ Builth

▲ Gwynedd

▲ Brycheiniog

▲ Other British kingdom or king

■ Early Anglo-Saxon royal centre

Kingdom of Rhodri Mawr 844–78

Linear earthwork

Battle

DYFED British kingdoms 6th–9th centuries

KENT Anglo-Saxon kingdoms 7th–9th centuries

Map labels

Dumbarton

Arran

Edinburgh (638)

GODODDIN (*c*. 638)

Clyde

Tweed

Bamburgh (547)

Yeavering

(BERNICIA) ❻

North Sea

STRATHCLYDE

Degsastan 603

NORTHUMBRIA

RHEGED (*c*. 642–70)

Solway Firth

Eden

Tees

Tyne

Isle of Man

Scot's Dyke

Catterick *c*. 600 ❷

(DEIRA) ❻

York

Goodmanham

Becca Banks

ELMET (*c*. 617–33)

Roman Ridge

Degannwy 822

Rhuddlan 796

Anglesey

GWYNEDD

Aberffraw

Llangadwaladr

Dinas Emrys

Irish Sea

Dee

Chester (616)

Wat's Dyke

Llangollen

Bangor-is-y-Coed

POWYS

Child's Ercall

High Ercall

Peak District

Trent

MERCIA

The Fens ❸

EAST ANGLIA

Offa's Dyke ❺

Baschurch

The Wrekin

Lichfield

Newtown

WALES

CYNDDYLAN'S KINGDOM

Devil's Ditch

Rendlesham

CEREDIGION

BUILTH

△ Builth

Wye

ERGYNG

Severn

Northampton

Hatton

Mathri

Cenarth

Llandeilo

Llandeilo'r Fan

Llan-Gors

Weston-under-Penyard

EAST SAXONS

Castelldwyran

SEISYLLWG

Dinefwr

Talgarth

Gloucester (577)

DYFED

Penally

GOWER

Llanfihangel Cwm Du

Caerwent

Cirencester (577)

Dorchester-on-Thames

Canterbury

Tenby

Llanddowror

BRYCHEINIOG

GWENT

GLWYSING

Dinas Powys

Dyrham 577 ❶

Wansdyke

Thames

KENT

Bristol Channel

Bath (577)

Glastonbury

WESSEX (WEST SAXONS)

Winchester

SOUTH SAXONS

Parrett

Taunton 722

Salisbury 552

Netley (508)

Pevensey (491)

DEVON

Exeter (*c*. 675)

Bokerly Ditch

Cerdic's Ford 519

Wareham ❹

Tintagel

DUMNONIA (*c*. 710–814)

Isle of Wight

CORNWALL

St Cleer

Giant's Hedge

Castle Dore 629

English Channel

0   50 miles

0   100 km

Early Christian Ireland

AD 400 – 700

MAP NOTES

❶ In pagan times Crúachain (Rathcroghan) was believed to be one of the entrances to the Otherworld.
❷ The prestige of Tara resulted from its role in pagan mythology as the seat of the god Lug.
❸ The Uí Néill dynasties originated in Connacht and founded their kingdoms in the 5th century.
❹ The Eóganacht dynasties claimed to have ruled in Britain. The name of their capital, Cashel, is derived from Latin castellum.
❺ The ogam alphabet originated in southeast Ireland, the region most open to Roman influence.
❻ Traditionally the place of St Patrick's death: like most traditions associated with the saint, it cannot be substantiated.

Peaceful trade contacts between Ireland and Roman Britain began as early as the 1st century AD. As Roman power declined in the late 4th century, raiding Britain for loot and slaves became attractive and in the 5th century permanent settlements were made. Ireland did not experience any great degree of Romanization as a result of these contacts, but they did lead to the development of the Irish ogam alphabet and the first contacts with Christians.

SOME OF THE FIRST CHRISTIANS to live in Ireland were British slaves. St Patrick was one: captured in his youth, around the end of the 4th century, he escaped after six years and returned as a missionary bishop *c.* 435. Patrick's mission to Ireland may have been the most successful but it was not the first. The earliest missions were sent from Gaul in the late 4th or early 5th century and by 431 there were enough converts for Pope Celestine to appoint Palladius of Auxerre as bishop of the Irish. While the early missionary work was concentrated in southeastern Ireland, Patrick's mission was to begin the conversion of the still entirely pagan northern half. The distribution of early churches with the name *Domnach Pátraic* ('church building of Patrick') may give some idea of the area evangelized by Patrick, though probably not all were actually founded by him. After Patrick's arrival Gaulish missionaries were gradually superseded by ones from Britain. By the 6th century Christianity was well established and paganism soon died out. According to Irish tradition, no martyrs were made, suggesting that the conversion was accomplished with relative ease.

By the 6th century, the basic political structure of seven over-kingdoms and a multitude of sub-kingdoms and minor dynasties was in place in Ireland, which lasted until the Viking Age. The kingdoms of the Northern and Southern Uí Néill were dominated by single dynasties; Laigin was dominated by the Uí Dúnlainge and Uí Chennselaig; Munster by the Eóganacht ; Connacht by the Uí Briúin and Uí Fiachrach; Ulaid by the Dál Fiatach; Airgialla was a confederation of minor dynasties. Both Ulaid and Laigin were declining in the face of the rising power of the Uí Néill dynasties. The Southern Uí Néill kings enjoyed enhanced prestige as rulers of the prehistoric ritual centre of Tara, but there was no High Kingship as yet. Many early missionary churches, such as St Patrick's see at Armagh, were founded close to pagan ritual centres associated with Irish kingship. This was probably a deliberate policy as the church pursued a similar course elsewhere in Europe.

An important feature of the period was the proliferation throughout Ireland of small-scale fortifications such as ringforts, crannogs and souterrains. Crannogs and souterrains have marked regional distributions, but ringforts are found everywhere: over 45,000 are known.

The Kilnasaggart Stone, Co. Armagh, marks the land given as a burial ground 'by Ternóc, son of Ciarán the Little', to St Peter. The earliest datable cross inscribed monument in Ireland, the stone dates to c. 700.

Medieval church on the Hill of Slane, Co. Meath. It was here that St Patrick is said to have lit the paschal fire in defiance of Lóegaire, the king of Tara, and his Druids.

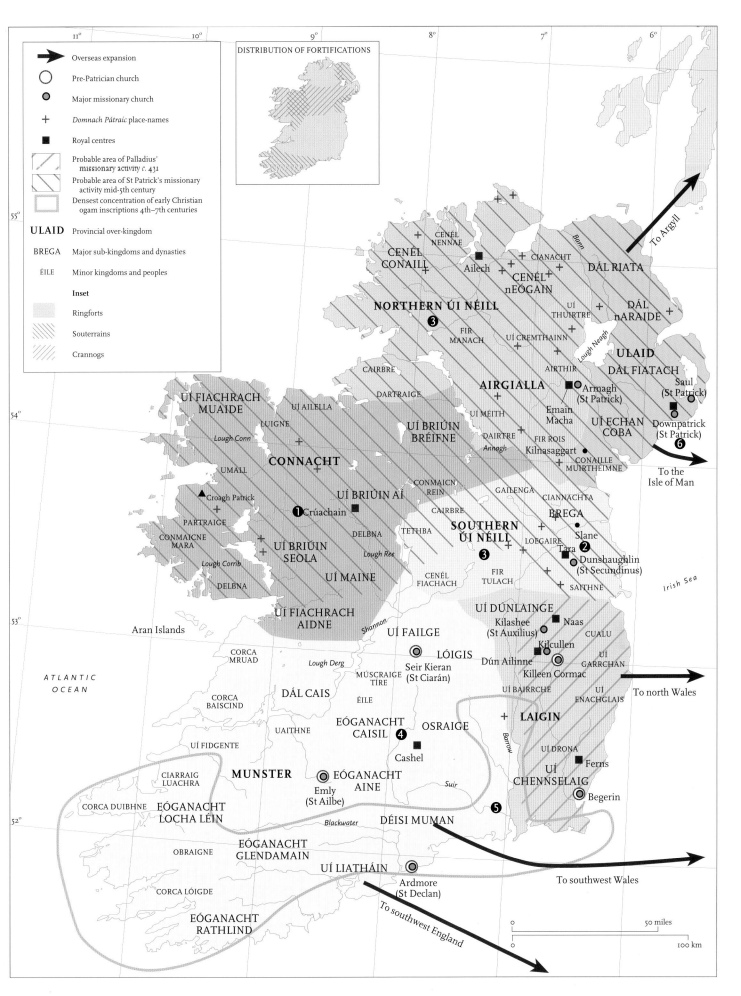

Legend

- Overseas expansion
- ○ Pre-Patrician church
- ● Major missionary church
- + *Domnach Pátraic* place-names
- ■ Royal centres
- Probable area of Palladius' missionary activity c. 431
- Probable area of St Patrick's missionary activity mid-5th century
- Densest concentration of early Christian ogam inscriptions 4th–7th centuries

ULAID Provincial over-kingdom
BREGA Major sub-kingdoms and dynasties
ÉILE Minor kingdoms and peoples

Inset
- Ringforts
- Souterrains
- Crannogs

DISTRIBUTION OF FORTIFICATIONS

To Argyll
To the Isle of Man
To north Wales
To southwest Wales
To southwest England

CENÉL NENNAE
CENÉL CONAILL
Ailech
CIANACHT
DÁL RIATA
CENÉL nEÓGAIN
NORTHERN ÚI NÉILL ❸
UÍ THUIRTRE
DÁL nARAIDE
FIR MANACH
UÍ CREMTHAINN
Lough Neagh
ULAID
CAIRBRE
UÍ MÉITH
AIRTHIR
DÁL FIATACH
DARTRAIGE
AIRGIALLA
Armagh (St Patrick)
Saul (St Patrick)
UÍ FIACHRACH MUAIDE
UÍ AILELLA
UÍ BRIÚIN BRÉIFNE
DAIRTRE
Emain Macha
UÍ ECHACH COBA
Downpatrick (St Patrick) ❻
LUIGNE
Lough Conn
FIR ROIS
Annagh
Kilnasaggart
CONAILLE MUIRTHEIMNE
CONNACHT
UMALL
CONMAICN REIN
GAILENGA
CIANNACHTA
Croagh Patrick
UÍ BRIÚIN AÍ ❶ Crúachain
CAIRBRE
BREGA
Slane
PARTRAIGE
DELBNA
TETHBA
SOUTHERN ÚI NÉILL ❸
LOEGAIRE
Tara ❷
CONMAICNE MARA
UÍ BRIÚIN SEOLA
Lough Ree
Dunshaughlin (St Secundinus)
Lough Corrib
UÍ MAINE
CENÉL FIACHACH
FIR TULACH
SAITHNE
Irish Sea
DELBNA
UÍ FIACHRACH AIDNE
Shannon
UÍ DÚNLAINGE
Aran Islands
UÍ FAILGE
Kilashee (St Auxilius)
Naas
CUALU
CORCA MRUAD
LÓIGIS
Kilcullen
UÍ GARRCHAN
Lough Derg
Seir Kieran (St Ciarán)
Dún Ailinne
Killeen Cormac
MÚSCRAIGE TÍRE
UÍ BAIRRCHE
UÍ ENACHGLAIS
CORCA BAISCIND
DÁL CAIS
ÉILE
EÓGANACHT CAISIL ❹
OSRAIGE
LAIGIN
UÍ FIDGENTE
Cashel
UÍ DRONA
Ferns
CIARRAIG LUACHRA
MUNSTER
EÓGANACHT ÁINE
Emly (St Ailbe)
Suir
UÍ CHENNSELAIG
CORCA DUIBHNE
EÓGANACHT LOCHA LÉIN
Begerin
Blackwater
DÉISI MUMAN ❺
OBRAIGNE
EÓGANACHT GLENDAMAIN
UAITHNE
UÍ LIATHÁIN
Ardmore (St Declan)
CORCA LÓIGDE
EÓGANACHT RATHLIND

ATLANTIC OCEAN

Barrow

0 50 miles
0 100 km

Ireland in the Golden Age

In the 7th century, Ireland saw the development of a remarkable monastic civilization at a time when cultural life in much of Europe was languishing in the so-called Dark Ages. This distinctive Irish Christian culture flourished for two centuries, and was exported to Britain and the continent, but the Viking invasions of the 9th century brought Ireland's Golden Age to an end.

THOUGH BISHOPS WERE RESPECTED and influential, the early Irish church did not develop a diocesan structure like that on the continent and pastoral care for the laity was often provided by monastic communities. Monasteries which were believed to share a common founder were grouped in loose associations called *paruchiae* (parishes). *Paruchiae* were not territorial units like dioceses but they did roughly reflect their founders' areas of missionary activity. Beginning in the 6th century, Irish monks enthusiastically took up the task of assimilating patristic and Classical literature. Irish scholars were soon producing a wide range of literature in both Latin and Gaelic, including biblical commentaries, hagiography, law, grammar, computation, annals and verse, of a quality comparable to the best being produced anywhere in western Europe at the time. Significantly, Irish scholars paid considerable attention to providing works suitable for the beginner, so ensuring a high average standard of education for monks. It was this, rather than works of individual genius, that earned Irish monks their high reputation abroad for learning.

Early medieval Ireland had no truly urban settlements, but major monastic centres, such as Armagh, Clonmacnois and Kildare, fulfilled many of the functions of towns. As great landowners, monasteries became administrative centres and centres for the collection of the surplus food production of the surrounding countryside, delivered as rent by the monasteries' tenants. As wealthy centres of consumption, monasteries attracted merchants and craftsmen to service their needs and also those of the pilgrims who flocked to them in search of cures or forgiveness for sins. Because they were protected by the saints, important monasteries became royal treasuries, and kings and their retainers became frequent visitors. The patronage of the church resulted in superb works of craftsmanship in stone and metal, but the works of art most associated with the Golden Age – the marvellous illuminated manuscripts, such as the *Book of Durrow* – were created by the monks themselves. The art of the Golden Age combined late Insular La Tène geometrical patterns with interlaced animal ornament borrowed from the Anglo-Saxons to produce decorations of astonishing intricacy.

The Irish church had a strong tradition of asceticism and the lives of monks at isolated monasteries such as the Atlantic island of Skellig Michael must have been hard indeed. However, the wealth and secular involvement of others led to the rise of the Culdees (from *Céile Dé*, 'Client of God'), an ascetic reform movement, in the 8th century. Though its achievements were limited, the movement remained influential into the 12th century.

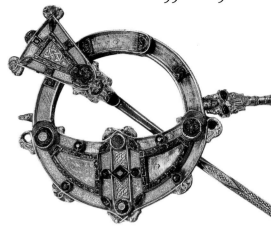

The so-called Tara brooch, from Bettystown, Co. Meath (c. 700). Made of cast silver-bronze, it shows the influence of Anglo-Saxon art styles and craftsmanship in its intricate animal interlace decoration executed in gold filigree.

MAP NOTES

❶ *A cluster of stone huts clinging to a precipitous islet, Skellig Michael is the most spectacular representative of the ascetic ideals of Irish monasticism.*

❷ *Armagh was recognized as the ecclesiastical capital of Ireland because of its links with St Patrick.*

❸ *Situated at a strategic junction of river and land routes, Clonmacnois became one of the richest and most influential of Irish monasteries.*

❹ *One of the best preserved of monastic round towers: built from the 9th to the 12th centuries they served as bell towers, treasuries and refuges from Viking raids.*

❺ *St Brigit was probably a Christianized pagan deity, but her shrine was the focus of the growth of a monastic proto-town in the 7th century.*

The Oratory of Gallarus, Co. Kerry, a small stone church built sometime during the early Middle Ages. The distinctive corbelling technique was commonly used for Irish monastic buildings.

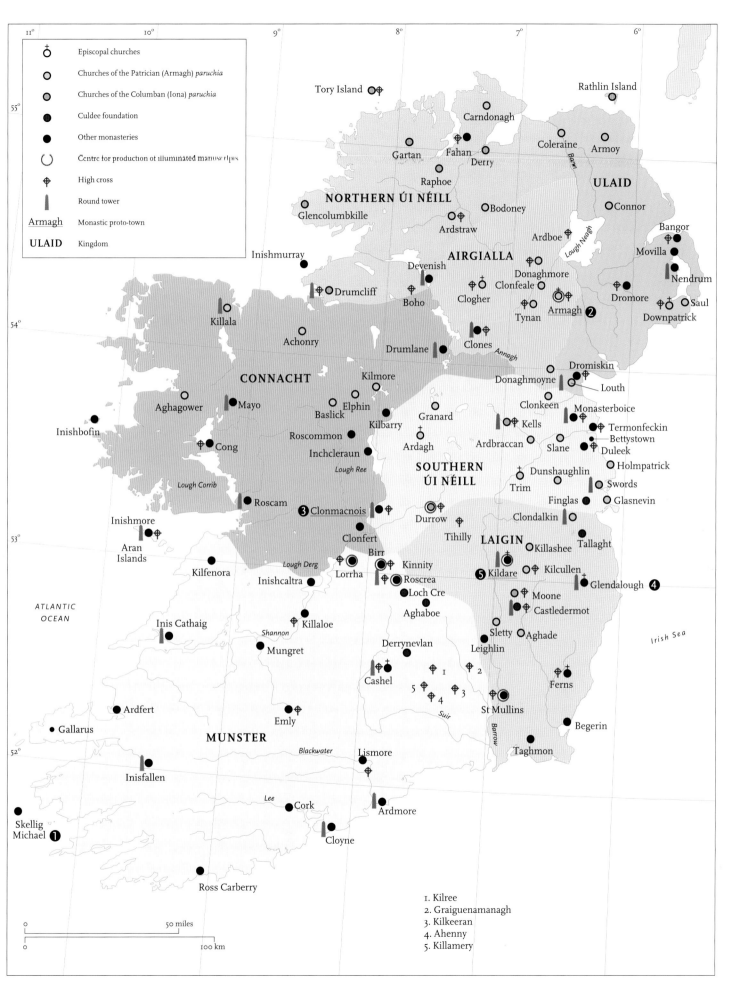

Episcopal churches ⊕

Churches of the Patrician (Armagh) *paruchia* ⊙

Churches of the Columban (Iona) *paruchia* ⊙

Culdee foundation ●

Other monasteries ●

Centre for production of illuminated manuscripts ◡

High cross ⊕

Round tower ▮

Armagh   **Monastic proto-town**

ULAID   **Kingdom**

Tory Island

Rathlin Island

Carndonagh

Gartan   Fahan   Coleraine   Armoy

Derry

Raphoe   **ULAID**

NORTHERN ÚI NÉILL   Bodoney   Connor

Glencolumbkille   Bangor

Ardstraw   Movilla

Ardboe   Nendrum

Inishmurray   Devenish   **AIRGIALLA**   Dromore   Saul

Donaghmore   Downpatrick

Drumcliff   Boho   Clonfeale

Killala   Clogher

Achonry   Tynan   Armagh ②

Drumlane   Clones

Annagh

Kilmore   Dromiskin

CONNACHT   Donaghmoyne   Louth

Elphin   Clonkeen   Monasterboice

Aghagower   Mayo   Baslick   Granard   Kells   Termonfeckin

Inishbofin   Roscommon   Kilbarry   Ardbraccan   Slane   Bettystown

Cong   Inchcleraun   Ardagh   Duleek

Holmpatrick

Lough Ree   Dunshaughlin

SOUTHERN   Swords

Roscam   **ÚI NÉILL**   Trim   Finglas   Glasnevin

Lough Corrib   Clonmacnois ③   Durrow

Inishmore   Clondalkin

Aran   Tihilly   **LAIGIN**   Tallaght

Islands   Clonfert   Killashee

Kilfenora   Birr   Kinnity   Kildare ⑤   Kilcullen   Glendalough ④

Lorrha   Roscrea

Inishcaltra   Loch Cre   Moone

Lough Derg   Aghaboe   Castledermot

ATLANTIC   Inis Cathaig   Killaloe   Derrynevlan   Sletty   Aghade

OCEAN   *Shannon*   Mungret   Leighlin   *Irish Sea*

Ardfert   Cashel   Ferns

Gallarus   Emly   1   2   Begerin

MUNSTER   5   3   St Mullins

Skellig   *Suir*   Taghmon

Michael ❶   Lismore   *Barrow*

Inisfallen

Lee   Cork   Ardmore

Cloyne

Ross Carberry

0   50 miles

0   100 km

1. Kilree
2. Graiguenamanagh
3. Kilkeeran
4. Ahenny
5. Killamery

Celtic Missionaries and Scholars in Europe
AD 400 – 1200

Early medieval Ireland was famous abroad as 'the island of saints and scholars'. Irish monks and scholars were great travellers, some seeking ultimate solitude in long sea voyages, others going to study, teach and evangelize in Britain and on the continent. Less well known are the activities of British missionaries in Brittany and Spain.

'THE IRISH FASHION OF GOING AWAY' began as part of the ascetic tradition of early Irish monasticism. Monks seeking solitude for contemplation settled in small communities or hermitages on remote islands, at first around the Irish coasts, then increasingly further afield, in the Hebrides, Orkney and Shetland islands and then beyond into unknown waters. The Irish called this practice *peregrinatio* – 'travelling for God'. Many *peregrini* must have disappeared never to be seen again, but some made safe landfalls and returned to tell the tale. By *c.* 800 Irish monks had become the first visitors to the Faroe Islands and Iceland. The *Voyage of St Brendan* is thought by some to describe a voyage to North America, but the account's mixture of the plausible and the fantastic makes it a very difficult work to interpret.

Not all *peregrini* wanted to turn their backs on the world completely. Columba sought isolation on Iona, in the Hebrides, in 563, but became closely involved in the conversion of the Picts to Christianity. St Aidan, another monk from Iona, played a major role in the conversion of the Anglo-Saxon kingdom of Northumbria. Missionaries such as Fursa and Columbanus took the Irish brand of monasticism to the continent. Although Irish influence extended as far as southern Italy, it was concentrated in the area between the Seine and the Rhine – the economic and political heartland of the powerful Frankish kingdom. The tradition of *peregrinatio* gradually died out after the 8th century as the influence of Benedictine monasticism, with its emphasis on stability, increased, but Irish monasteries (*Schottenklöster*) remained influential in southern Germany up to the Reformation.

In the 8th and 9th centuries, Irish scholars followed the missionaries to the continent. Many found a welcome at the court of the Frankish king Charlemagne (768–814) at Aachen. Charlemagne fostered a revival of learning, known as the Carolingian Renaissance, bringing together representatives of the three main scholarly traditions of the early medieval west: the Irish, English and Italian. Among the most important Irish scholars contributing to the renaissance were the poet Sedulius Scottus, the geographer Dicuil and the philosopher John Eriugena, one of the few genuinely original thinkers of the period.

The activities of British missionaries in Europe have attracted less attention. They were mainly active in areas of British settlement overseas, primarily in Brittany but also in a little-known colony in Galicia, known as Britonia. Unlike the Irish, the Britons played no role in converting their English neighbours. The Anglo-Saxon scholar Bede regarded this as an unspeakable crime; presumably he saw it as a malicious policy, to keep the English out of Heaven.

❶ *A major centre for Irish missionaries, Péronne was known as Peronna Scottorum ('Péronne of the Irish').*

❷ *Bretoña was probably the seat of the British bishop Mailoc in the 6th century.*

❸ *The palace school at Aachen was a centre for scholars from Ireland, England and Italy in the late 8th–9th centuries.*

❹ *Columbanus was expelled from Luxeuil in 609 after an argument with King Theuderic II: he settled at Bobbio in 613 where he died in 615.*

❺ *Iona was the most influential Irish foundation in Britain, playing a leading role in the conversion of the Picts and Northumbrians.*

(Above) A page from the Gospel-book of St Gall, Switzerland, showing St Mark surrounded by symbols of the four evangelists. The book is entirely Irish in style and was most likely illuminated by an Irish monk living in Switzerland.

Charlemagne, king of the Franks, used Irish monks in his plans to revive learning and improve standards of Christian worship.

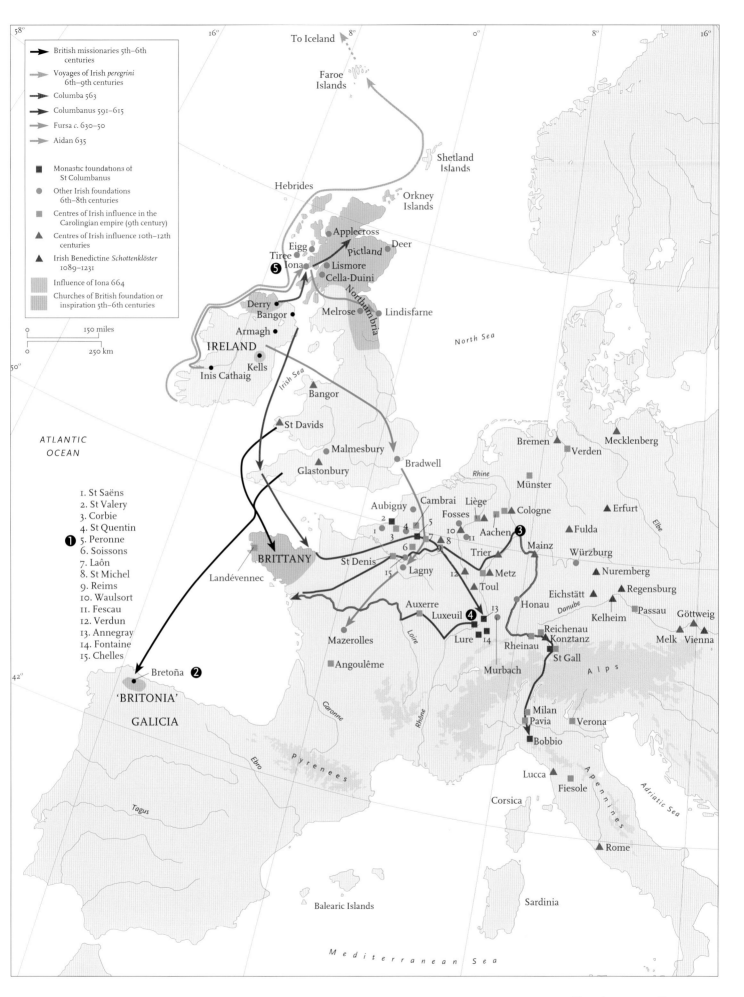

Legend:

British missionaries 5th–6th centuries

Voyages of Irish *peregrini* 6th–9th centuries

Columba 563

Columbanus 591–615

Fursa *c.* 630–50

Aidan 635

■ Monastic foundations of St Columbanus

● Other Irish foundations 6th–8th centuries

■ Centres of Irish influence in the Carolingian empire (9th century)

▲ Centres of Irish influence 10th–12th centuries

▲ Irish Benedictine *Schottenklöster* 1089–1231

Influence of Iona 664

Churches of British foundation or inspiration 5th–6th centuries

150 miles

250 km

1. St Saëns
2. St Valery
3. Corbie
4. St Quentin
5. Peronne
6. Soissons
7. Laôn
8. St Michel
9. Reims
10. Waulsort
11. Fescau
12. Verdun
13. Annegray
14. Fontaine
15. Chelles

To Iceland

Faroe Islands

Shetland Islands

Hebrides

Orkney Islands

Applecross

Deer

Eigg

Pictland

Tiree

Iona

Lismore

Cella-Duini

Derry

Bangor

Melrose

Lindisfarne

Northumbria

Armagh

IRELAND

Kells

North Sea

Inis Cathaig

Irish Sea

Bangor

ATLANTIC OCEAN

St Davids

Malmesbury

Bradwell

Glastonbury

Aubigny

Cambrai

Liège

Fosses

Cologne

Bremen

Verden

Mecklenberg

Münster

Erfurt

Rhine

Aachen

Fulda

Trier

Mainz

Würzburg

BRITTANY

St Denis

Lagny

Metz

Nuremberg

Regensburg

Landévennec

Toul

Eichstätt

Passau

Göttweig

Auxerre

Honau

Kelheim

Danube

Luxeuil

Reichenau

Melk

Vienna

Mazerolles

Loire

Lure

Konztanz

Rheinau

St Gall

Angoulême

Murbach

Alps

Bretoña

'BRITONIA'

GALICIA

Ebro

Milan

Pavia

Verona

Pyrenees

Bobbio

Tagus

Rhône

Garonne

Lucca

Fiesole

Apennines

Adriatic Sea

Corsica

Sardinia

Balearic Islands

Mediterranean Sea

Celt and Viking in Ireland

AD 795 – 1014

Attracted by the wealth of its relatively undefended monasteries, Vikings began raiding Ireland in the late 8th century. Though they caused much destruction and brought the 'Golden Age' to an end, they also founded the country's first towns and bound it more closely into the European economy than it had ever been before.

THE VIKINGS – Scandinavian pirates – first struck in 795. For more than 30 years the Vikings confined their attacks to monasteries and other places within easy reach of the coast, snatching treasure, captives and livestock and withdrawing before the Irish could organize a defence. Ireland's fragmented political structure aided the Vikings as there was little co-operation between kingdoms. In the 830s the Vikings became more confident and began to sail inland along navigable rivers and build fortified camps from which they could raid all year round. Some of these, such as Dublin, became trading centres and developed into Ireland's first true towns. Once they had established permanent settlements it became easier for the Irish to launch effective counter-attacks and the Viking threat was gradually contained. The Vikings became just one more factor in the complex internecine struggles of the Irish kingdoms, often allying with native rulers against their mutual enemies. In this way Osraige became briefly a leading kingdom in the 9th century.

In 902 the Irish expelled the Vikings, but they returned in 914, soon re-establishing themselves at Dublin, Waterford, Wexford, Cork and Limerick and resuming raiding with a vengeance. But the Irish successfully contained the Vikings in their coastal towns and by the end of the century they had all been forced to acknowledge Irish kings as their overlords. There was no attempt to expel the Vikings, or Ostmen as they were now called. Irish kings recognized the commercial benefits the Ostman towns brought and they profited personally from the tribute they paid to preserve their independence. The Ostmen were becoming less alien too, having adopted Christianity.

Ireland's Viking Age is traditionally reckoned to have ended with Brian Boru's victory at Clontarf in 1014. Brian became king of Dál Cais in 976 and soon won control of all of Munster. In 984 he began to bring the rest of Ireland under his authority by imposing tributary status on Osraige. Brian became High King in 1002, and by 1004 all the Irish kingdoms and the Ostman towns were tributary to him (hence his nickname *bóraime*, 'of the tributes'), making him the most successful of early Irish kings. Triumphant 'circuits' of Ireland in 1005 and 1006 paraded Brian's authority, but Laigin and Dublin rebelled in 1013 and called in Viking allies from Man and Orkney. It was this coalition which Brian defeated at Clontarf, though he was killed. Brian's tributaries rebelled and the Munster hegemony collapsed. Other kings would try to emulate Brian's achievement, but none came close before 1169.

Monastic round tower on Devenish Island, Lower Lough Erne, Co. Fermanagh. Such towers were built as belfries and treasuries but they also served as short-term refuges from Viking raiders.

MAP NOTES

❶ *The poor and sparsely populated west coast was least affected by Viking raids.*

❷ *Armagh, Ireland's leading ecclesiastical centre, was sacked three times in 840 alone.*

❸ *Dublin was founded in 841 as a Viking fleet base and slave market.*

❹ *Osraige briefly became a leading kingdom in the 9th century thanks to an alliance with the Dublin Vikings.*

❺ *Dál Cais was named after its ruling dynasty. In the 11th century the dynasty changed its name to Uí Briain after its most famous king, Brian Boru.*

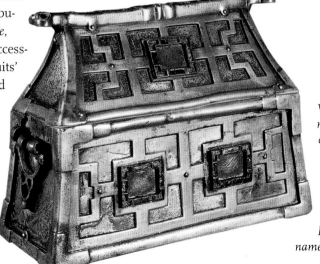

Viking raiders hacked up most of their loot to make it easier to share out fairly. This reliquary found its way intact from Ireland or Scotland back to Norway where it was used as a jewel box by a woman called Ranvaik, who scratched her name in runes on its base.

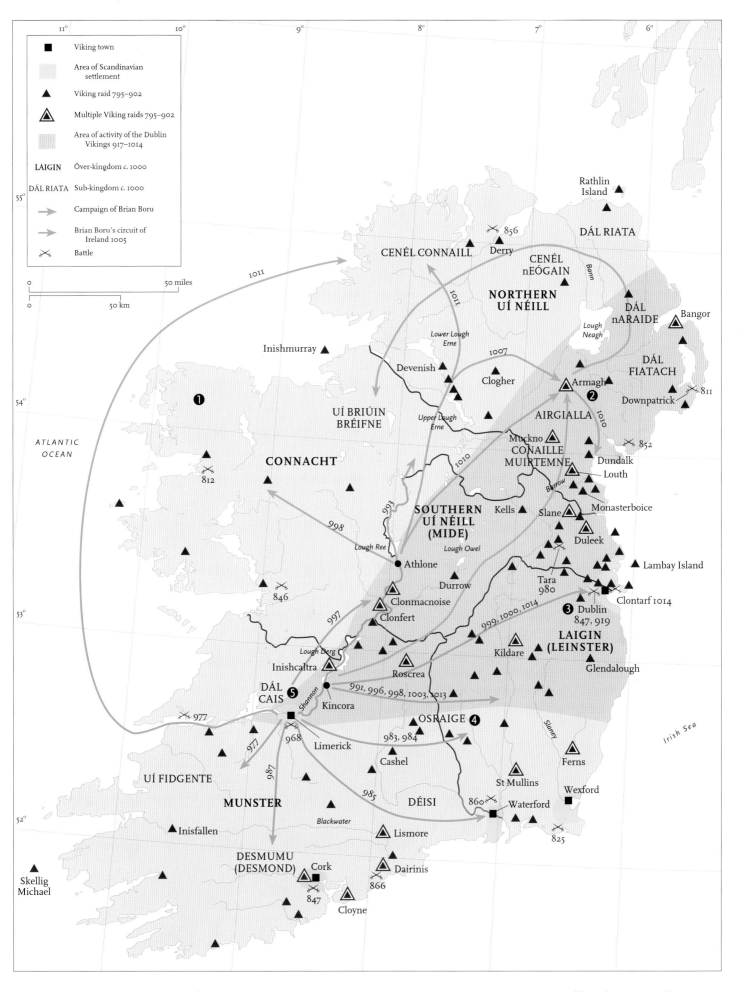

Legend

- ■ Viking town
- Area of Scandinavian settlement
- ▲ Viking raid 795–902
- ◬ Multiple Viking raids 795–902
- Area of activity of the Dublin Vikings 917–1014
- **LAIGIN** Over-kingdom c. 1000
- DÁL RIATA Sub-kingdom c. 1000
- → Campaign of Brian Boru
- → Brian Boru's circuit of Ireland 1005
- ⚔ Battle

0   50 miles
0   50 km

❶

ATLANTIC OCEAN

CENÉL CONNAILL

Derry

Rathlin Island

DÁL RIATA

CENÉL nEÓGAIN

NORTHERN UÍ NÉILL

Inishmurray

Devenish

Lower Lough Erne

Clogher

Upper Lough Erne

Lough Neagh

DÁL nARAIDE

Bangor

Armagh **❷**

DÁL FIATACH

Downpatrick

811

CONNACHT

UÍ BRIÚIN BRÉIFNE

AIRGIALLA

852

Muckno

CONAILLE MUIRTEMNE

Dundalk

Louth

812

Kells

Slane

Monasterboice

SOUTHERN UÍ NÉILL (MIDE)

Lough Ree

Lough Owel

Duleek

846

Athlone

Durrow

Tara 980

Lambay Island

Clonmacnoise

Clonfert

Kildare

Dublin 847, 919 **❸**

Clontarf 1014

LAIGIN (LEINSTER)

Lough Derg

Inishcaltra

Roscrea

Glendalough

DÁL CAIS ❺

Shannon

Kincora

991, 996, 998, 1003, 1013

999, 1000, 1014

977

Limerick

983, 984

OSRAIGE **❹**

Cashel

Ferns

Slaney

UÍ FIDGENTE

MUNSTER

985

St Mullins

Wexford

Waterford

860

825

Blackwater

DÉISI

Lismore

Irish Sea

Inisfallen

DESMUMU (DESMOND)

Cork

Dairinis

866

847

Skellig Michael

Cloyne

998

997

993

1010

1007

1010

1011

1011

968

977

987

The Kingdom of the Scots

c. AD 900 – 1300

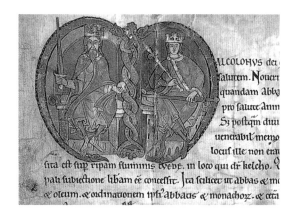

When Kenneth MacAlpin conquered the Picts in 843, the Scots had no sense of being a distinct nation; they saw themselves as being culturally and linguistically one people with the Irish. It was only after Scotland achieved roughly its modern borders in the 13th century that a sense of Scottish national identity developed.

THE PRESENCE OF THE VIKINGS on the west coast encouraged the MacAlpin dynasty to base itself in the old Pictish heartland around Perth and Strathearn. The first king to use the title 'King of Scotland' (Gaelic *rí Alban*) was Donald II (889–900). 'Scotland' (*Alba*) at this time referred only to the lands between the Forth and Moray and it was not until the 13th century that the word came to be used to describe the whole of what is today mainland Scotland. The influence of the kings of Scotland began to expand steadily in the 10th century. Weakened by Viking attacks, the British kingdom of Strathclyde became a satellite of Scotland before it was finally annexed *c.* 1018. Lothian, with its English-speaking population, was gained in 973. In the 11th century a long struggle for dominance began with the rival Scots kingdom of Moray. After Malcolm Canmore (1058–93) defeated and killed Macbeth in 1057, Moray declined and became part of the kingdom of Scotland by 1130. In the 12th century, Scotland conquered Galloway and the Scandinavian-dominated area of Caithness. Most of the Hebrides came under the rule of Somerled, a Gaelic chieftain, in 1156, but they remained under Norwegian overlordship until 1266. With this Scotland had achieved almost its modern borders; its last territorial acquisitions were Orkney and Shetland, ceded by Denmark in 1468–69.

In 1100, 'Scotland' was still a kingdom without a nation: Scots still saw themselves as Irish, their English and British subjects still retained their own identities. After David I (1124–53) began to encourage Anglo-Norman settlement in Scotland, English gradually became the language of the court and the church, replacing Welsh in Strathclyde and Gaelic in Fife and Angus. Traditional Gaelic lordship survived in the Highlands, where royal authority was weak, but the Lowlands became feudalized. A result of these changes was that in the 13th century, Scots began consciously to reject their Irish origins as they became aware of themselves as a separate people. This emerging national identity was emphatically confirmed by the experience of the wars of independence against England (1296–1328). Scottish identity was not homogeneous, as a division remained between the English-speaking Lowlands and the Gaelic-speaking Highlands until the 19th century. Coming late to Scottish rule, the Orkney and Shetland islanders did not share in this nation-building process and they continued to look to their Scandinavian origins; even today they retain a distinct identity.

Initial showing kings David I and Malcolm IV from a charter of the latter to Kelso Abbey, 1159. It was during the reign of David I that Scottish kingship began to lose its Celtic character.

MAP NOTES

❶ *Strathclyde never fully recovered after the Dublin Vikings sacked its capital Dumbarton in 870.*

❷ *Round towers built at Brechin and Abernethy c. 1100 are evidence of continuing Irish influence in Scotland.*

❸ *Perth was Scotland's capital from c. 1100 to 1436, when Edinburgh became the capital.*

❹ *The battle of Largs was the last attempt by Norway to end growing Scots influence in the western isles.*

❺ *Defeat of a rebel army confirmed Scottish control of Moray in 1130 but further rebellions followed in 1142, 1156, 1221 and 1228.*

❻ *Despite being much fought over, the present Anglo-Scottish border is little different from that established in 1092.*

Showing Irish and Anglo-Saxon influences, the Hunterston brooch from Ayrshire was made c. 700. Looted by Vikings it then belonged to a woman with an Irish name, Melbrigda, who wrote her name on it in Scandinavian runes.

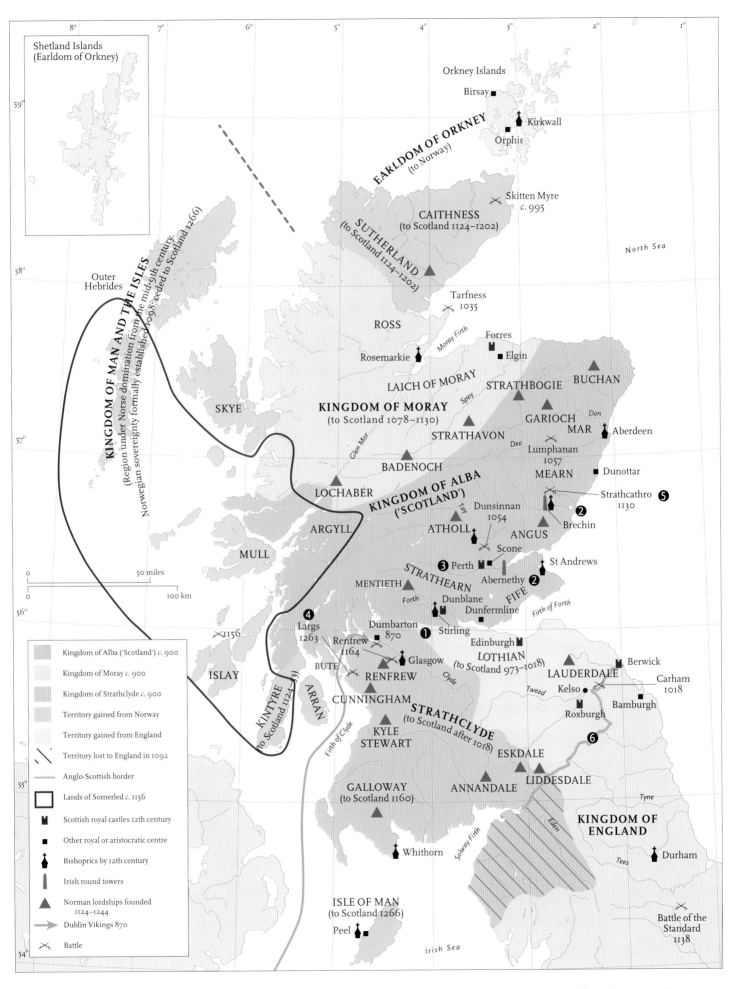

Shetland Islands
(Earldom of Orkney)

Orkney Islands

Birsay ■

✝
🏰 Kirkwall
Orphir ■

EARLDOM OF ORKNEY
(to Norway)

North Sea

Skitten Myre
⚔ c. 995

CAITHNESS
(to Scotland 1124–1202)

SUTHERLAND
(to Scotland 1124–1202) 🔺

Tarfness
⚔ 1035

KINGDOM OF MAN AND THE ISLES
(Region under Norse domination from the mid-9th century.
Norwegian sovereignty formally established 1098; ceded to Scotland 1266)

Outer
Hebrides

ROSS

Forres ■
Rosemarkie ✝
Moray Firth
Elgin ■

LAICH OF MORAY

STRATHBOGIE 🔺

BUCHAN 🔺

SKYE

KINGDOM OF MORAY
(to Scotland 1078–1130)

Spey
STRATHAVON 🔺

GARIOCH 🔺
Don
MAR
🏰 Aberdeen

Glen Mor

BADENOCH

Dee
Lumphanan
⚔ 1057

Dunottar ■

LOCHABER

KINGDOM OF ALBA
('SCOTLAND')

MEARN

Strathcathro ❺
1130

ARGYLL

Tay
Dunsinnan
⚔ 1054

ATHOLL
🏰

🔺
ANGUS
✝🏰
Brechin ❷

MULL

Scone
🏰❸ Perth 🏰
St Andrews ✝

MENTIETH 🔺
STRATHEARN
Abernethy ✝ ❷

Forth
Dunblane 🏰
FIFE
Dunfermline

Firth of Forth

❹
Largs
1263 ⚔
Dumbarton ■
❶ Stirling
Edinburgh ■

Renfrew ⚔
1164
Glasgow ✝

LOTHIAN
(to Scotland 973–1018)

Berwick ■

LAUDERDALE 🔺

BUTE

RENFREW 🔺

Clyde

CUNNINGHAM

Kelso ●
Roxburgh 🏰

Carham
1018

Bamburgh ■

KINTYRE
(to Scotland 1124–33)

ARRAN

STRATHCLYDE
(to Scotland after 1018)

Tweed

ISLAY

KYLE
STEWART

Firth of Clyde

ESKDALE 🔺
LIDDESDALE 🔺
❻

Tyne

GALLOWAY
(to Scotland 1160)

ANNANDALE 🔺

**KINGDOM OF
ENGLAND**

Whithorn ✝

Solway Firth
Eden

Durham ✝

Tees

ISLE OF MAN
(to Scotland 1266)

Peel ✝ ■

Irish Sea

⚔
Battle of the
Standard
1138

Legend

▨	Kingdom of Alba ('Scotland') c. 900
▨	Kingdom of Moray c. 900
▨	Kingdom of Strathclyde c. 900
▨	Territory gained from Norway
▨	Territory gained from England
▨	Territory lost to England in 1092
—	Anglo-Scottish border
▢	Lands of Somerled c. 1156
🏰	Scottish royal castles 12th century
■	Other royal or aristocratic centre
✝	Bishoprics by 12th century
▮	Irish round towers
🔺	Norman lordships founded 1124–1244
→	Dublin Vikings 870
⚔	Battle

⚔ 1156

Dumbarton
■ 870

Dublin Vikings 870 (→)

The Lordship of the Isles   AD 1266 – 1545

The most successful of the traditional Gaelic lordships of Highland Scotland was the MacDonald Lordship of the Isles. In the 15th century the Lords of the Isles became dangerous over-mighty subjects whose ambitions threatened the security of the kingdom of Scotland as a whole and led to their downfall.

THE ORIGINS OF the lordship go back to 1266 when Norway ceded the Isles to Scotland, though the change of sovereignty did not have dramatic effects on local lordship. Most of the Western Isles had already been brought under effective Gaelic rule by Somerled in 1156, and his descendants simply acknowledged the king of Scots as their overlord instead of the king of Norway. The people of the Isles were now thoroughly Gaelic too, the Norse settlers having been assimilated to the Gaelic-speaking population through intermarriage and conversion to Christianity.

The growth of the lordship began with Angus Og MacDonald, a descendant of Somerled's grandson Donald. Angus was made lord of Islay in 1307 by Robert Bruce for his support in his struggle with the Comyns for the Scottish throne. Angus led the men of the Isles at Bannockburn in 1314 and was further rewarded with Ardnamurchan, Morvern and Lochaber. Angus' son and successor John of Islay greatly expanded his inheritance through diplomacy and advantageous marriages. By 1354, when he adopted the formal title 'Lord of the Isles', John had gained control of all the Isles except Skye, together with the mainland areas of Kintyre, Knapdale and Garmoran. The lordship reached its greatest extent when Alexander, the third lord, acquired the Earldom of Ross by inheritance from his mother in 1424.

Royal authority, Norwegian or Scots, had never been strong in the Isles and the lords were able to rule in virtual independence. The main political centre of the lordship was Finlaggan Castle on Islay, where the Council of the Isles met. Gaelic was the language of

MAP NOTES

❶ Finlaggan Castle was built on an island in a loch: the Council of the Isles met on a second island connected to the castle by a causeway.

❷ The Isles and west coast of Scotland had the densest concentration of stone castles in Britain. Most were situated to control sea lanes.

❸ His defeat by a royal army at Harlaw dashed the 2nd lord Donald's hopes of controlling Ross: it was later acquired by his son Alexander.

❹ John II's son Angus defeated his father in a naval battle in an attempt to seize the lordship: he was murdered before he could benefit from his victory.

❺ John II, the 4th and last Lord of the Isles, died in prison in Dundee in 1503.

❻ By the 15th century, Scots English had begun to spread through northeast Scotland. Most of Scotland's towns were in the English-speaking area.

(Left) A 15th-century grave slab from Kilmory Knap chapel, Argyll. The Highland galley, a common symbol of power on grave slabs in this maritime region, shows the lasting influence of Viking shipbuilding traditions.

(Below) Tioram Castle, situated on a tidal island at the head of Loch Moidart, was one of the most important strongholds on the west coast of Scotland. Built in the 13th century, the castle and its lands were held from the Lords of the Isles in return for galley service, the maritime equivalent of feudal knight's service.

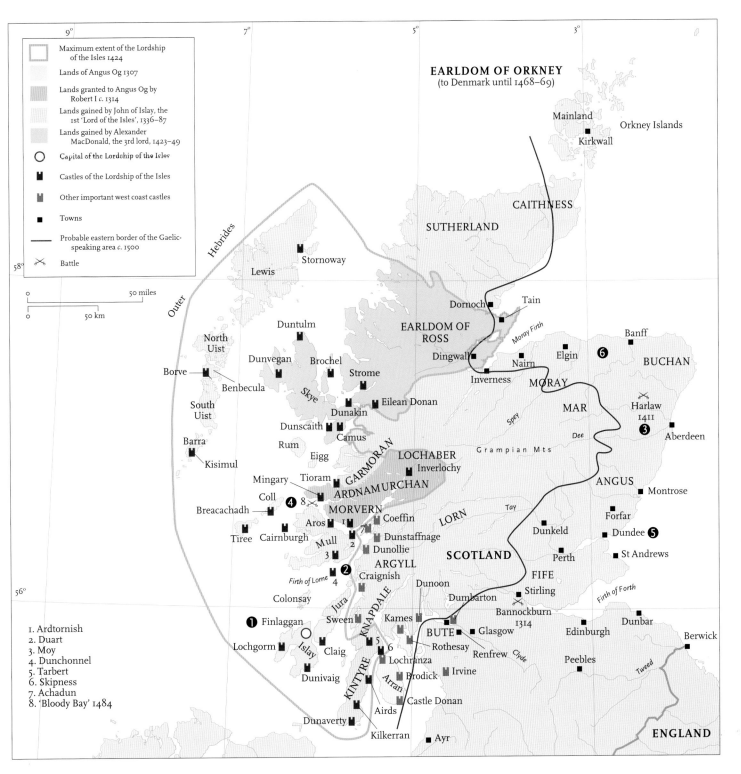

Legend:
- Maximum extent of the Lordship of the Isles 1424
- Lands of Angus Og 1307
- Lands granted to Angus Og by Robert I c. 1314
- Lands gained by John of Islay, the 1st 'Lord of the Isles', 1336–87
- Lands gained by Alexander MacDonald, the 3rd lord, 1423–49
- Capital of the Lordship of the Isles
- Castles of the Lordship of the Isles
- Other important west coast castles
- Towns
- Probable eastern border of the Gaelic-speaking area c. 1500
- Battle

government. The lords were effective rulers in the Isles, but they failed to prevent clan feuding in their mainland territories.

This vast lordship was seen as a threat by the Scottish crown after Donald, the second lord, allied with Henry IV of England in 1405 in an attempt to win the Earldom of Ross. John II, the fourth lord, allied with Edward IV of England in 1462, for which he forfeited Kintyre, Knapdale and the Earldom of Ross in 1476. In 1493 John was imprisoned by James IV and the lordship abolished. Its lands were divided between local clan chiefs and no clan was ever allowed to build up such a large lordship. But local loyalty was strong, and in 1545 John's grandson Donald Dubh received support when he acknowledged Henry VIII of England as king in an attempt to restore the lordship.

Wales in the Age of Llywelyn the Great

AD 1066 – 1274

Following the Norman conquest of England, Norman lords began to seek new opportunities for territorial expansion in Wales in the late 11th century. Yet a hundred years later they had still only gained secure control of the southern third of the country. In the 13th century even that achievement was threatened when Llywelyn the Great of Gwynedd and his successors took advantage of the political weakness of England to unite the Welsh and lay the basis of a national polity.

PROGRESS TOWARDS ACHIEVING political unification of Wales was slow. In the 10th and 11th centuries several rulers succeeded in bringing most, or in the case of Gruffydd ap Llywelyn (d. 1063), all of Wales under their rule. However, their achievements did not long outlive them. No king ever exercised direct authority throughout his dominions, but had to rule through vassal kings who had usually not submitted willingly. At any sign of weakness they would try to recover their independence. Also, the Welsh frequently practised partible inheritance, making it difficult for any lordship to remain intact.

Cross-border warfare with the English remained common in the 10th and 11th centuries. Massive English raids often forced Welsh kings to submit and pay tribute: these submissions formed the basis of later English claims to sovereignty over Wales. After the Norman conquest of England, Anglo-Norman lords began a piecemeal encroachment on Welsh territory. Though the smaller southern kingdoms succumbed, early Anglo-Norman advances in the north and west were defeated. Welsh rulers, such as Rhys ap Gruffydd, king of Deheubarth (d. 1197), adopted many Norman ways, including castle building and siege-warfare techniques, and encouraged church reform and monasticism to bring the Welsh church fully into line with Roman practices.

The most successful of Welsh rulers was Llywelyn ab Iorwerth of Gwynedd (1195–1240). Llywelyn took advantage of a civil war in England to conquer all the independent Welsh kingdoms, an achievement for which he became known as Llywelyn the Great. Punitive campaigns kept the English marcher barons on the defensive during his reign. To try to ensure that Welsh unity survived him, Llywelyn broke with custom by making his son Dafydd (d. 1246) his sole heir. However, Dafydd proved a weak ruler and the kingdom collapsed through internal dissent and English invasion. Unity was restored by Llywelyn ap Gruffydd (1246–82) who adopted the title 'Prince of Wales' in 1258. An ambitious ruler, Llywelyn pursued an expansionist policy, reconquering areas which had been under English rule for over a century. Despite forcing Henry III of England to grant formal recognition of his lands and title in 1267, Llywelyn's rule was unpopular in Gwynedd and his own brother Dafydd even defected to the English. Welsh unity was far from secure.

Hywel Dda (Hywel the Good), king of Deheubarth, c. 900–50, pictured in a 13th-century manuscript. Hywel was famous for his consolidation of the Laws of Wales.

MAP NOTES

❶ *Powys declined in importance after it was divided in 1160 and came under the domination of Gwynedd.*
❷ *The kingdom of Deheubarth was formed by the union of Dyfed and Seisyllwg in the 10th century: its capital was at Dinefwr.*
❸ *A long-lived linguistic border between Welsh and English was created by Flemish and English settlement around Haverfordwest in the early 12th century.*
❹ *Site of the court of the kings of Gwynedd.*
❺ *The senior bishopric of Wales, the pope decreed two pilgrimages to St Davids to be equivalent to one pilgrimage to Rome.*

Dolbadarn Castle, near Llanberis, Gwynedd, was built by Llywelyn the Great before 1230 to control a major north–south route through the mountains of Snowdonia.

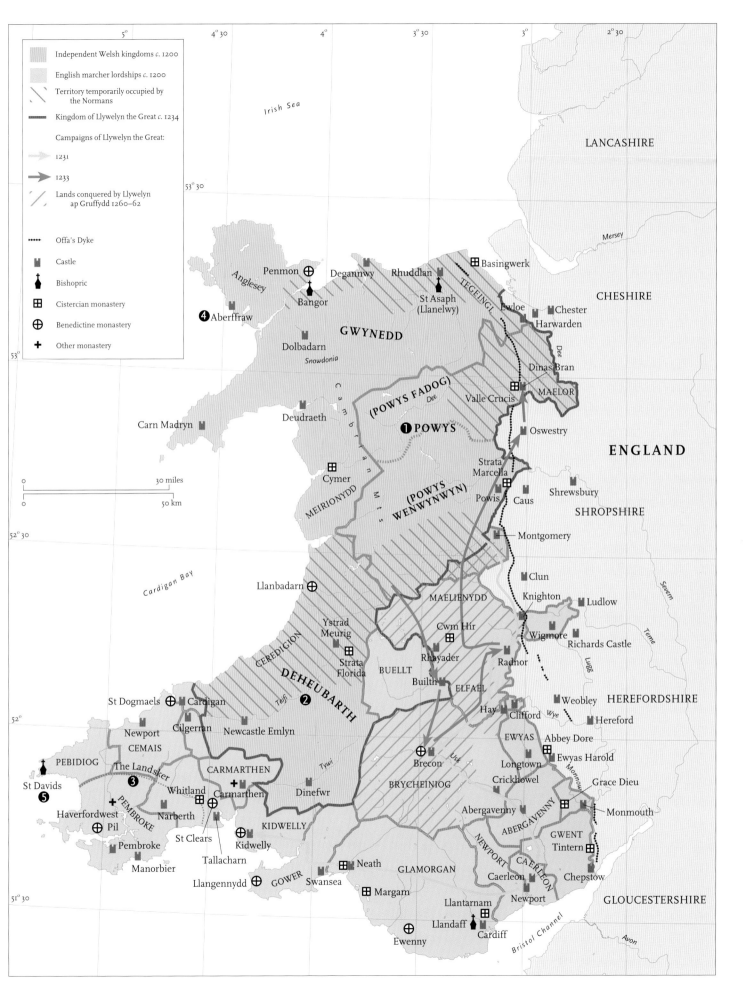

Legend

Independent Welsh kingdoms *c.* 1200

English marcher lordships *c.* 1200

Territory temporarily occupied by the Normans

Kingdom of Llywelyn the Great *c.* 1234

Campaigns of Llywelyn the Great:

1231

1233

Lands conquered by Llywelyn ap Gruffydd 1260–62

Offa's Dyke

Castle

Bishopric

Cistercian monastery

Benedictine monastery

Other monastery

Map labels

Irish Sea

LANCASHIRE

CHESHIRE

Mersey

❹ Aberffraw

Penmon ⊕
Degannwy
Rhuddlan
⊞ Basingwerk
Bangor
St Asaph (Llanelwy)
TEGEINGL
Ewloe
⊞ Chester
Harwarden

Anglesey

GWYNEDD

Dolbadarn

Snowdonia

Carn Madryn

Deudraeth

(POWYS FADOG)
Dee
Dinas Bran
Valle Crucis
⊞
MAELOR
❶ POWYS
Oswestry

ENGLAND

Cymer ⊞

MEIRIONYDD

(POWYS WENWYNWYN)
Strata Marcella ⊞
Powis
Caus
Shrewsbury

SHROPSHIRE

Montgomery

Cardigan Bay

Llanbadarn ⊕

MAELIENYDD

Clun

Knighton
⊞ Cwm Hir
Ludlow

Ystrad Meurig
Strata Florida ⊞
Rhayader
BUELLT
Builth
Radnor
Wigmore
Richards Castle

CEREDIGION

DEHEUBARTH ❷

Teifi

ELFAEL

Weobley

HEREFORDSHIRE

St Dogmaels ⊕
Cardigan
Cilgerran
Newcastle Emlyn
Hay
Clifford
Wye
Hereford

Newport
CEMAIS
The Landsker ❸
CARMARTHEN
Tywi
Brecon ⊕
EWYAS
Abbey Dore
Abergavenny

St Davids ✝
❺
PEBIDIOG
Whitland
Carmarthen
Dinefwr
BRYCHEINIOG
Longtown
Ewyas Harold
Grace Dieu

Haverfordwest
Pil ⊕
Narberth
KIDWELLY
Crickhowel
Monmouth

Pembroke
St Clears
Kidwelly ⊕
Abergavenny
ABERGAVENNY

Manorbier
Tallacharn
Neath ⊞
GLAMORGAN
NEWPORT
GWENT
Tintern ⊞

Llangennydd ⊕
GOWER
Swansea
Margam ⊞
CAERLEON
Caerleon
Chepstow

Llantarnam ⊞
Llandaff ✝
Newport
GLOUCESTERSHIRE

Ewenny ⊕
Llandaff
Cardiff

Bristol Channel
Avon

The End of Welsh Independence

The Treaty of Montgomery in 1267, whereby Henry III of England recognized Llywelyn ap Gruffydd as Prince of Wales, represented the apogee of medieval Wales. But, as with all earlier attempts to create a united Welsh state, Llywelyn's principality was soon torn apart by a combination of English aggression and internal disunity.

IT WAS LLYWELYN HIMSELF who precipitated the crisis which destroyed his principality. Llywelyn's successes against Henry III had made him overconfident and he fatally underestimated Henry's son Edward I, who succeeded him in 1272. Summoned, as established custom dictated, to attend Edward's coronation in London in 1274, Llywelyn refused. Llywelyn compounded the fault by refusing also to pay homage to Edward and by planning to marry the daughter of Simon de Montfort, the leader of a major baronial revolt against Henry III. Llywelyn's power already posed a threat to the security of the marcher barons so in 1276 Edward began preparing a full-scale invasion of Wales. Edward himself led a force into north Wales in the summer of 1277, smaller armies invaded mid- and southwest Wales. English sea power was exploited to outflank the main Welsh force at Conwy and ravage Anglesey, the bread basket of Wales. Within a few months, Llywelyn was forced to negotiate terms to stave off further attacks. By the Treaty of Aberconwy, Llywelyn's principality was dismembered. Native rulers were restored to independence and Llywelyn's brother Dafydd was rewarded for supporting Edward with lands in north Wales.

The first war of Welsh independence left many issues unsettled and disputes between the Welsh princes and the English crown were common. Dafydd was particularly unhappy with his treatment and he rebelled in March 1282 and attacked Hawarden. When Llywelyn decided to answer his brother's appeal for help, the second and final war of Welsh independence broke out. Despite massive retaliation by Edward, the Welsh initially enjoyed considerable success, but Llywelyn's death in battle near Builth in December 1282 was a disaster from which they did not recover. Dafydd took over leadership of the Welsh, but he had made many enemies in his treacherous career and he was betrayed to the English in June 1283 and executed at Shrewsbury. Edward proceeded to dispossess all the Welsh rulers who had supported Llywelyn. Only Powys Wenwynwyn remained under a native family, though they were now direct subjects of the crown. By the Statute of Rhuddlan in 1284, English law was imposed on Wales as the first stage towards its absorption into England (completed by the Act of Union in 1536). To consolidate his conquest, Edward began an ambitious programme of castle building. It was needed, for the English hold on Wales was shaken by a major rebellion in 1294–95 which was suppressed only with difficulty.

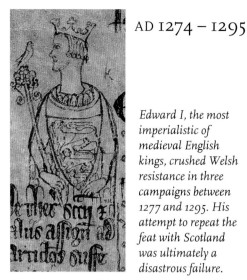

Edward I, the most imperialistic of medieval English kings, crushed Welsh resistance in three campaigns between 1277 and 1295. His attempt to repeat the feat with Scotland was ultimately a disastrous failure.

MAP NOTES

❶ The most important agricultural area of Wales, Anglesey was vulnerable to English sea power.

❷ The mountains of Snowdonia were ideal country for guerrilla warfare but lacked the resources to support prolonged resistance: English strategy aimed at cutting the area off from outside supplies.

❸ Llywelyn was killed after an English force captured Irfon Bridge in a surprise attack.

❹ The last stronghold in Welsh hands, Castell-y-Bere, fell in March 1283.

Edward I watches the execution of Dafydd ap Gruffydd, the last independent Prince of Wales, at Shrewsbury in 1283, depicted in a 14th-century manuscript.

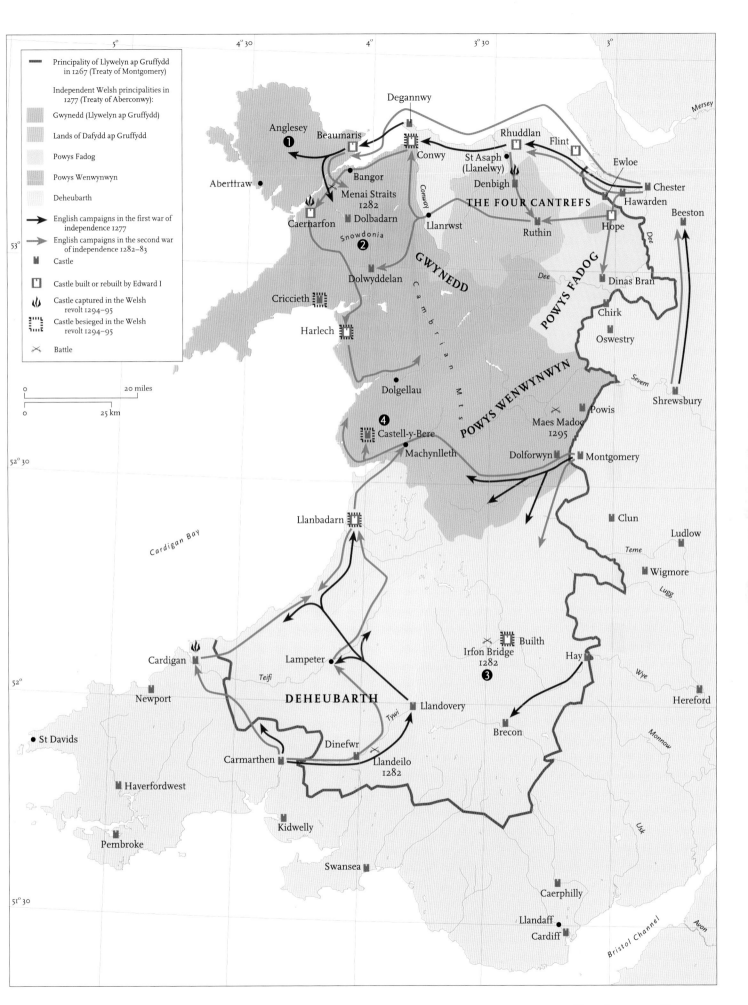

Principality of Llywelyn ap Gruffydd in 1267 (Treaty of Montgomery)

Independent Welsh principalities in 1277 (Treaty of Aberconwy):

Gwynedd (Llywelyn ap Gruffydd)

Lands of Dafydd ap Gruffydd

Powys Fadog

Powys Wenwynwyn

Deheubarth

English campaigns in the first war of independence 1277

English campaigns in the second war of independence 1282–83

Castle

Castle built or rebuilt by Edward I

Castle captured in the Welsh revolt 1294–95

Castle besieged in the Welsh revolt 1294–95

Battle

0   20 miles
0   25 km

Mersey

Degannwy

Anglesey ❶

Beaumaris

Aberffraw

Bangor

Menai Straits 1282

Caernarfon

Dolbadarn ❷

Snowdonia

Conwy

Conway

St Asaph (Llanelwy)

Denbigh

THE FOUR CANTREFS

Llanrwst

Ruthin

Hope

Rhuddlan

Flint

Ewloe

Chester

Hawarden

Beeston

Dee

Dee

POWYS FADOG

Dinas Bran

Chirk

Oswestry

Dolwyddelan

GWYNEDD

Cambrian Mts

Criccieth

Harlech

Dolgellau

❹

Castell-y-Bere

Machynlleth

POWYS WENWYNWYN

Severn

Powis

Maes Madog 1295

Dolforwyn

Montgomery

Shrewsbury

Clun

Ludlow

Teme

Wigmore

Lugg

Cardigan Bay

Llanbadarn

Lampeter

Teifi

DEHEUBARTH

Tywi

Llandovery

Dinefwr

Llandeilo 1282

Carmarthen

Cardigan

Newport

St Davids

Haverfordwest

Kidwelly

Pembroke

Swansea

Irfon Bridge 1282

Builth

❸

Hay

Brecon

Wye

Hereford

Monnow

Usk

Caerphilly

Llandaff

Cardiff

Bristol Channel

Avon

5°   4°30   4°   3°30   3°

53°

52°30

52°

51°30

Glyndŵr's Revolt

MAP NOTES

❶ *After he was captured at Pilleth, Edmund Mortimer, the Earl of March, became an ally of Glyndŵr's. The mass grave of those slain in the battle has been discovered at a local church.*

❷ *Henry IV's victory at Shrewsbury prevented northern English rebels uniting with the Welsh.*

❸ *Glyndŵr called the first Welsh parliament at Machynlleth in 1404.*

❹ *After its fall in 1404, Harlech became Glyndŵr's headquarters: here he was crowned Prince of Wales. It was recaptured by the English in 1408, with Glyndŵr's wife, daughter and grandchildren.*

❺ *Monnington Court, near Vowchurch in Herefordshire, is thought to be Glyndŵr's most likely burial place.*

In the century following the Edwardian conquest, the English did little to make their rule acceptable to the Welsh. In 1400 the accumulation of Welsh grievances led to the outbreak of a general rebellion which for several years reduced the English hold on Wales to a few castles and fortified towns.

THE LEADER OF THE REVOLT was Owain Glyndŵr (b. 1359), the lord of Glyndyfrdwy in northeast Wales. Though descended from a Welsh princely family, Glyndŵr was an unlikely rebel, having studied law at the Inns of Court, served as a squire to the earl of Arundel and fought loyally in Richard II's army in Scotland. Richard's deposition by Henry IV in 1399 may have strained Glyndŵr's loyalty, but it was an apparently trivial property dispute with Lord Grey of Ruthin which finally caused him to rebel in September 1400. Glyndŵr's supporters pronounced him Prince of Wales and he began raiding English border towns. The late 14th century had seen many small Welsh revolts as English landowners had increased their exactions in the economic chaos which followed the Black Death, and support for Glyndŵr spread rapidly. By 1405 no part of Wales was unaffected by the rising. Glyndŵr generally avoided open battle, preferring to use guerrilla tactics, and English counter-attacks achieved little.

Glyndŵr laid ambitious plans for an independent Welsh principality, with a parliament, civil service, universities, and an independent Welsh church with an archbishopric at St Davids. Glyndŵr found English allies in the Percy and Mortimer families, both of which opposed Henry IV's usurpation, and the three agreed on a tripartite division of England in 1405 which would have added the English border shires to the Principality of Wales. Glyndŵr also negotiated an alliance with the French, who sent an expeditionary force in 1405.

The French captured Worcester but failed to hold it. This proved the turning point of Glyndŵr's fortunes. The French withdrew in 1406 and without the prospect of any further foreign intervention, support for the rebellion began to waver. By 1408, the English had recovered control of most of south and mid-Wales, but resistance continued in the mountains of north Wales for several more years. Glyndŵr himself went into hiding in 1410, and after he refused an offer of pardon from Henry V in 1415 he disappeared from history into the realms of folklore.

The effect of the revolt on Wales was serious. Years of warfare had devastated both towns and countryside and repressive anti-Welsh legislation remained in force until the accession of the Welsh Tudor dynasty to the English throne in 1485. The failure of the revolt to all intents and purposes ended Welsh aspirations for independence: future Welsh political aspirations aimed at achieving equal treatment with the English.

(Below left) Seal of Owain Glyndŵr showing him enthroned as Prince of Wales.

(Below right) The reign of Richard II saw English exploitation of Wales increase dramatically, turning the country into a hotbed of discontent, ripe for rebellion.

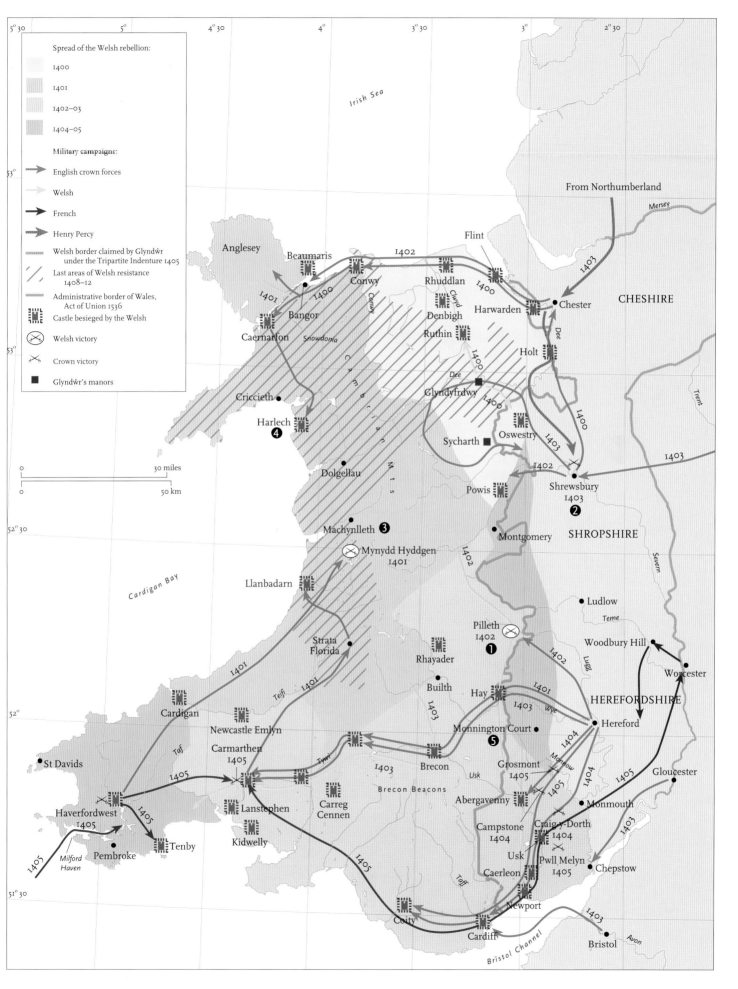

Spread of the Welsh rebellion:

1400
1401
1402–03
1404–05

Military campaigns:

→ English crown forces
→ Welsh
→ French
→ Henry Percy

Welsh border claimed by Glyndŵr under the Tripartite Indenture 1405
Last areas of Welsh resistance 1408–12
Administrative border of Wales, Act of Union 1536
Castle besieged by the Welsh
Welsh victory
Crown victory
Glyndŵr's manors

Irish Sea

30 miles
50 km

Anglesey
Beaumaris
Conwy 1402
Bangor 1401
Caernarfon 1400
Snowdonia

Rhuddlan 1400
Denbigh
Ruthin
Harwarden
Chester 1403
CHESHIRE
Mersey

From Northumberland
Flint

Holt

Glyndyfrdwy 1400
Sycharth
Oswestry 1403
Shrewsbury 1403 **②**
1402
SHROPSHIRE
Powis
Montgomery
Trent

Cambrian Mts

Criccieth
Harlech **④**
Dolgellau
Machynlleth **③**

Mynydd Hyddgen 1401

Cardigan Bay

Llanbadarn

Strata Florida
1401

Pilleth 1402 **①**

Ludlow
Teme

Woodbury Hill
Worcester

Rhayader
Builth
Hay 1401 1403 Wye
Monnington Court **⑤**
HEREFORDSHIRE
Hereford

St Davids
Cardigan
Newcastle Emlyn
Carmarthen 1405
Lanstephen
Brecon
1403
Carreg Cennen
Kidwelly

Grosmont 1405
Abergavenny
Campstone 1404
Craig-y-Dorth 1404
Usk
Pwll Melyn 1405
Caerleon
Monmouth
Gloucester
Chepstow

Haverfordwest 1405
Pembroke
Milford Haven
Tenby

Brecon Beacons

Coity
Cardiff
Newport
Bristol
Avon

Bristol Channel

Ireland and the Anglo-Normans

In 1183 Rory O'Connor, king of Connacht and the last High King of Ireland, abdicated in favour of his son Conchobar, his prestige and authority shattered by his failure to contain the power of the Anglo-Norman invaders.

THE CHAIN OF EVENTS which led to the Anglo-Norman invasion began in 1166 when the High King Rory O'Connor exiled Diarmait MacMurchada, the king of Leinster. Diarmait fled to the English king Henry II and was given permission to recruit soldiers among the Welsh marcher barons to help him recover his kingdom. Diarmait returned with a small force of Anglo-Norman knights and archers in 1167 and re-established his kingdom inside two years. In 1170 the marcher baron Richard FitzGilbert de Clare ('Strongbow') arrived with reinforcements and captured Waterford and Dublin. Diarmait rewarded Strongbow with marriage to his daughter Aoife, and when Diarmait died without legitimate male heirs in 1171 he inherited the kingdom of Leinster. This alarmed Henry, and to prevent his vassal founding an independent kingdom he came to Ireland with an army and forced Strongbow and most native Irish kings to acknowledge him as overlord. Rory O'Connor hesitated but in 1175 he conceded, bringing all Ireland, at least nominally, under English sovereignty.

The dramatic success of the Anglo-Normans lay in their use of a combination of armoured knights and archers, giving them military superiority over the Irish, whose troops fought unarmoured with spears, much as they had done since the Iron Age. The Anglo-Normans were also far superior at building fortifications. Earth-and-timber motte-and-bailey castles were thrown up by the hundred, gradually to be replaced by a smaller number of imposing stone castles and fortress towns. English settlement was encouraged to help consolidate the military conquests, but English settlers remained a small minority among the Irish, mostly confined to towns and the east coast. In those areas which they controlled, the Anglo-Norman lords established a degree of stability: Irish peasants, enjoying more favourable terms than their English counterparts, achieved considerable prosperity. The landscape was transformed as the area under cultivation expanded rapidly. Despite this, by the end of the 13th century it was clear that it would be impossible to dislodge all the native Irish dynasties. The Anglo-Normans' military superiority was undermined as the Irish turned to guerrilla tactics and used Scottish galloglasses – heavily armed infantry – so that they could fight on equal terms. The Anglo-Norman lords were also handicapped by their kings' lack of interest in Ireland, so that at times the royal government in Dublin virtually ceased to function.

Seal of Richard FitzGilbert de Clare, lord of Striguil in southwest Wales, better known as 'Strongbow'. Henry II's invasion of Ireland was precipitated when Strongbow inherited the throne of Leinster.

MAP NOTES

❶ *In 1170, just ten Anglo-Norman knights supported by 70 archers routed a 3000-strong Irish army near Waterford.*

❷ *The areas of densest Anglo-Norman settlement were in the fertile lands of Meath and between Wexford and Limerick.*

❸ *King John made Dublin the capital of English government in Ireland in 1204.*

❹ *English colonists defeated an attempt by Brian O'Neill to resurrect the high kingship in 1260.*

❺ *Hebridean galloglasses helped the Irish win a major victory over the English at Athankip in 1270.*

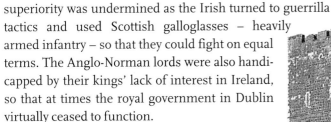

Carrickfergus Castle, Co. Antrim. Founded in 1180, Carrickfergus was the first stone castle to be built in Ireland. It remained the main centre of English power in Ulster until the 17th century.

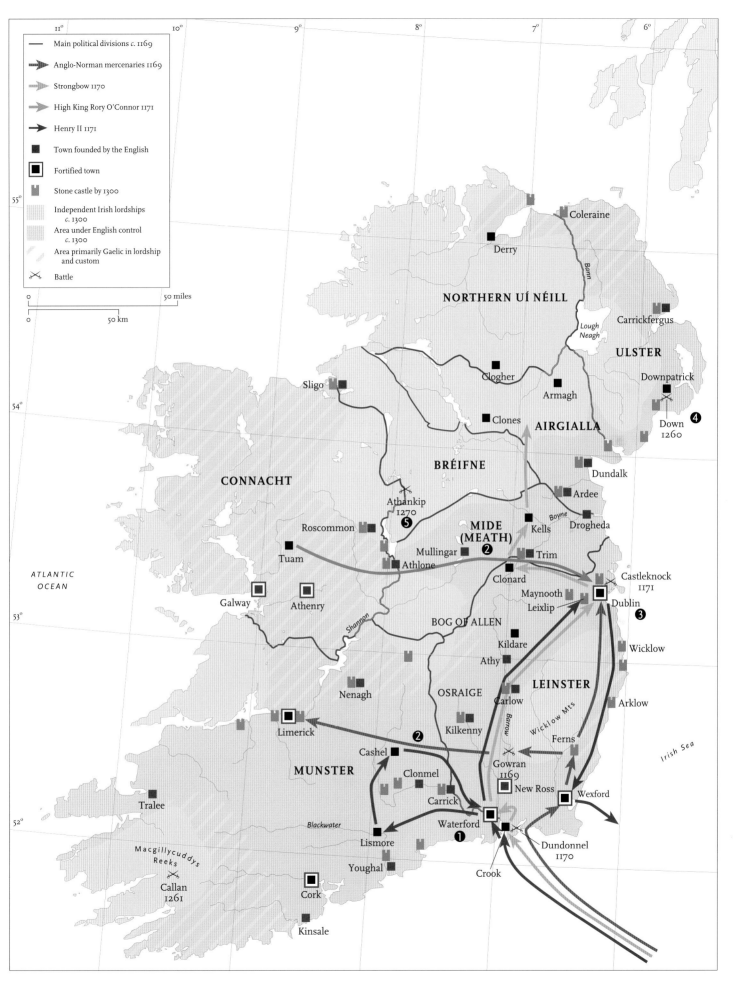

Legend

— Main political divisions *c.* 1169

➤ Anglo-Norman mercenaries 1169

➤ Strongbow 1170

➤ High King Rory O'Connor 1171

➤ Henry II 1171

■ Town founded by the English

▣ Fortified town

▮ Stone castle by 1300

Independent Irish lordships *c.* 1300

Area under English control *c.* 1300

Area primarily Gaelic in lordship and custom

✕ Battle

0   50 miles

0   50 km

ATLANTIC OCEAN

Irish Sea

NORTHERN UÍ NÉILL

ULSTER

AIRGIALLA

BRÉIFNE

CONNACHT

MIDE (MEATH)

LEINSTER

MUNSTER

OSRAIGE

BOG OF ALLEN

Wicklow Mts

Macgillycuddys Reeks

Coleraine

Derry

Carrickfergus

Downpatrick

Down 1260 ❹

Clogher

Armagh

Clones

Sligo

Dundalk

Ardee

Kells

Drogheda

Boyne

Bann

Lough Neagh

Athankip 1270 ❺

Roscommon

Tuam

Mullingar ❷

Athlone

Trim

Clonard

Galway

Athenry

Maynooth

Leixlip

Castleknock 1171

Dublin ❸

Wicklow

Shannon

Kildare

Athy

Nenagh

Carlow

Kilkenny

Barrow

Arklow

Ferns

Limerick

Cashel

Clonmel

Carrick

Gowran 1169 ❷

New Ross

Wexford

Waterford ❶

Dundonnel 1170

Crook

Tralee

Lismore

Blackwater

Youghal

Callan 1261

Cork

Kinsale

English and Gaelic Lordships in Later Medieval Ireland AD 1300 – 1500

The late Middle Ages saw English lordship in Ireland begin to crumble, until by the end of the 15th century only the Pale around Dublin was securely controlled by them. The decline in English power was accompanied by a strong revival of Gaelic culture.

BY 1300 NATIVE IRISH LORDS had turned back the English advance, but, strongly entrenched in their castles and walled towns, they were still able to beat off a major Scottish invasion under King Robert Bruce's brother Edward in 1315–18. The English faced a more insidious threat than military overthrow – that they would be assimilated by the Irish. This became ever more likely after the outbreak of the Black Death in 1348–50 killed 40 per cent of the mainly urbanized English settlers, while sparing the far more numerous rural Irish.

The increasing strength of Gaelic Ireland resulted in a resurgence of Gaelic culture led by a number of learned families, each of which had its own specialism – poetry, history, music, medicine or law. Irish kingship survived the Anglo-Norman invasion but declined as an institution. In the 14th century traditional inauguration ceremonies were revived and carried out at sites which in some cases, as at Tara and the Navan (Emain Macha), had been associated with kingship since the Iron Age. Despite this, 14th-century Irish kings were essentially warlords whose powers were not constrained by law or church. They were emulated by English lords who became increasingly difficult to distinguish from native rulers, especially as many were bilingual in English and Gaelic. Many of the ordinary English settlers had also begun to adopt Irish ways, often through intermarriage. In 1366 the English government introduced the Statutes of Kilkenny to try to keep the English in Ireland distinct from the Irish. Intermarriage was banned and the English were not to keep Irish minstrels or play Irish sports, and above all they were not to speak Gaelic.

The crown made great efforts in the late 14th century to support the settlers in Ireland, but little was achieved despite considerable expenditure. In the 15th century crown policy was changed and beyond the Pale power was devolved to the great English magnate families of the FitzGeralds in Kildare and Desmond and the Butlers in Ormond. The magnates enjoyed effectively 'self-government at the king's command' and in 1460 the Irish parliament, which they dominated, declared that it was not bound by laws passed in the English parliament unless it too passed them. The earl of Kildare ruled as viceroy until in 1494 King Henry VII sent Sir Edward Poynings to reassert direct crown control over Anglo-Ireland.

MAP NOTES

❶ The English Pale was the highly anglicized region which in the 15th century was firmly under the Dublin government's control. It had been fortified by 1495.

❷ Maynooth castle was the seat of the influential earls of Kildare in the 15th century.

❸ One of the most powerful Irish dynasties, the O'Neills dominated all of Ulster in the late 15th century.

❹ The MacMurroughs exacted 'black rent' (blackmail) from the Pale until the late 16th century.

❺ Low hills, 60–150 m (200–500 ft) high, such as Cnoc Buadha, with good views over the regal territory were favoured as inauguration sites.

Illustration from an early 15th-century manuscript depicting an encounter in 1399 between a party of heavily armoured English knights and Art MacMurchada, king of Leinster. Art rides in the usual Irish way, without stirrups.

A 15th-century tower house, Cloghmore Castle, Achill Island, Co. Mayo. A sign of general insecurity, tower houses were built in their thousands during the 15th and 16th centuries by both Gaelic and English lords.

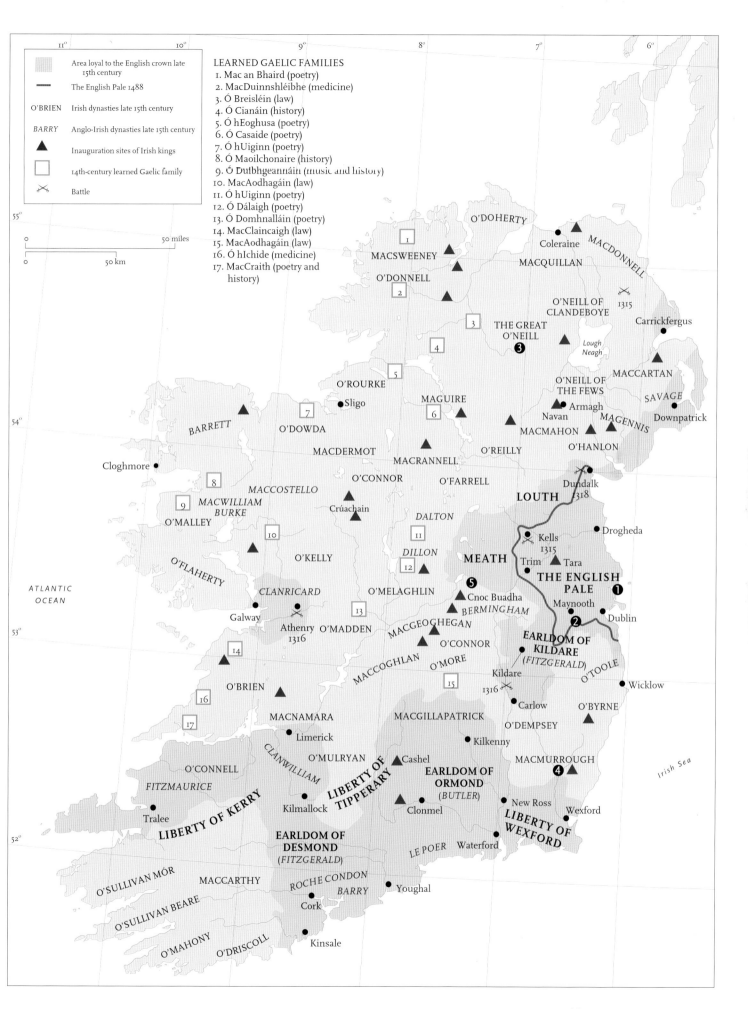

LEARNED GAELIC FAMILIES
1. Mac an Bhaird (poetry)
2. MacDuinnshléibhe (medicine)
3. Ó Breisléin (law)
4. Ó Cianáin (history)
5. Ó hEoghusa (poetry)
6. Ó Casaide (poetry)
7. Ó hUiginn (poetry)
8. Ó Maoilchonaire (history)
9. Ó Duibhgeannáin (music and history)
10. MacAodhagáin (law)
11. Ó hUiginn (poetry)
12. Ó Dálaigh (poetry)
13. Ó Domhnalláin (poetry)
14. MacClaincaigh (law)
15. MacAodhagáin (law)
16. Ó hIchide (medicine)
17. MacCraith (poetry and history)

Area loyal to the English crown late 15th century

The English Pale 1488

O'BRIEN Irish dynasties late 15th century

BARRY Anglo-Irish dynasties late 15th century

▲ Inauguration sites of Irish kings

□ 14th-century learned Gaelic family

✕ Battle

0   50 miles
0   50 km

O'Neill's Rising and the Fall of Gaelic Ireland   AD 1534 – 1603

When Ireland rejected the Protestant Reformation, English governments feared that the country would be used by the hostile Catholic powers of Europe as a base for an invasion of England. Reducing Ireland to obedience to the crown became an urgent necessity.

THE PROTESTANT REFORMATION was officially introduced into Ireland by the 'Reformation Parliament' of 1536 which was easily manouevred into recognizing Henry VIII as head of the church in Ireland. Henry further strengthened his position in 1541 by constituting Ireland as a separate kingdom and adopting the title 'King of Ireland' (previous English kings had used the title 'Lord of Ireland'). Dissolution of monasteries was begun, but no major doctrinal changes were introduced. Opposition grew under Henry's successor Edward VI, whose government began to introduce Protestant doctrines without consulting the Irish parliament. Anti-Catholic measures were stepped up in the 1580s but the 'Old English' (as the established English families in Ireland now began to be called) increasingly rejected the state church and opted for recusancy: in areas under Gaelic lordship, the state church had never been accepted to begin with.

The Tudor monarchs pursued policies to anglicize the government of Ireland and introduce local government based on English-style shires. This policy threatened the status of both Gaelic lords and the Old English, causing several rebellions. To promote anglicization English governments garrisoned the country and began a policy of plantations of 'New English' settlers on lands confiscated from rebels, beginning in Leix-Offaly in 1556. Most of these plantations failed because of guerrilla warfare waged by their dispossessed former owners.

Opposition to anglicization came to a head in 1593 when Hugh O'Neill, the earl of Tyrone, began a rebellion – known as the Nine Years War – with the support of the O'Donnells of Tyrconnell and the Maguires of Fermanagh. Though O'Neill's call for freedom of conscience failed to win over the Catholic Old English, Elizabeth I recognized the seriousness of the revolt, proclaiming O'Neill a traitor in 1595 and sending a large army under the earl of Essex in 1598: O'Neill ran rings around it. Essex was replaced by Lord Mountjoy who began to hem O'Neill in with forts and garrisons. A Spanish force arrived at Kinsale to support the revolt in 1601 but the English inflicted a decisive defeat on O'Neill and O'Donnell before they could join up with it. In 1603 O'Neill finally admitted defeat and signed a peace treaty. Four years later O'Neill, Rory O'Donnell and Cúchonnacht Maguire fled their earldoms to go into exile on the continent. With 'the Flight of the Earls' the days of Gaelic lordship in Ireland were ended and though the Gaelic language survived, without the patronage of Gaelic lords, Gaelic cultural traditions began a long decline.

Hugh O'Neill, earl of Tyrone. For many years O'Neill successfully played a double game against Elizabeth I, feigning loyalty while secretly supporting rebellion and negotiating with Spain.

MAP NOTES

❶ *The Munster plantation was begun on lands confiscated by the crown in 1583 after a rebellion by the earl of Desmond.*

❷ *The division of Monaghan between Irish supporters of the crown was one of the main causes of the Nine Years War.*

❸ *An English column on its way to Enniskillen lost its food supplies in an ambush, giving the battle its unusual name.*

❹ *The worst English defeat of the Nine Years War left the plantations exposed to attack by O'Neill.*

❺ *The Flight of the Earls: Hugh O'Neill and his supporters fled to the continent from Rathmullan in 1607.*

A contemporary representation of the Irish siege of Enniskillen during the Nine Years War. Lack of artillery hampered Irish siege operations throughout the war.

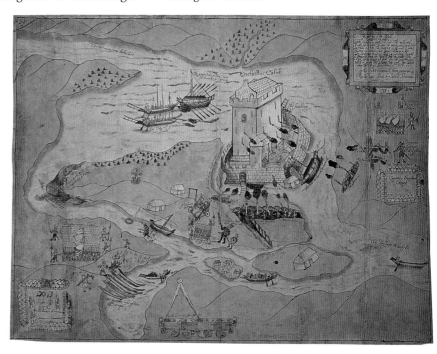

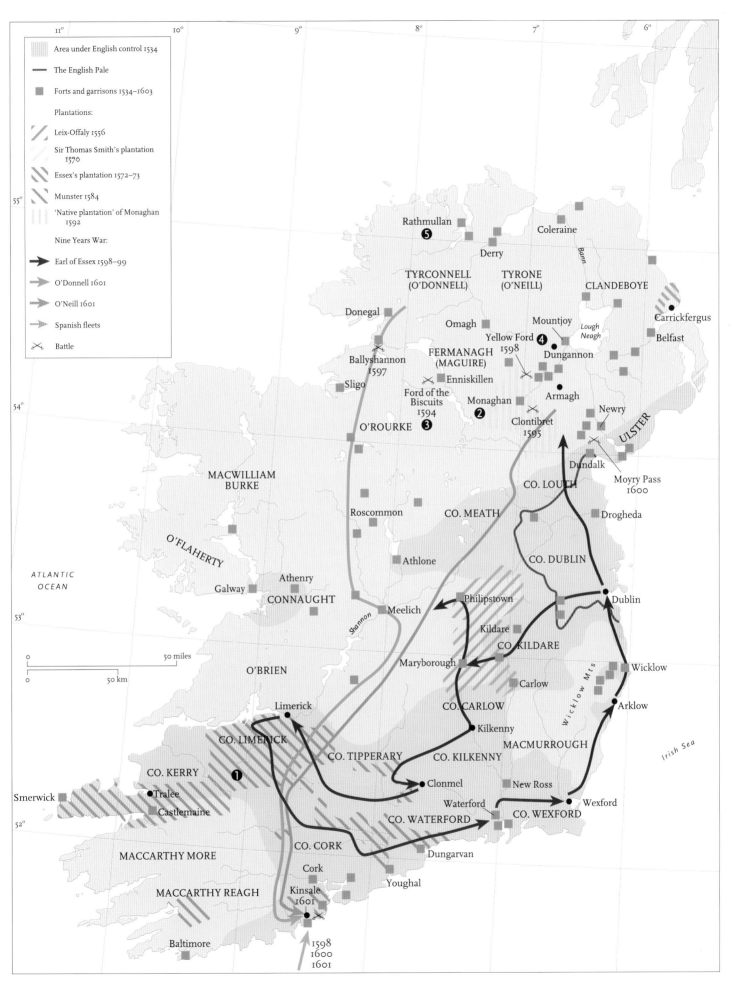

Legend:

Area under English control 1534

The English Pale

Forts and garrisons 1534–1603

Plantations:

Leix-Offaly 1556

Sir Thomas Smith's plantation 1570

Essex's plantation 1572–73

Munster 1584

'Native plantation' of Monaghan 1592

Nine Years War:

Earl of Essex 1598–99

O'Donnell 1601

O'Neill 1601

Spanish fleets

Battle

Map labels:

TYRCONNELL (O'DONNELL)

TYRONE (O'NEILL)

CLANDEBOYE

Rathmullan ⑤

Coleraine

Derry

Carrickfergus

Omagh

Mountjoy

Belfast

Yellow Ford 1598 ④

Lough Neagh

Dungannon

FERMANAGH (MAGUIRE)

Enniskillen

Armagh

Ballyshannon 1597

Sligo

Donegal

Ford of the Biscuits 1594 ③

Monaghan ②

Clontibret 1595

Newry

ULSTER

Dundalk

Moyry Pass 1600

O'ROURKE

MACWILLIAM BURKE

Roscommon

CO. LOUTH

Drogheda

CO. MEATH

O'FLAHERTY

Athlone

CO. DUBLIN

ATLANTIC OCEAN

Galway

Athenry

CONNAUGHT

Meelich

Shannon

Philipstown

Kildare

Dublin

CO. KILDARE

Maryborough

Wicklow

O'BRIEN

Carlow

Wicklow Mts

Arklow

Limerick

CO. CARLOW

Kilkenny

CO. LIMERICK

CO. TIPPERARY

CO. KILKENNY

MACMURROUGH

Irish Sea

CO. KERRY ①

Clonmel

New Ross

Wexford

Smerwick

Tralee

Castlemaine

Waterford

CO. WEXFORD

CO. WATERFORD

MACCARTHY MORE

CO. CORK

Dungarvan

Cork

Youghal

MACCARTHY REAGH

Kinsale 1601

Baltimore

1598 1600 1601

Scale:

0 — 50 miles

0 — 50 km

The Plantations in Ireland

AD 1605 – 1657

The failure of O'Neill's rebellion was followed by the imposition of a new Protestant ruling class, large-scale land confiscations and the plantation of English and Scottish Protestant settlers: the Irish problem would be solved by getting rid of the Irish.

THE TUDOR PLANTATIONS began as grants of confiscated lands of rebellious Irish or Old English magnates to small numbers of New English or, in some cases, loyal Irish landowners: in Munster they turned into attempts at ethnic cleansing. A short-lived rebellion in Donegal in 1608 persuaded the government of the Stuart king James I (James VI of Scotland) to adopt the same policy in Ulster. The Articles of Plantation of 1609 provided for the removal of most of the Irish population to designated reservations to release the country's best land for plantation with Protestant Scots or English tenant farmers. The scheme failed for the same reasons that plans to encourage settlement in Ireland had always failed – its reputation as a violent rebellious province. The undertakers (chief planters) appointed by the government to oversee the plantations found that it was not just necessary but highly profitable to retain Irish tenants as they were willing to pay high rents to stay on the land. Only in Antrim and Down was a majority Protestant population – mainly of Lowland Scots – established.

The combination of religious discrimination, land confiscations, high rents and resulting poverty caused seething discontent, but the government was still caught unprepared when the Irish rebelled in 1641. Civil war broke out between Charles I and Parliament in 1642 and it was ten years before Oliver Cromwell restored English rule in the name of the new republican government. Approximately one-third of Ireland's population had died during the rebellion, most from disease and starvation rather than the massacres which both sides committed with equal conviction in the justness of their actions. The lands of what was left of the native and Old English aristocracy were confiscated and all Catholics were ordered to resettle in Connacht to make way for veterans of the Parliamentary army. But England's prosperous New World colonies were a more attractive prospect for would-be settlers, so Catholics continued to occupy, if no longer own, the land.

For all that the plantations of the 17th century did not achieve what English governments hoped for, they did complete the destruction of the traditional order of Gaelic Ireland begun by the Tudors. For over 200 years a minority Protestant land-owning and ruling class lorded it over the majority Catholic population which was politically, economically and culturally marginalized. United by their Catholicism, the Old English and the Irish closed ranks and the old division between Gael and English-speaker was replaced by one based on religion.

Monea Castle, Co. Fermanagh, a Scottish-style plantation castle. Founded by the Scot Malcolm Hamilton in 1616, the castle held out throughout the Catholic Rising of 1641.

MAP NOTES

❶ *The Ulster plantation was decided upon after Derry was burned by Sir Cahir O'Doherty, a minor chieftain from Donegal, in 1608.*

❷ *The plantation of Antrim and Down was a private venture carried out by local Catholic aristocrat Sir Randal McDonnell.*

❸ *Destroyed in the Nine Years War, the Munster plantations were revived and prospered in the early 1600s.*

❹ *The Catholic Confederation of Kilkenny controlled most of Ireland from 1642 until Cromwell's invasion 1649–50.*

❺ *A 1-mile wide coastal strip of Connacht was assigned to army veterans by Cromwell, to isolate the Irish from the sea.*

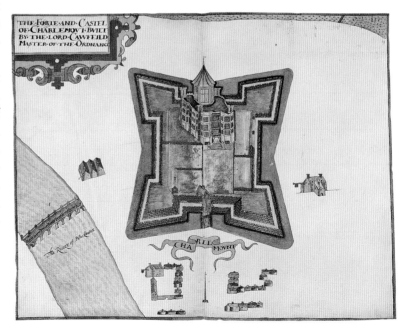

Charlemont Castle, a Tudor artillery fort which played an important role in the Nine Years War and the Catholic Rising of 1641, became the site of a country house in more peaceful times.

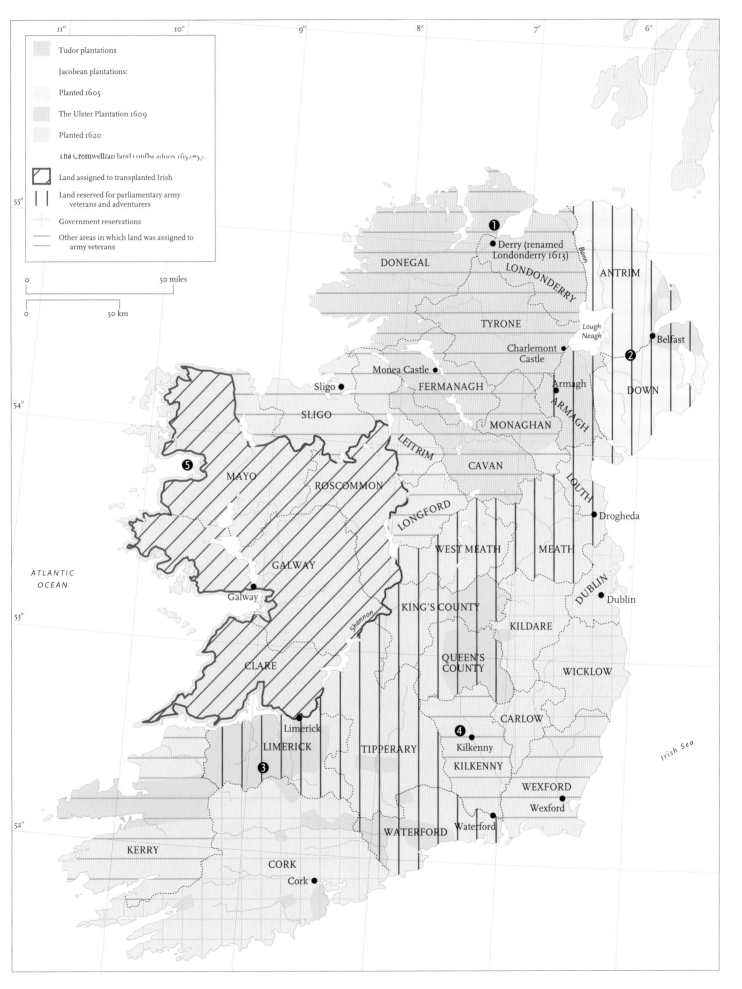

Legend

Tudor plantations

Jacobean plantations:

Planted 1605

The Ulster Plantation 1609

Planted 1620

The Cromwellian land confiscations 1652–57.

Land assigned to transplanted Irish

Land reserved for parliamentary army veterans and adventurers

Government reservations

Other areas in which land was assigned to army veterans

0   50 miles

0   50 km

DONEGAL

❶

Derry (renamed Londonderry 1613)

Bann

LONDONDERRY

ANTRIM

TYRONE

Lough Neagh

Charlemont Castle

Belfast

❷

DOWN

Monea Castle

FERMANAGH

Armagh

ARMAGH

Sligo

SLIGO

MONAGHAN

LEITRIM

CAVAN

LOUTH

MAYO

❺

ROSCOMMON

LONGFORD

Drogheda

WEST MEATH

MEATH

ATLANTIC OCEAN

GALWAY

Galway

Shannon

KING'S COUNTY

DUBLIN

Dublin

KILDARE

QUEEN'S COUNTY

WICKLOW

CLARE

Limerick

LIMERICK

❸

TIPPERARY

CARLOW

❹

Kilkenny

KILKENNY

WEXFORD

Wexford

WATERFORD

Waterford

KERRY

CORK

Cork

Irish Sea

The Highlands and the Jacobite Rebellions

AD 1688 –1746

Highland clans – Gaelic societies based on real or imaginary kinship – are known from the early 12th century onwards, but it was only after the suppression of the Lordship of the Isles in 1493 that they came to the fore. The writ of the Edinburgh government scarcely ran in the Highlands and clan chiefs preserved an essentially medieval social order into the 18th century. The chiefs exercised hereditary rights of private jurisdiction over their tenants, who owed them military service. Thus equipped with private armies, clan chiefs feuded constantly with their neighbours: inter-clan warfare and cattle raiding were endemic.

THE DESTRUCTION of this social order was indirectly brought about by the overthrow of the Catholic Stuart king James II/VII in 1688 in favour of the Protestant William of Orange. James' supporters, known as Jacobites, actively sought his restoration and, after his death in 1701, that of his son James and grandson Charles Edward ('Bonnie Prince Charlie'). Of the three Jacobite rebellions, 1689–90, 1715 and 1745–46, the last was the most serious and most nearly successful, but the overwhelming victory of government forces at Culloden in 1746 ended Jacobitism as a military force.

The Jacobite cause had supporters in all parts of the British Isles but, because of the leading role they played in the rebellions, it has become particularly closely associated with the Highland clans. Because the Stuarts were a Scottish dynasty, support for Jacobitism was stronger in Scotland than England and, especially after the Act of Union in 1707, it was a convenient focus for anti-English sentiment. But Jacobitism was indelibly tainted by Catholicism and this ensured that it had little appeal for most Scots. Support

Charles Edward Stuart, 'the Young Pretender'. Charles' self-confidence was not matched by ability, and his muddled leadership of the '45 was a disaster both for the Jacobite cause and the Highlands in general. Despite this, his wanderings after Culloden made 'Bonnie Prince Charlie', quite undeservedly, into a romantic figure.

Corgarff Castle, Grampian: a 16th-century tower house converted into a barracks for Hanoverian troops in 1748. The garrison was finally withdrawn in 1831 after it had spent several years trying, unsuccessfully, to suppress the smuggling of illegal whisky.

Tower at Glenfinnan marking the spot where Charles Edward Stuart raised his father's standard in August 1745, beginning the '45 Jacobite Rising.

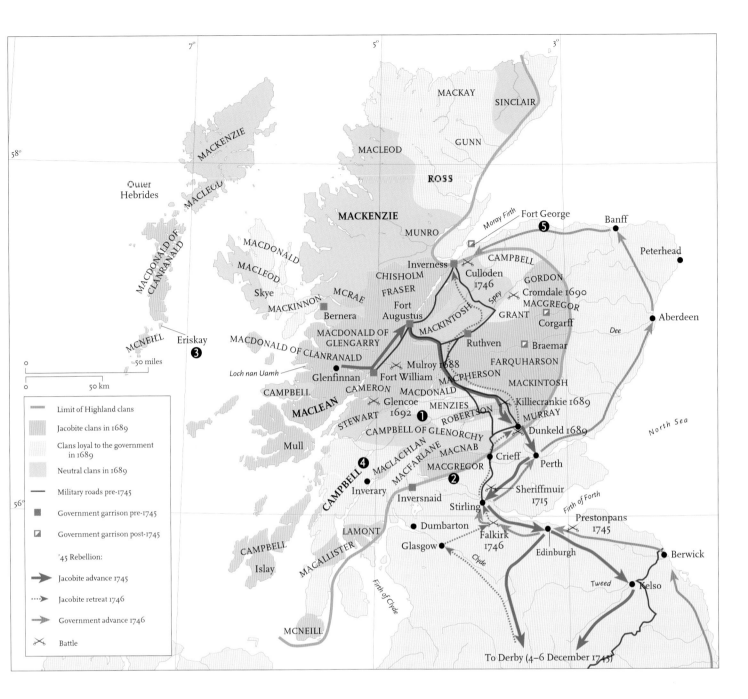

for the Jacobites was not even universal in the Highlands: some clans tried to remain neutral in the rebellions, others, such as the Campbells, supported the government. What made the Highlands so important to the Jacobites was not so much the strength of support there but that, thanks to the clan system, it was the only place in Britain where their supporters could raise large bodies of fighting men easily.

The aftermath of Culloden saw an all out assault on the clan system to ensure that the Highlands would never again be a centre of rebellion. No distinction was made between Jacobite clans and those which had remained loyal. The lands of Jacobite chiefs were confiscated and the powers of other clan chiefs curtailed by the abolition of hereditary jurisdictions. Bearing arms, playing bagpipes, wearing highland dress and speaking Gaelic were banned, though all but the first proved unenforceable. The system of military roads, begun by General Wade in the 1720s, was extended and the Highlands remained garrisoned into the 19th century, long after any real Jacobite threat had ended.

MAP NOTES

❶ *Mulroy: the last clan battle, fought between the Mackintoshes and the MacDonalds of Keppoch.*

❷ *The clan of Rob Roy MacGregor (d. 1734), posthumously romanticized as a Scottish Robin Hood, in reality a notorious cattle rustler and protection racketeer.*

❸ *Charles Edward Stuart first set foot in Scotland on Eriskay in July 1745 in a French ship.*

❹ *The most important of the anti-Jacobite clans, the Campbells fought with the government army at Culloden.*

❺ *Massive artillery fort built after the '45 to secure the Highlands, now the best preserved 18th-century fortress in Britain.*

The Highland Clearances AD 1763 – 1886

After the '45 Rebellion the Highland clan chiefs rejected their traditional responsibilities to subordinate clan members and became, in effect, ordinary landowners. Tenants who had been an asset when the chiefs needed as many men as they could raise for their private armies, now became an economic burden. As estates were reorganized with profit rather than manpower the first priority, tens of thousands of Highlanders were cleared from the land. The resulting dislocation completed the destruction of the clan system and created the 'natural' wilderness of the modern Highland landscape.

THE CLEARANCES fell into three phases. In the first phase it was former tacksmen (clan gentry who had acted as the chiefs' military lieutenants) who were the main sufferers. Tacksmen had leased land from the clan chiefs and sublet it to peasant farmers, but even before the '45 they were becoming seen as unnecessary middlemen: faced with massive rent increases many now emigrated to North America. The second phase began in the last decades of the 18th century as landowners started to evict farming tenants to create large, single-tenant sheep farms. There was considerable popular resistance to clearance and landowners sometimes resorted to force to evict their tenants. Evicted tenants were helped to emigrate or resettled in planned villages, most

of which were on the coast, where they were expected to make a living from crofting, fishing and kelping (making fertilizer from seaweed). Despite emigration, the overall Highland population actually increased steadily during this phase of the Clearances as a result of health-care improvements such as inoculation and the introduction of new crops such as the potato.

Crofters evicted from Glencalvie (Easter Ross) in 1845 sought temporary shelter in the churchyard at Croick. Many scratched farewell messages on the church's windows before leaving the glen.

MAP NOTES

❶ *The earliest sheep farms in the Highlands were created around Arrochar and Lochgoilhead in 1752.*
❷ *Cheviot sheep from the Borders were introduced to Perthshire in 1765: they become the dominant breed in the Highlands*
❸ *Troops were called to Kildermorie in 1792 – the 'Year of the Sheep' – after locals drove sheep off the hills.*
❹ *Resistance to clearance on the Countess of Sutherland's estates at Kildonan continued for 6 months.*
❺ *In the first major incident of the land war, crofters fought police sent to evict rent strikers.*

Restored blackhouse (above and below) at Arnol, Isle of Lewis, the typical Highland dwelling before the late 19th century. Windowless and lacking chimneys, blackhouses were dark (hence the name) and smoky, but also warm and easy to maintain.

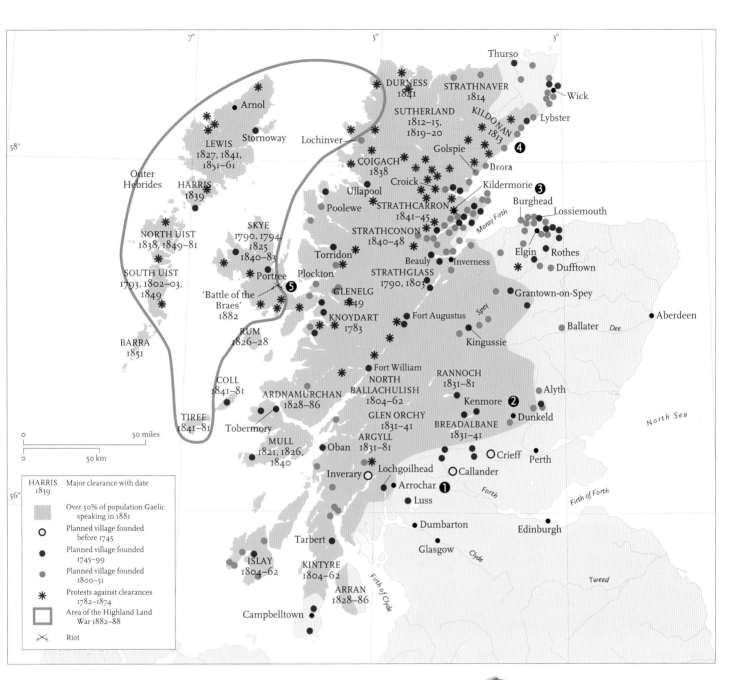

Thurso
DURNESS 1841
STRATHNAVER 1814
Wick
SUTHERLAND 1812–15, 1819–20
KILDONAN 1813
Lybster
Arnol
LEWIS 1827, 1841, 1851–61
Stornoway
Lochinver
Golspie
Brora
❹
COIGACH 1838
Croick
Kildermorie
❸
Outer Hebrides
HARRIS 1839
Ullapool
Poolewe
STRATHCARRON 1841–45
Burghead
Lossiemouth
NORTH UIST 1838, 1849–81
SKYE 1790, 1794, 1825 1840–83
STRATHCONON 1840–48
Elgin
Rothes
Torridon
Beauly
Inverness
Dufftown
SOUTH UIST 1793, 1802–03, 1849
Portree
Plockton
STRATHGLASS 1790, 1803
'Battle of the Braes' 1882
❺
GLENELG 1849
Grantown-on-Spey
Spey
KNOYDART 1783
Fort Augustus
Aberdeen
Ballater
Dee
BARRA 1851
RUM 1826–28
Kingussie
COLL 1841–81
Fort William
NORTH BALLACHULISH 1804–62
RANNOCH 1831–81
Alyth
ARDNAMURCHAN 1828–86
GLEN ORCHY 1831–41
Kenmore
❷
Dunkeld
North Sea
TIREE 1841–81
Tobermory
BREADALBANE 1831–41
MULL 1821, 1826, 1840
ARGYLL 1831–81
Oban
Crieff
Perth
Inverary
Lochgoilhead
Callander
Arrochar
❶
Forth
Firth of Forth
Luss
Dumbarton
Edinburgh
Tarbert
Glasgow
Clyde
ISLAY 1804–62
KINTYRE 1804–62
Tweed
ARRAN 1828–86
Campbelltown

50 miles
50 km

HARRIS 1839   Major clearance with date

Over 50% of population Gaelic speaking in 1881

○   Planned village founded before 1745

●   Planned village founded 1745–99

●   Planned village founded 1800–51

✳   Protests against clearances 1782–1874

▢   Area of the Highland Land War 1882–88

⚔   Riot

Cheaper foreign imports made kelping unprofitable after 1815 and shortly after wool prices began to decline too because of competition from Australia and New Zealand. A further blow came in the 1840s, when potato blight brought famine to the Highlands (potato blight affected all of Europe, not just Ireland). Voluntary mass emigration and migration to the industrial towns of Lowland Scotland began to reverse the population growth of the previous 60 years. This influx of Highlanders was a major factor in the 'celticizing' of the Lowland Scottish identity in modern times. In the 1860s a third wave of Clearances began as landowners cashed in on the fashion for deer-stalking and the remainder of the 19th century was a time of dramatic population decline across the Highlands. Inspired by the success of the Irish Land League, the residual crofting population founded the Highland Land League (the forerunner of the Scottish National Party) in 1882 to campaign for greater security of tenure. Popular protests, known as the Highland Land War, spread, bringing major reforms in 1886, but population decline continued well into the 20th century.

Statue of George Granville Leveson-Gower, First Duke of Sutherland, at Golspie, Sutherland. Leveson-Gower acquired the Sutherland estates through his wife Elizabeth, Countess of Sutherland. The scale of his evictions in 1812–20 made him notorious, but he preserved the Sutherland estates intact at a time when declining rents forced more humane landowners to sell up.

By the 18th century the days of Celtic independence were all but over, and any concept of a Celtic identity had long since ceased to exist. Today, millions of people all over the world consider themselves to be Celtic and millions of others are rediscovering Celtic roots. This remarkable revival of the Celtic identity is one of the most fascinating developments of modern times: its causes are intimately linked to major developments in European cultural and political life, such as Romanticism and nationalism.

PART 3

(Above) A modern brooch inspired by the Celtic art styles of the early Middle Ages, by a contemporary jeweller on North Uist, Scotland.

(Left) The modern-day Druids celebrating the summer solstice at Stonehenge, a Neolithic monument with no historical connections to ancient Druidism. Though modern Druidism is a synthetic religion, it has become an emblem of the revival of Celtic identity.

THE MODERN CELTS

THE CELTIC REVIVAL did not originate as a popular movement: indeed it could not have not have done so, as there was no continuous tradition of self-conscious Celticness on which to draw. Though some at least of the ancient Celtic-speaking peoples – all of them on the continent – called themselves Celts and recognized a degree of wider Celtic or Gallic identity, this consciousness did not survive into the Middle Ages. Despite the survival of Celtic-speaking communities in Britain, Ireland and Brittany, for more than a thousand years there had been no one in Europe who regarded him- or herself as being a Celt. It was only the rediscovery of the ancient Celts by late 17th- and early 18th-century antiquarians that made the rebirth of a self-conscious Celtic identity possible. Ironically, most of this work took place far from Celtic-speaking areas, though many of the leading figures were expatriate native Celtic-speakers.

The rediscovery of the ancient Celts began at a time that was witnessing the development of a recognizably modern, rationalistic approach to history. Antiquarians began to look beyond a view of the past which for centuries had been dominated by the Bible and ancient Greece and Rome and construct a prehistory of Europe. Pioneer antiquarians, such as John Aubrey in the 17th century, began to study the ancient monuments that littered the European countryside and artifacts dug out of barrows and bogs, and to take a more critical attitude to legendary traditions such as the tales of King Arthur. In this age before scientific archaeological excavation and dating techniques were developed, the true antiquity of humankind was still not conceived of and historians had to work within the established Classical and biblical chronologies in which the creation in 4004 BC and the Deluge in 2348 BC were fixed points. Antiquarians attempted to relate prehistoric monuments and artifacts to the little that was known about pre-Roman Europe from Classical texts; not surprisingly, most of their conclusions have not stood the test of time. Megalithic monuments are not now regarded as Druidic temples, as William Stukeley and Jacques Cambry supposed, but the works of these two pioneers were both popular and influential and led to a growing awareness that Europe had a Celtic as well as a Classical past.

Although the 16th-century Scot George Buchanan and the 18th-century Breton Paul-Yves Pezron had approached the subject, the scholar who first defined the Celtic language family, and so who made the greatest contribution to modern ideas about who the Celts were and are, was Edward Lhuyd. In his *Archaeologia Britannica* (published 1707) Lhuyd, a native Welsh-speaker, recognized the similarities between the language of ancient Gaul and the Welsh, Cornish, Breton and Gaelic languages of his own day, and described them all as the 'Celtic' languages. Up to that time, following the usage of the Classical authors, the Celts had

been thought of only as a continental people. Lhuyd never used the term Celt to describe any of the modern Celtic-speaking peoples themselves, but the connection between language and identity is a close one and within a few years educated Welsh people had begun to describe themselves as Celts. This is not surprising. One of Lhuyd's purposes in writing had been to demonstrate that the Welsh had a historical identity that was distinct from the English. The Welsh had always regarded themselves as the Britons – after all they were their direct descendants – but after the Act of Union between England and Scotland in 1707 that identity was appropriated for the new kingdom of Great Britain. The Welsh therefore had need of a new means of asserting their difference from the English.

Romanticism and Celtomania

Humankind's growing mastery over the natural environment led in the late 18th century to the growth of the Romantic movement, a cultural rebellion against materialism and rationalism. The movement led to major aesthetic shifts, in particular a new appreciation of wild nature, previously seen as threatening. The same aesthetic changes also influenced attitudes to the Celts. In the Classical world, the word 'Celt' had been synonymous with 'barbarian'. Wishing to present them in an unfavourable light, Classical writers had constructed a stereotype of the Celt as violent, proud, undisciplined and superstitious. In the Middle Ages, Celts had also been described in similarly unflattering terms by their French or English neighbours. Now that they had been conquered and pacified, the Celts' archaic codes of honour,

A Celtic warfare re-enactment society prepares for a mock battle.

valour and hospitality actually began to seem rather attractive to comfortable, secure European intellectuals.

The result of the Celt's transformation from dangerous savage into noble savage was Celtomania, a literary and artistic craze for all things Celtic. Celtomania can be said to have begun with the publication of the Ossianic poems by the Scot James Macpherson in the 1760s. Macpherson claimed that the poems were translations of the works of Ossian, a semi-legendary Gaelic bard of the early Middle Ages. Even though they were soon exposed as forgeries, the poems were hugely influential best-sellers, not just in Britain but throughout Europe. Despite their dubious origin, the Ossianic poems at least helped to stimulate interest in genuine Celtic literature. Intellectuals who were disillusioned with organized religion and dismayed by the ugliness of industrialization were drawn to the nature worship of the Druids. Druids loomed large in the poems of William Blake and William Wordsworth, and several societies were founded to 'revive' the Druidic religion. Most of the revived Druidic ceremonies, such as Edward Williams' Maen Gorsedd bardic ceremony, first celebrated in London in 1792, were – could only have been – pure invention: virtually nothing was known about real Druidic ceremonies.

Inevitably, the romanticization of the ancient Celts rubbed off on the modern Celtic-speaking peoples. This can be seen most clearly in Scotland. Prior to the suppression of the '45 Rebellion, Gaelic-speaking Highlanders had usually been portrayed as savages. The pacification of the Highlands which followed allowed Lowlanders the luxury of romanticizing the Gael, a process triumphantly completed by Walter Scott's novel *Rob Roy* (1818), which turned a real-life 18th-century cattle-thief and protection-racketeer into a Celtic Robin Hood. The rehabilitation of the Highlander was also greatly aided by the magnificent fighting record of Highland regiments in the British army during the Napoleonic wars. The spectacular scenery of the Highlands attracted increasing numbers of tourists, whose experiences helped cast a romantic aura over the whole region.

Lowland Scots found the Highlanders' Celtic identity increasingly attractive, not only because it was romantic but also because it helped to accentuate the differences between the Scots and the English. This did not reflect a desire for independence – 19th-century Scots saw partnership in the British empire as very much in their interests – so much as a fear of cultural assimilation by the English. As the English language spread into the Highlands and Highlanders migrated to the Lowlands, the old division between the two regions began to blur and a more homogeneous Scottish identity began to emerge.

Celtic Identity and Irish Nationalism

In Ireland the Celtic revival made a defining contribution to the development of Irish nationalism but, in contrast to the Scottish experience, it had the effect of sharpening rather than blurring the country's already deep divisions. Modern Irish nationalism and republicanism began to develop at the end of the 18th century, with support from both Catholics and Protestants. The first society for the preservation of the Gaelic language was even founded by Ulster Protestants in 1795. A century later, however, Protestants had come to see Gaelic as a threat. In the course of the 19th century, nationalism came increasingly to be defined by the majority Catholic population. Centuries of English influence on Ireland and the Irish were rejected as nationalists sought the roots of Irishness in an idealized Celtic past. The growing sense of nationality manifested itself not only in political action but in popular recreational and cultural organizations such as the Gaelic Athletic Association and the Gaelic League, and in an influential literary and artistic 'renaissance'. This dominant Catholic-Celtic Irish national identity quite literally alienated the Irish Protestant minority, most of whom were the descendants of Lowland Scots and English settlers. Protestant support for Unionism steadily increased, so that by 1900 most Irish Protestants identified themselves as British and were prepared to oppose home rule by any means, including rebellion against the state to which they professed allegiance. Faced with a rising tide of violence, the British government's response was the partitioning of Ireland in 1922 – the greater part of Ireland achieving independence as the Irish Free State (now the Republic of Ireland), while six counties of Ulster which had a Protestant majority became the province of Northern Ireland. Today, after 30 years of bombings and murders, it is manifestly clear that Northern Ireland is a failed state. The 1998 Good Friday Agreement began a peace process, but at the time of writing it is still too soon to guess where that will ultimately take Northern Ireland. Nationalists have always placed the blame for Northern Ireland's 'Troubles' squarely at the feet of the British government. Few enough, perhaps, would argue with this, but the failure of nationalism to create an inclusive Irish identity has both contributed to the circumstances which led to partition and stood in the way of rapprochement between Ireland's two traditions ever since.

By the 1970s a second period of Celtomania was underway and is still continuing. The causes are similar to those of the first period of Celtomania – the appeal of the noble savage to an increasingly materialistic world. Environmental concerns, post-imperial guilt and the rapid decline of organized religion have all contributed to this renewed fascination, not so much with the real Celts of history but with the idealized Celts created in the Romantic era. This new Celtomania has seen a surge of interest in their Celtic heritage among both modern Celtic-speakers and by people all over the world who trace their descent back to the Celtic peoples. While the innate attractiveness of the idealized Celt and the increasing importance of identity in today's 'global village' have played their part in this, it is also closely linked to wider political developments in Europe. In Scotland and Wales the growth of Celtic consciousness is associated with the growth of political nationalism (though the main nationalist parties in both countries officially reject ethnic nationalism in favour of an inclusive civic nationalism). In Cornwall it is a sense of neglect by central government that has led to a growth of Celtic identity; in Brittany it has been the struggle to maintain a non-French identity. Political nationalism remains weak in both Cornwall and Brittany, however. Thanks to the European Union, minorities in member states have gained confidence by being able to appeal over the heads of central government for recognition, cultural funding and economic aid, resulting in a resur-

gence of regional identities. This has been very striking in Galicia, where a new awareness of the Celtiberian past has contributed to a growing sense of nationality.

The Decline of the Celtic Languages

Language preservation or revival movements have been central to the resurgence of the Celtic identity over the last two centuries, yet there has been an inexorable decline in the numbers of people speaking Celtic languages on an everyday basis. In Ireland and the Scottish Highlands, Gaelic-speaking communities have been diminished by the mass emigration which followed the Potato Famine (1845–49) and the Clearances (1763–1886). In the South Wales industrial area, Welsh-speaking communities have been diluted by immigration of English-speakers. Immigration of French-speakers has had the same effect in Brittany. Exclusion of Celtic languages from administration and education has been a major factor: in the case of the latter this has often had the support of Celtic-speaking parents, who believed that an English- or French-language education would serve their children's interests best. Though active government hostility has played a part, chiefly in Brittany, simple indifference to the fate of the languages has been much more usual. But these factors alone cannot be the complete explanation for the decline of the Celtic languages.

Since independence in 1922, the Irish government has pursued policies which have been highly supportive of Gaelic. Teaching of Gaelic in schools has been compulsory and the Gaeltachts have had considerable financial support to try to stem the tide of emigration of Gaelic-speakers into

English-speaking areas. These policies have produced an apparent increase in the numbers of people able to speak some Gaelic, from around 550,000, mostly first-language speakers, around the time of independence to more than a million in 1991. But this figure includes only around 20,000 people who speak Gaelic as a first language. Even in some Gaeltachts, habitual Gaelic-speakers now constitute little more than half the population. Irish people consistently voice high levels of support for Gaelic, but this does not translate into a willingness to speak it. In recent years Welsh, Scottish Gaelic and Breton have all achieved higher levels of recognition in education, local government and broadcasting, but, with the possible exception of Welsh, these languages continue to decline in everyday use.

Campaigners for the Celtic languages believe that it is still possible to reverse the decline and re-establish them as truly national languages. The successful revival of Hebrew in modern Israel is claimed as support for this belief, but the circumstances are not comparable. After independence, Israel was a nation of immigrants who lacked a common language. All modern Celts already share a common language – English or French. Though many will continue to learn Celtic languages as a means of understanding and expressing commitment to their cultural identity, in reality few will invest the considerable amount of time and effort necessary to attain fluency in a language for which they will have little practical everyday use. The future for the Celtic languages must, therefore, be a bleak one.

The Future of the Celts

For some, the very survival of the Celtic identity depends upon the continued survival of the Celtic languages. This may be an overly pessimistic view. Language is obviously not the central issue for most modern Celts – there are other cultural, historical and political aspects of identity which are far more important. This is readily apparent in the remarkable revival of Celtic identity in Galicia, which owes nothing to the Celtic languages. For today's Galician Celts, folklore, building traditions, music, costume and social values form just as valid a basis for Celtic identity as language. However, it is worth remembering that the Celtic identity has been quite self-consciously revived by communities as a response to long-standing social, economic and political marginalization and could, therefore, be just as self-consciously abandoned. It is not impossible to imagine a time when, perhaps as a result of increased political empowerment or prosperity, an identity rooted in the distant past may seem less appropriate to those communities, and the Celts may be relegated, as in France, to the role of honoured ancestors.

High-school Welsh language lesson at Ystrad Mynach, Glamorgan, South Wales. Though it does not enjoy universal support, compulsory teaching of Welsh has led to an increase in the numbers of people able to speak the language in recent years.

Celtomania and European Nationalism

By 1700 Celtic-speakers were confined to Europe's Atlantic fringe. Only in the Highlands of Scotland did a semi-independent Celtic-speaking society survive and this would soon be destroyed in the repression which followed the Jacobite Rebellions. But, as the last vestiges of independent Celtdom were being extinguished, European scholars were for the first time beginning to show a serious and methodical interest in the Celtic peoples and their history, language and literature.

AT FIRST THIS ACTIVITY took place in centres which were mostly remote from Celtic-speaking areas, notably in London, Paris and Edinburgh, and was conducted largely by English, French and Lowland Scots academics, though one of the most notable figures, Edward Lhuyd, was a native Welsh-speaker. Much early research was misguided. The antiquarian William Stukeley, for example, popularized the idea that Stonehenge was a Druidic temple: it is now known to pre-date the Druids by thousands of years.

The mysterious Celtic past evoked by antiquarians captured the public imagination across Europe, causing a craze for all things Celtic which has been called the Celtomania. Celtomania was just one manifestation of the Romantic movement of the later 18th–early 19th centuries, a cultural rebellion against materialism and rationalism. The wild Celt was the ideal noble savage, while the nature worship of the Druids had an irresistible appeal to intellectuals disillusioned with organized religion and industrialization. Druids appeared in English poetry and Italian operas. Societies were even founded to 'revive' the religion of the Druids. The most influential works of the Celtomania were the 'translations' of the poems of the ancient bard Ossian published by James Macpherson in 1760–63. Though quickly denounced as forgeries, they were wildly popular – admirers included Goethe and Napoleon. The novelist Walter Scott completed the romanticization of the Celt with his novel *Rob Roy* (1818), which turned a real-life Highland cattle-thief into a noble hero. Societies sprang up in Britain and Ireland to promote the use of Celtic languages and in Wales the Eisteddfod was revived to promote Welsh language and culture.

By the mid-19th century, the Celtic past had been pressed into the service of nationalism. The Celtic leaders of resistance to Roman domination were presented as national heroes in art and sculpture, for example, Vercingetorix in France, Ambiorix in Belgium and Viriathus in Spain and Portugal. In Ireland the nationalist Fenian Society drew its inspiration from Irish myths. At the same time a more scientific understanding of the ancient Celts was emerging thanks to the development of methodical archaeological excavation and recording techniques, with archaeologists in France taking the lead. Nationalism had a role to play here too. Napoleon III sponsored excavations of the *oppida* at Alesia and Bibracte, scenes of heroic Gallic resistance to Caesar, as part of a campaign to foster national spirit at a time when France was threatened by the rise of Prussian power.

A romantic statue of Vercingetorix, the Gaulish chief who led resistance to Caesar, erected at Alesia by Napoleon III: concerned by the growth of Prussian power, the emperor hoped this heroic Celt would inspire national resistance.

Ossian receiving the Warriors of the Revolution into Paradise (1803), by A.-L. Girodet, blends nationalism with Celtomania.

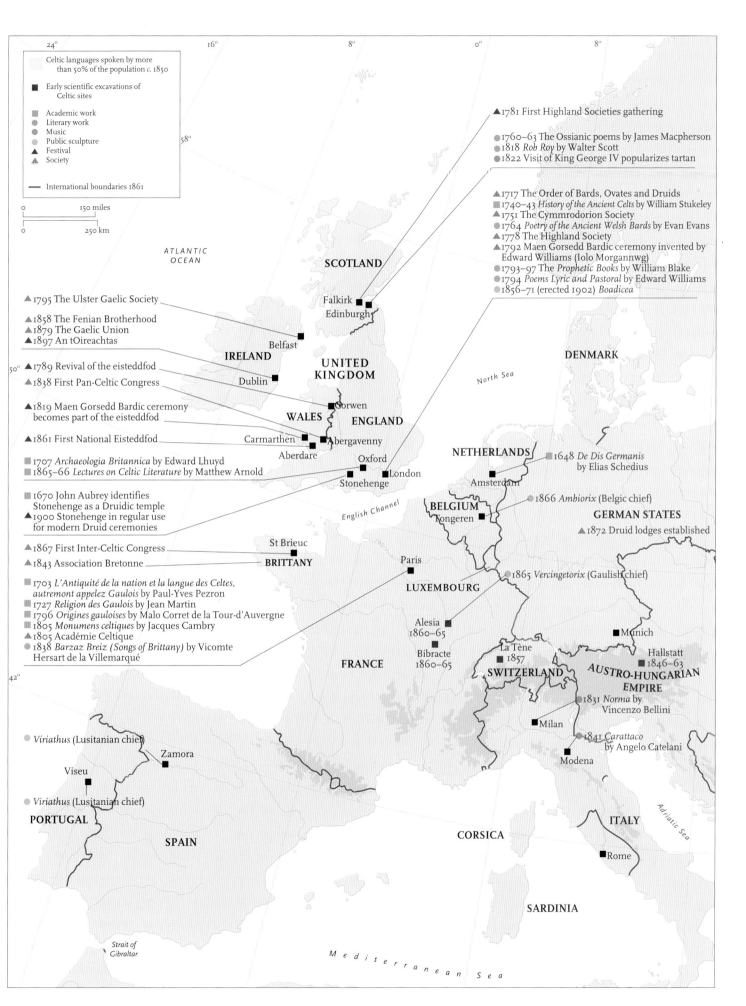

Celtic languages spoken by more than 50% of the population *c.* 1850

■ Early scientific excavations of Celtic sites

▪ Academic work
● Literary work
● Music
● Public sculpture
▲ Festival
▲ Society

— International boundaries 1861

0   150 miles
0   250 km

ATLANTIC OCEAN

▲1781 First Highland Societies gathering

●1760–63 The Ossianic poems by James Macpherson
●1818 *Rob Roy* by Walter Scott
●1822 Visit of King George IV popularizes tartan

▲1717 The Order of Bards, Ovates and Druids
▪1740–43 *History of the Ancient Celts* by William Stukeley
▲1751 The Cymmrodorion Society
●1764 *Poetry of the Ancient Welsh Bards* by Evan Evans
▲1778 The Highland Society
▲1792 Maen Gorsedd Bardic ceremony invented by Edward Williams (Iolo Morgannwg)
●1793–97 The *Prophetic Books* by William Blake
●1794 *Poems Lyric and Pastoral* by Edward Williams
●1856–71 (erected 1902) *Boadicea*

SCOTLAND

Falkirk
Edinburgh

DENMARK

North Sea

▲1795 The Ulster Gaelic Society

▲1858 The Fenian Brotherhood
▲1879 The Gaelic Union
▲1897 An tOireachtas

Belfast

IRELAND

UNITED KINGDOM

Dublin

▲1789 Revival of the eisteddfod

▲1838 First Pan-Celtic Congress

Gorwen

WALES   ENGLAND

▲1819 Maen Gorsedd Bardic ceremony becomes part of the eisteddfod

▲1861 First National Eisteddfod

Carmarthen   Abergavenny
Aberdare

Oxford

NETHERLANDS   ▪1648 *De Dis Germanis* by Elias Schedius

Amsterdam

▪1707 *Archaeologia Britannica* by Edward Lhuyd
▪1865–66 *Lectures on Celtic Literature* by Matthew Arnold

Stonehenge   London

BELGIUM   ●1866 *Ambiorix* (Belgic chief)

Tongeren   GERMAN STATES

▪1670 John Aubrey identifies Stonehenge as a Druidic temple
▲1900 Stonehenge in regular use for modern Druid ceremonies

English Channel

▲1872 Druid lodges established

▲1867 First Inter-Celtic Congress

▲1843 Association Bretonne

St Brieuc

BRITTANY

Paris

●1865 *Vercingetorix* (Gaulish chief)

▪1703 *L'Antiquité de la nation et la langue des Celtes, autremont appelez Gaulois* by Paul-Yves Pezron
▪1727 *Religion des Gaulois* by Jean Martin
▪1796 *Origines gauloises* by Malo Corret de la Tour-d'Auvergne
▪1805 *Monumens celtiques* by Jacques Cambry
▲1805 Académie Celtique
●1838 *Barzaz Breiz (Songs of Brittany)* by Vicomte Hersart de la Villemarqué

LUXEMBOURG

Alesia
1860–65

Bibracte
1860–65

FRANCE

La Tène
1857

SWITZERLAND

Munich

Hallstatt
1846–63

AUSTRO-HUNGARIAN EMPIRE

●1831 *Norma* by Vincenzo Bellini

Milan

●1841 *Carattaco* by Angelo Catelani

Modena

●*Viriathus* (Lusitanian chief)

Zamora

Viseu

●*Viriathus* (Lusitanian chief)

PORTUGAL

SPAIN

CORSICA

ITALY

Adriatic Sea

Rome

Strait of Gibraltar

Mediterranean Sea

SARDINIA

The Celtic Diaspora

The Celtic Diaspora is a term which has been used to describe the global migrations of millions of people from the 'Celtic' countries between the late 18th and early 20th centuries. Although only two long-lived Celtic-speaking communities resulted from these migrations, because emigrants preserved a strong awareness of their origins they did create the conditions in which the modern Celtic identity could develop an intercontinental dimension.

THE EXACT NUMBERS of emigrants cannot be known with certainty, as accurate records were not always kept either at ports of departure or arrival. The United States was far the most popular destination, but large numbers also went to England, Canada, Australia and New Zealand and smaller numbers to southern Africa and South America. The common view of Celtic emigration is that of a desperate flight from destitution, but the dreadful famine ships of the 1840s were not typical: for most emigration was a positive choice which brought increased opportunities and improved living standards.

The Irish were the most numerous emigrants from the Celtic countries: about 8 million people left Ireland between 1801 and 1921. From the 17th century a steady stream of exiles had left Ireland for the continent, many to serve in the armies of England's enemies. Large-scale emigration began in the mid-18th century with an exodus of 'Ulster Scots' (northern Irish Protestants) for North America. Catholic emigration began in the early 19th century and became a flood after the Potato Famine of the 1840s. The Catholic Irish faced the same discrimination in Protestant America as they had at home, contributing greatly to the emergence of the assertive, anglophobic, overwhelmingly Catholic, Irish-American identity.

Canada became an important area of settlement for Gaelic-speaking Scottish Highlanders in the Clearance period. It is claimed that more Gaelic is spoken in Canada than in Scotland, but the number of habitual speakers is now probably fewer than 2000, most of them in Cape Breton. Bretons were among the earliest European settlers in Canada and Breton immigration

MAP NOTES

❶ Catholic Irish settlement in the USA was urban – concentrated in the industrial cities of Pennsylvania, New Jersey, New York and New England.

❷ The most important settlements of Scottish Gaelic-speakers were on Prince Edward Island, Cape Breton Island and around Pictou and Antigonish.

❸ Nearly a quarter of immigrants to Australia in the 19th century were Irish, among them transported nationalist rebels.

❹ Cornish tin and copper miners emigrated to mining areas on every continent.

❺ The main destination of Manx emigrants was the northeast USA.

❻ In 1851, 22% of Liverpool's population was born in Ireland, 6% in Wales and 4% in Scotland.

(Below left) A positive view of emigration: Irish emigrants react to their first sighting of America. Illustrated London News, 1871. Shipboard conditions for emigrants improved considerably during the 19th century.

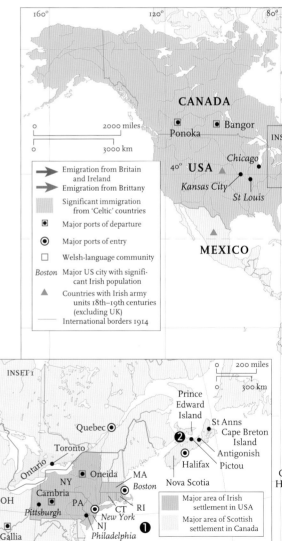

continued after French Canada came under British rule in 1763.

Welsh emigration did not involve the sheer numbers of that from the Scottish Highlands and Ireland but, uniquely, much of it was specifically motivated by the desire to preserve the Welsh language. Several Welsh-speaking communities were founded in North America but they were soon swamped by English-speaking settlers. This led to attempts to found settlements outside the English-speaking world, in Brazil and Russia, and most successfully in 1865 in the Chubut Valley in Argentinean Patagonia. The founders hoped Y Wladfa ('The Colony') could remain independent, but the Argentine government insisted its authority was recognized (though otherwise was supportive of the settlers). After years of decline, Welsh has staged a modest recovery in recent years and the old colony has become a tourist attraction.

A Welsh teahouse at Trelew, Patagonia. Long outnumbered by Spanish-speakers, the Patagonian Welsh still celebrate their culture with eisteddfods.

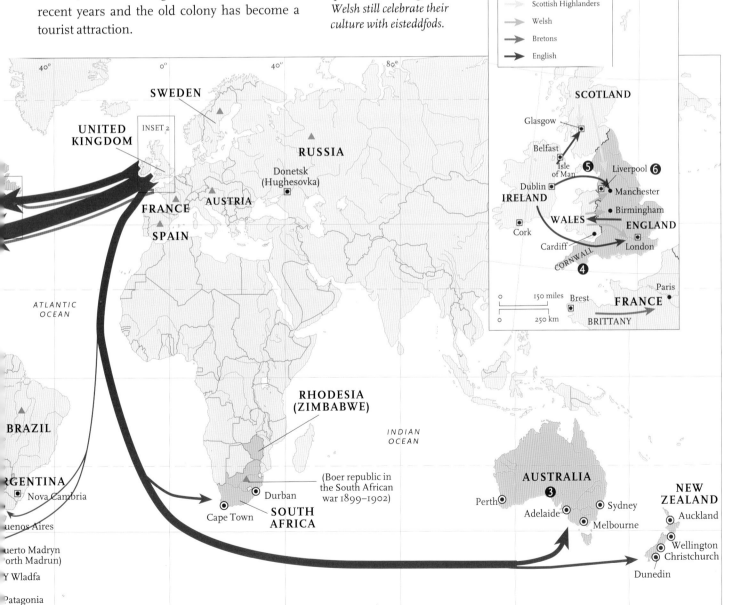

The Celtic Languages Today

Four Celtic languages – Welsh, Breton, Irish Gaelic and Scottish Gaelic – are still spoken on an everyday basis today. Over two million people claim to be able to speak Celtic languages but the number of habitual speakers is much lower, possibly fewer than 500,000. Despite efforts to support and promote the Celtic languages, their long-term survival as spoken languages in an age of globalized business and culture must be in doubt.

Newspapers on sale at a Welsh newsagents: a healthy publishing industry is essential for the long-term survival of the Celtic languages. However, because of its small readership, much Celtic-language publishing is viable only with state subsidies.

SUPERFICIALLY, IRISH GAELIC is the most flourishing of the Celtic languages – over a million people claim to able to speak it. Gaelic has official status in the Irish Republic where it is taught in all schools. The state gives substantial economic aid to the Gaeltachts (Gaelic-speaking areas) but, despite this, the number of habitual speakers is the smallest for any Celtic language. Gaelic is extinct as a spoken language in Northern Ireland but its close association with Irish nationalism still makes it a source of political contention there.

Though it was never the language of all Scotland, Scottish Gaelic is in a slightly better state than its Irish counterpart. Though its decline on the mainland is now probably irreversible, there are still healthy Gaelic-speaking communities in the Hebrides. Almost half of all Scottish Gaelic-speakers live in the Lowlands, having migrated there for economic reasons.

Welsh has the highest numbers of habitual speakers of the Celtic languages: over 300,000. Compulsory Welsh-language teaching in schools has led to a slight increase in those able to speak Welsh, but the numbers doing so habitually are probably still declining. The map gives a slightly misleading impression of the distribution of Welsh-speakers, around half of whom live in the densely populated but mainly English-speaking South Wales region. There are also still significant numbers of Welsh-speakers in the English border county of Shropshire and, due to recent migration, in the Liverpool area.

Breton has been described as a hidden language. Because of the demands of the important tourist industry and the growing monoglot French-speaking population, Breton speakers increasingly use their language only with people they know and it is often not heard by visitors. Estimates for the numbers of habitual speakers vary considerably and the figure given on the map may actually be wildly optimistic.

Currently, there are attempts to revive two extinct Celtic languages, Manx Gaelic and Cornish. Cornish never became a fully-fledged literary language and knowledge of its pronunciation, vocabulary and grammar is incomplete. Revived Cornish is actually an artificial language containing elements adopted from Welsh and Breton. The numbers who have attained fluency in Revived Cornish were estimated in the 1990s as fewer than one hundred. Realistically, the future for Cornish and Manx is probably as 'hobby languages' for enthusiasts.

A primary school class on the Isle of Skye: there is considerable support for teaching in Gaelic in the Isles, not only among Gaelic-speaking parents but also among incomers who want their children to be able to integrate with the local community.

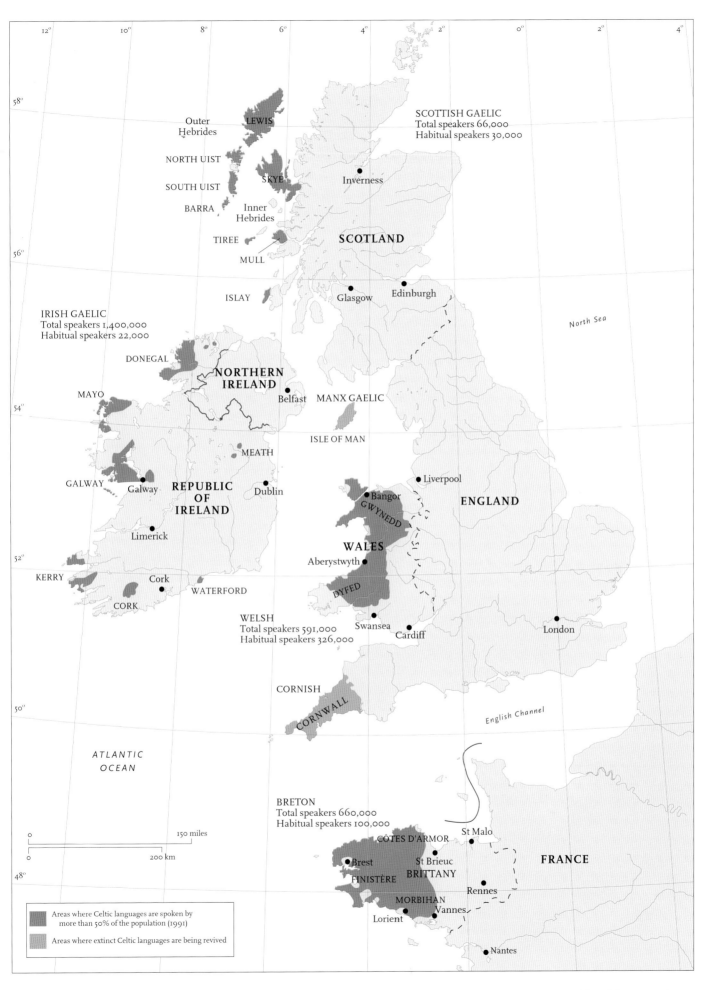

SCOTTISH GAELIC
Total speakers 66,000
Habitual speakers 30,000

Outer
Hebrides

LEWIS

NORTH UIST

SOUTH UIST

SKYE

BARRA

Inner
Hebrides

Inverness

TIREE

MULL

SCOTLAND

ISLAY

Glasgow

Edinburgh

North Sea

IRISH GAELIC
Total speakers 1,400,000
Habitual speakers 22,000

DONEGAL

NORTHERN
IRELAND

MAYO

Belfast

MANX GAELIC

ISLE OF MAN

MEATH

GALWAY

Galway

REPUBLIC
OF
IRELAND

Dublin

Liverpool

Bangor

GWYNEDD

ENGLAND

Limerick

WALES

Aberystwyth

KERRY

Cork

WATERFORD

DYFED

CORK

WELSH
Total speakers 591,000
Habitual speakers 326,000

Swansea

Cardiff

London

CORNISH

CORNWALL

English Channel

ATLANTIC
OCEAN

150 miles

200 km

BRETON
Total speakers 660,000
Habitual speakers 100,000

CÔTES D'ARMOR

St Malo

Brest

St Brieuc

FRANCE

FINISTÈRE

BRITTANY

MORBIHAN

Rennes

Lorient

Vannes

Areas where Celtic languages are spoken by
more than 50% of the population (1991)

Areas where extinct Celtic languages are being revived

Nantes

The Celtic Countries

The Celtic League, an influential pan-Celtic organization, recognizes six Celtic countries – Ireland, Scotland, Wales, the Isle of Man, Cornwall and Brittany – on the basis that Celtic languages are, or have been in the recent past, spoken there. In all these countries, a self-conscious sense of Celtic identity is a relatively recent historical phenomenon and in none of them is it universally accepted as part of a national identity.

THE MODERN SENSE of Celtic identity originated in 18th-century Wales as a reaction against Britishness. The Welsh had always regarded themselves as the Britons, the descendants of Britain's original inhabitants, but after the Act of Union with Scotland in 1707 the name was appropriated to describe the entire population of the new nation of Great Britain. It was to reassert their prior claim to the land, that the Welsh began to describe themselves as Celts.

In Ireland and Scotland the growth of Celtic identity in the 19th century was also a reaction against Britishness and Englishness. For Irish nationalists, the Celtic identity was a way of drawing a line between the Irish people and their colonial masters. However, the close association which developed between the Celtic identity, the Gaelic language, Catholicism and Republicanism has made it unacceptable to a large minority of Irish people – the Protestant Unionist majority of Northern Ireland whose cultural roots lie elsewhere. The celticizing of Scotland was less overtly political. As a result of the migration of Gaelic Highlanders to the Lowlands and a fear of assimilation by the English, Lowland Scots adopted much of the Highlanders' increasingly romanticized Celtic identity. Not all modern Scots are comfortable with this 'tartan' identity and it is not shared by the Orkney and Shetland islanders, who still look to their Norse past.

Brittany was not completely absorbed into France until 1790 and Breton identity has remained strong. By stressing their Celticness, Bretons help to maintain a non-French identity. Both the Isle of Man and Cornwall have small Celtic nationalist groups which have raised awareness of Celtic language, culture and history. The Manx are a self-governing nation but, though the Cornish have a strong local identity, there is little sense of Cornish nationality. The majority of the people of both Man and Cornwall are, in any case, now of English origin.

One of the most significant recent developments is the growth of Celtic consciousness in Galicia. Culturally and linguistically distinct from the rest of Spain, it has not been a Celtic-speaking region for over a thousand years (Galician is a Portuguese language). Galicians do not seem to feel that it is essential to speak a Celtic language to be Celtic – a sign that the Celtic identity is developing independently of its linguistic roots.

(Above) The Interceltic Festival at Lorient in Brittany is one of the most successful pan-Celtic cultural events with an international reputation.

(Right) Detail of a traditional Breton costume from Finistère. Such costumes are now only worn for festivals.

(Below) Pipers at a Galician festival. An icon of Celtic music, bagpipes originated in the Middle East and were once popular throughout Europe.

(Left) Throwing the hammer at a Highland games. Modern games are a product of the romanticizing of the Highlander in the early 19th century.

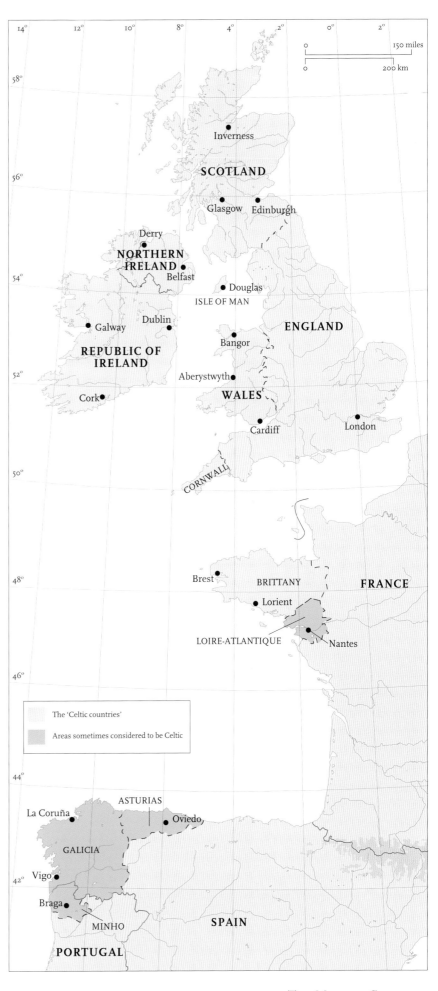

The 'Celtic countries'

Areas sometimes considered to be Celtic

Further Reading

This is a selective bibliography, limited exclusively to works in English, most of which have been published recently and should be readily available to the non-academic reader. Included in the bibliography are the main sources of material for the maps. I would like to take the opportunity here to acknowledge, in a general way, my debt to the archaeologists and historians upon whose research this book has been based.

Aalen, F. H. A., Whelan, K. & Stout, M. (eds), *Atlas of the Irish Rural Landscape* (Cork, 1997)
Alcock, L., *Arthur's Britain* (Harmondsworth, 1971)
Audouze, F. & Büchsenschütz, O., *Towns, Villages and Countryside of Celtic Europe* (London & Bloomington, 1991)
Ball, M. J. (ed.), *The Celtic Languages* (London & New York, 1993)
Berresford-Ellis, P., *The Celtic Revolution* (Talybont, 1985)
Black, R., Gillies, W. and Ó Maolalaigh, R. (eds), *Celtic Connections, Vol. 1, Language, Literature, Culture, History* (East Linton, 1999)
Chadwick, N., *The Celts* (Harmondsworth, 1970)
Chapman, M., *The Celts: the Construction of a Myth* (Basingstoke & London, 1992)
Clyde, R., *From Rebel to Hero: The Image of the Highlander 1745–1830* (East Linton, 1995)
Coffey, M. & Golway, T. (eds), *The Irish in America* (London & New York, 2000)
Collis, J., *The European Iron Age* (London, 1984)
Cowan, E. J. & McDonald, R. A. (eds), *Alba: Celtic Scotland in the Medieval Era* (East Linton, 2000)
Craig, D., *On the Crofters' Trail: In Search of the Clearance Highlanders* (London, 1990)
Cunliffe, B., *The Ancient Celts* (Oxford & New York, 1997)
Cunliffe, B., *The Oxford Illustrated Prehistory of Europe* (Oxford & New York, 1994)
Cunliffe, B., *Iron Age Communities in Britain* (3rd ed., London & New York, 1991)
Curchin, L. A., *Roman Spain: Conquest and Assimilation* (London, 1991)
Davies, J., *A History of Wales* (London, 1993)
Davies, R. R., *The Revolt of Owain Glyn Dwr* (Oxford, 1995)
Davies, W., *Wales in the Early Middle Ages* (London & New York, 1982)
De Paor, M. & L., *Early Christian Ireland* (London, 1965)
Drinkwater, J. F., *Roman Gaul* (London, 1983)
Duffy, S. (ed.), *Atlas of Irish History* (Dublin, 1997)
Durkacz, V. E., *The Decline of the Celtic Languages* (Edinburgh, 1983)
Ellis, S. G., *Ireland in the Age of the Tudors* (London, 1998)
Eluère, C., *The Celts: First Masters of Europe* (London, 1993)
Filip, J., *Celtic Civilisation and its Heritage* (Prague, 1962)
Frere, S., *Britannia* (3rd ed., London, 1987)
Galliou, P. & Jones, M., *The Bretons* (Oxford, 1991)
Grant, A., *Independence and Nationhood: Scotland 1306–1469* (London, 1984)
Green, M. J. (ed.), *The Celtic World* (London & New York, 1995)
Green, M. J., *Exploring the World of the Druids* (London & New York, 1997)

Haywood, J., *The Penguin Historical Atlas of the Vikings* (London, 1995)
Haywood, J., *Encyclopaedia of the Viking Age* (London & New York, 2000)
James, S., *The Atlantic Celts: Ancient People or Modern Invention* (London, 1999)
James, S., *Exploring the World of the Celts* (London & New York, 1993)
Jones, M., *Ducal Brittany* (Oxford, 1970)
Jones, M., *The Creation of Brittany* (London, 1988)
King, A., *Roman Gaul and Germany* (London, 1990)
Kinvig, R. H., *The Isle of Man: A Social, Cultural and Political History* (Liverpool, 1975)
Kruta, V., et al. (eds), *The Celts* (London, 1991)
Laing, L., *The Archaeology of Late Celtic Britain and Ireland* c. 400–1200 AD (London, 1975)
Laing, L. & J., *The Picts and the Scots* (Stroud, 1994)
Macinnes, A., *Clanship, Commerce and the House of Stuart* (East Linton, 1996)
McDonald, R. A., *The Kingdom of the Isles: Scotland's Western Seaboard, c. 1100–c. 1336* (East Linton, 1997)
MacNeill, P. G. B. & MacQueen, H. L. (eds), *Atlas of Scottish History to 1707* (Edinburgh, 1996)
Mallory, J. P., *In Search of the Indo-Europeans* (London & New York, 1989)
Megaw, R. & Megaw, V., *Celtic Art* (rev. ed., London & New York, 2001)
Moody, T. W. et al. (eds), *A New History of Ireland Vol. IX, Maps, Genealogies and Lists* (Oxford, 1984)
Morris, J., *The Age of Arthur* (London, 1973)
Morris, J. E., *The Welsh Wars of Edward I* (Oxford, 1901, reprint Stroud, 1996)
Ó Cróinín, D., *Early Medieval Ireland 400–1200* (London & New York 1995)
Piggott, S., *The Druids* (London, 1968)
Pittock, M. G. H., *Celtic Identity and the British Image* (Manchester & New York, 1999)
Raftery, B., *Pagan Celtic Ireland: The Enigma of the Irish Iron Age* (London & New York, 1994)
Rankin, D., *Celts and the Classical World* (London, 1987)
Rees, W., *An Historical Atlas of Wales* (2nd ed., London, 1972)
Renfrew, C., *Archaeology and Language* (London, 1987)
Ross, A., *Druids* (Stroud, 1999)
Salway, P., *Roman Britain* (Oxford, 1981)
Smyth, A. P., *Warlords and Holy Men: Scotland AD 80–1000* (London, 1984)
Snyder, C. A., *An Age of Tyrants, Britain and the Britons AD 400–600* (Stroud, 1998)
Snyder, C. A., *Exploring the World of King Arthur* (London & New York, 2000)
Szabó, M., *The Celtic Heritage in Hungary* (Budapest, 1971)
Todd, M., *The Southwest to AD 1000* (London, 1987)
Walker, D., *Medieval Wales* (Cambridge, 1990)
Webster, B., *Medieval Scotland, The Making of an Identity* (London & Basingstoke, 1997)
Webster, G., *Boudica: the British Revolt against Rome AD 60* (London, 1978)
Williams, G., *The Welsh in Patagonia* (Cardiff, 1991)
Withers, C. W. J., *Gaelic Scotland* (London & New York, 1988)
Whyte, I. & K., *On the Trail of the Jacobites* (London & New York, 1990).

Illustration Credits

Index